John Paul II & St. Thomas Aquinas

To William Riordan

John Paul II & St. Thomas Aquinas

edited by

MICHAEL DAUPHINAIS &
MATTHEW LEVERING

EX CORDE ECCLESIAE
VERITATIS SPLENDOR
·AVE·
MARIA
UNIVERSITY

Sapientia Press
of Ave Maria University

Sapientia Press
of Ave Maria University
24 Frank Lloyd Wright Drive
Ann Arbor, MI 48106
888-343-8607

Cover Design: Eloise Anagnost

Printed in the United States of America.

Library of Congress Control Number: 2006921772

ISBN-10: 1-932589-28-7

ISBN-13: 978-1-932589-28-3

Table of Contents

Introduction

MICHAEL DAUPHINAIS &
MATTHEW LEVERING

ONE WAY OF HONORING the work and memory of John Paul II, John Paul the Great, is to call attention to his relationship to the great saints and doctors who have gone before him and with whom he is now rejoicing. Thus by way of celebrating the philosophical and theological contributions of the pope, we wish to draw special attention to his relationship to one of his teachers and friends in Christ, St. Thomas Aquinas.

The question that interests us is not whether the pope was a "Thomist," but rather how the pope's teachings have instructed the new movements in Thomistic theology that took shape during his papacy. In a book that has important affinities with the pope's approach to Aquinas, Aidan Nichols has recently suggested that "a new Thomistic renaissance" may be underway.[1] Nichols states that this "new renaissance (if the phrase be not premature) proceeds most characteristically by laymen and laywomen finding out certain qualities of St. Thomas for themselves. In search of intellectual, moral, and spiritual coherence, they find that his writing has a winning power to keep together things that most people either separate or confuse."[2] He names four examples of this "winning power" of integration: theology and spirituality (united in Aquinas's *exitus-reditus* pattern), revelation and ethics (integrating the natural and the supernatural in virtue theory), the social and the individual (through the account of charity and justice), and philosophy and doctrine (metaphysical clarity). As regards the fourth, Nichols comments, "Its clarity is refreshing in a post-modern world where parodistic allusiveness, randomness and incoherence are frequently erected into pseudo-virtues that make reflective life an intellectual mess."[3]

---

1 Aidan Nichols, OP, *Discovering Aquinas: An Introduction to His Life, Work and Influence* (London: Darton, Longman and Todd, 2002): 142.

2 Ibid.

3 Ibid., 143.

Why is a "renaissance" needed? The neo-scholastic theology that predominated before the Second Vatican Council came under criticism for deficient attention to biblical themes, lack of interest in the theology of the Fathers, lack of practical relevance because of over-sophisticated philosophical structures, failure to discern any insights in the work of modern philosophers, and the inadequate pedagogy of the theological manuals. On all counts, Nichols observes that familiarity with the actual texts and practice of Thomas manifests that Aquinas himself embodies the opposite. As regards theological integration of biblical themes, "Thomas himself passes such a test with flying colours"; as regards the Fathers, "[i]n large part Thomas's output had been patristic synthesis"; and as regards inspirational relevance, Aquinas's "key notions" possess a "liberating and evangelical charge."[4]

The new Thomistic theology thus seeks to draw out Aquinas's biblical, patristic, and evangelical profundity, and thereby to contribute constructive and contemporary Thomistic theology. For Nichols, such theology remains indispensable because:

> Thomas constitutes the classic theological moment of Latin Christendom. This is not only because he had a pre-eminent gift of synthesising the materials of Scripture and patristic Tradition, revelation's witnesses. It is also because he honed a metaphysic that was up to the job of being that revelation's philosophical instrument—in the traditional language, its serviceable "handmaid." It is hardly surprising, then, that any major derogation from Thomas's achievement (to be carefully distinguished from enrichment of it by the provision of complementary insights) will tend to create difficulties for the articulation of Catholic faith.[5]

Nichols here agrees, as we will see, with the insights of John Paul II regarding the contribution of St. Thomas Aquinas.

We might begin with John Paul's bestselling 1994 book, *Crossing the Threshold of Hope*. Here he places Aquinas within the tradition of Christian mysticism.[6] For the pope, Aquinas's theology develops not only an account of intellect, but also an account of will and of the affective desire for God, that serves the pattern of mystical ascent to God inscribed in the structure of *exitus-reditus*. He explains, "I think that it is wrong to maintain that Saint Thomas's position [on God] stands up only in the realm of the rational. One must, it is true, applaud Etienne Gilson when he agrees

---

[4] Ibid., 140–42.

[5] Ibid., ix.

[6] John Paul II, *Crossing the Threshold of Hope,* ed. Vittorio Messori, trans. Jenny McPhee and Martha McPhee (New York: Alfred A. Knopf, 1995), 87.

with Saint Thomas that the intellect is the most marvelous of God's creations, but that does not mean that we must give in to a unilateral rationalism. Saint Thomas celebrates all the richness and complexity of each created being, and especially of the human being."[7] The view of neo-scholasticism as a rationalism, lacking appreciation for the richness of the person, does not hold up as regards Aquinas's writings. Because of Aquinas's insight into God and into the human being, Aquinas's thought has far more than historical value. As John Paul II remarks, "It is not good that his thought has been set aside in the post-conciliar period; he continues, in fact, to be the *master of philosophical and theological universalism*."[8] Earlier the pope regrets the fact that "today, unfortunately, the *Summa Theologica* has been somewhat neglected."[9]

In *Crossing the Threshold of Hope*, John Paul II points especially to Aquinas's metaphysical profundity. After discussing the anthropocentric thought of Descartes, the pope writes, "How different from the approach of Saint Thomas for whom it is not *thought which determines existence, but existence,* 'esse,' *which determines thought*! I think the way I think because I am that which I am—a creature—and because He is He who is, *the absolute uncreated Mystery*. If He were not Mystery, there would be no need for Revelation, or, more precisely, there would be no need for *God to reveal Himself*."[10] The entirety of *sacra doctrina* depends, in short, on recognizing this metaphysical point (Creator-creature) that Aquinas explicates most profoundly, just as Aquinas's account of the human being exposes the depth of "richness and complexity" that characterizes the human creature.

The pope wrote these words just as he was promulgating what is widely recognized, by admirers and detractors alike, as among the most significant of his encyclicals, *Veritatis Splendor*. That encyclical, it could be argued, marks a transition in his body of encyclicals toward a deeper appropriation and use of the theology of Aquinas. The profound engagement with Aquinas's theological perspective in *Veritatis Splendor* is incontestable.[11]

---

[7] Ibid., 31.

[8] Ibid.

[9] Ibid., 29.

[10] Ibid., 38; cf. the same point on 51. See also John Paul II's *Memory and Identity: Conversations at the Dawn of the Millennium* (New York: Rizzoli, 2005), 7–12, where the pope makes this point regarding the significance of Aquinas's metaphysics for the future of the west, and of the world, in even stronger terms. This book unfortunately appeared too late for us to include a full discussion of it here.

[11] See, e.g., the articles collected in *Veritatis Splendor and the Renewal of Moral Theology*, ed. J. A. DiNoia, OP, and Romanus Cessario, OP (Chicago, IL: Midwest Theological Forum, 1999); Servais Pinckaers, OP, *Pour une lecture de Veritatis splendor* (Paris: Mame, 1995).

Of the encyclicals that followed—*Evangelium Vitae* (1995), *Ut Unum Sint* (1995), *Fides et Ratio* (1998), and *Ecclesia de Eucharistia* (2003)—only *Ut Unum Sint* does not draw significantly from Thomas. Furthermore, *Fides et Ratio* and *Ecclesia de Eucharistia* owe a heavy debt to Aquinas's thought. The themes treated in these encyclicals have a long tradition in earlier papal and conciliar documents, which themselves bear the strong mark of Thomistic approaches (Vatican I in the background of *Fides et Ratio* and Trent in the background of *Ecclesia de Eucharistia*).[12] Thus it is not particularly surprising that John Paul II's analyses of faith, reason, and the Eucharist, like his account of the moral life in *Veritatis Splendor*, follow Thomistic argumentation at so many crucial points.

In these encyclicals the pope takes pains, as we have seen him do also in *Crossing the Threshold of Hope*, to reject the notion of Aquinas as a rationalist. *Ecclesia de Eucharistia*, for instance, concludes with Aquinas's *poetry*: "Let us make our own the words of Saint Thomas Aquinas, an eminent theologian and an impassioned poet of Christ in the Eucharist, and turn in hope to the contemplation of the goal to which our hearts aspire in their thirst for joy and peace: *Bone pastor, panis vere, /Iesu, nostri miserere. . . .*"[13] John Paul recognizes that Aquinas's writings on the Eucharist flow from a mystical desire for Truth, faith seeking understanding. Thus he writes, "*Adoro te devote, latens Deitas,* we shall continue to sing with the Angelic Doctor. Before this mystery of love, human reason fully experiences its limitations. One understands how, down the centuries, this truth has stimulated theology to strive to understand it ever more deeply."[14] Similarly, John Paul's remarks in the penultimate paragraph of the encyclical take up Aquinas's panoramic view of the Eucharist, easily forgotten by those who reduce his contribution solely to the doctrine of transubstantation: "There can be no danger of excess in our care for this mystery," the pope writes, since, as Aquinas makes clear, " 'in this sacrament is recapitulated the whole mystery of our salvation.' "[15]

Along with countering the notion of a rationalist Aquinas, the pope's encyclicals resist the move that some have made to contrast Aquinas the metaphysician with Aquinas the theologian, as if metaphysical analysis were in some way opposed to the evangelical expression of the gospel. Thus,

---

12 On *Fides et Ratio*, see e.g., the articles collected in *The Two Wings of Catholic Thought: Essays on* Fides et Ratio, ed. David Ruel Foster and Joseph W. Koterski, SJ (Washington, DC: The Catholic University of America Press, 2003).

13 *Ecclesia de Eucharistia,* §62.

14 Ibid., §15.

15 Ibid., §61. He later cites a similar text from Aquinas: "the Eucharist is 'as it were the summit of the spiritual life and the goal of all the sacraments' " (§38).

whereas some commentators have sought to draw an opposition between the more philosophical second part of *Veritatis Splendor* and its more theological first and third parts, the pope unites the three parts by appealing to the integrative (evangelical and metaphysical) wisdom of Aquinas's account of law: "Going to the heart of the moral message of Jesus and the preaching of the Apostles, and summing up in a remarkable way the great tradition of the Fathers of the East and West, and of Saint Augustine in particular, Saint Thomas was able to write that *the New Law is the grace of the Holy Spirit given through faith in Christ*."[16] The New Law does not displace the natural law, but rather heals and elevates our soul so that we may live out the self-giving life of love required by the ten commandments, thereby fulfilling (not negating) in Christ the gift to Moses. Similarly, *Evangelium Vitae,* with its biblically centered argumentation, draws upon Aquinas's theology of law at the very hinge of its discussion: "The doctrine on the necessary *conformity of civil law with the moral law* is in continuity with the whole tradition of the Church. . . . This is the clear teaching of Saint Thomas Aquinas, who writes that 'human law is law inasmuch as it is in conformity with right reason and thus derives from the eternal law. But when a law is contrary to reason, it is called an unjust law; but in this case it ceases to be a law and becomes instead an act of violence.' "[17]

The same approach characterizes *Fides et Ratio*. Arguing that both the relationship of faith and reason, and the nature of each, find superb expression in Aquinas's theology, John Paul affirms, "This is why the Church has been justified in consistently proposing St. Thomas as a master of thought and a model of the right way to do theology."[18] But in thus presenting Aquinas as "a model of the right way to do theology," John Paul emphasizes Aquinas's stature as a mystical theologian:

> Another of the great insights of St. Thomas was his perception of the role of the Holy Spirit in the process by which knowledge matures into wisdom. From the first pages of his *Summa Theologiae*, Aquinas was keen to show the primacy of the wisdom which is the gift of the Holy Spirit and which opens the way to a knowledge of divine realities. His theology allows us to understand what is distinctive of wisdom in its close link with faith and knowledge of the divine. This wisdom comes to know by way of connaturality; it presupposes faith and eventually formulates its right judgment on the basis of the truth of faith itself.[19]

---

[16] *Veritatis Splendor,* §24.

[17] *Evangelium Vitae,* §72.

[18] *Fides et Ratio,* §43.

[19] Ibid., §44.

Having discarded the rationalist Aquinas, the pope in the same paragraph resists any supposed antinomy between the philosophical modes of discourse in Aquinas and Aquinas's contemplative theology: "Yet the priority accorded this wisdom [the gift of the Holy Spirit] does not lead the Angelic Doctor to overlook the presence of two other complimentary forms of wisdom—philosophical wisdom, which is based upon the capacity of the intellect, for all its natural limitations, to explore reality, and theological wisdom, which is based upon revelation and which explores the contents of faith, entering the very mystery of God."[20]

It comes as no surprise that the pope made the very same points in his personal memoir, *Gift and Mystery: On the Fiftieth Anniversary of My Priestly Ordination*, published two years before *Fides et Ratio*. Discussing the importance of study for the Christian, John Paul first recalls Aquinas's theology of the gifts of the Holy Spirit. As he notes, "Saint Thomas Aquinas explains how, with the gifts of the Holy Spirit, a person's whole spiritual being becomes responsive to God's light, not only the light of knowledge but also the inspiration of love. I have prayed for the gifts of the Holy Spirit since my youth and I continue to do so."[21] In the very next paragraph he adds, "But of course Saint Thomas also teaches that 'infused knowledge,' which is the fruit of a special intervention by the Holy Spirit, does not free us from the duty of gaining 'acquired knowledge.' "[22] Ultimately there will not only be no contradiction between the two, but indeed each will deepen the other. This integrative wisdom, that neither conflates nor opposes the gifts of nature and grace, is the path of a *sacra doctrina* adequate to the creating and the redeeming God. Summing up his perspective on Aquinas's theology, the pope writes in *Fides et Ratio*,

> Profoundly convinced that "whatever its source, truth is of the Holy Spirit". . . St. Thomas was impartial in his love of truth. He sought truth wherever it might be found and gave consummate demonstration of its universality. In him, the Church's Magisterium has seen and recognized the passion for truth; and precisely because it stays consistently within the horizon of universal, objective and transcendent truth, his thought scales "heights unthinkable to human intelligence." Rightly, then, he may be called an "apostle of the truth." Looking unreservedly to truth, the realism of Thomas could recognize the objectivity of truth and

20 Ibid.

21 Pope John Paul II, *Gift and Mystery: On the Fiftieth Anniversary of My Priestly Ordination* (New York: Doubleday, 1996), 92–93.

22 Ibid., 93.

> produce not merely a philosophy of "what seems to be" but a philosophy of "what is."[23]

The descriptions of Aquinas as scaling unthinkable heights and as an "apostle of truth" come from Popes Leo XIII and Paul VI, respectively, but John Paul II gives them his own stamp by means of his call for the renewal of theology that employs a metaphysical philosophy.

In sum, with a particular emphasis beginning in the early 1990s, but reaching back into his doctoral work on Aquinas and St. John of the Cross, the pope's depictions of Thomas's theology consistently return to three points: (1) Aquinas is not a rationalist, but rather a contemplative spiritual theologian whose work is profoundly evangelical; (2) Aquinas's theology has particular value especially because of his metaphysical profundity in apprehending the Creator-creature relationship; and (3) Aquinas provides an integrative wisdom that avoids the false antinomies, reductions, and conflations that lesser theologians fall into and that fail to do justice to the triune God as both Creator and Redeemer. It will be noticed at once that these are essentially the same points made by Nichols in his account of the demise of neo-scholastic theology and of the ongoing "new renaissance" of Thomistic theology.

John Paul's three programmatic points may provide significant inspiration to theologians who discern in Aquinas's thought crucial resources for the work of contemporary constructive theology. The question that arises today, after a generation in which the study of Aquinas's thought has largely (outside moral theology) been relegated to the provinces of historical theology, is how to develop anew Thomistic modes of theologizing about the central mysteries of faith. Various recommendations are emerging as regards this project, ranging from J. A. DiNoia, OP's account of the dialectical and metaphysical strength of Aquinas's approach to *sacra doctrina*, to Fergus Kerr, OP's emphasis on how the tensions and ambiguities present in competing readings of Aquinas may both validate and serve the outlook and goals of postmodern theological ventures, to Thomas O'Meara, OP's rather limited presentation of Aquinas's theology as a set of medieval thought-forms now transposed by Karl Rahner into anthropocentric forms suited to the "modern mind."[24]

---

23 *Fides et Ratio,* §44.

24 See J. A. DiNoia, OP, "Thomism after Thomism: Aquinas and the Future of Theology," in *The Future of Thomism*, ed. Deal W. Hudson and Dennis W. Moran (Mishawaka, IN: American Maritain Association, 1992), 231–45; Fergus Kerr, OP, After Aquinas: Versions of Thomism (Oxford: Blackwell, 2002); Fergus Kerr, OP, ed., *Contemplating Aquinas: On the Varieties of Interpretation* (London: SCM Press, 2003); idem, "Ambiguity in Thomas Aquinas: Reflections after Aquinas," *Providence* 8:

In light of such alternatives, the present collection of essays—with the exception of Francesca Murphy's, originally published as an issue of *Nova et Vetera*—asks whether the extensive theological contribution of John Paul II might serve as a model and an impetus for contemporary systematic reflection on the realities of faith. Inspired and renewed by the thought of John Paul II, perhaps indeed there is ongoing a "new renaissance" of Thomistic theology, in service of the new evangelization to which John Paul the Great has called believers.

(2003): 1–19; Thomas F. O'Meara, OP, *Thomas Aquinas Theologian* (Notre Dame, IN: University of Notre Dame Press, 1997). See also Serge-Thomas Bonino, OP, ed., *Thomistes, ou de l'actualité de saint Thomas d'Aquin* (Paris: Parole et Silence, 2003).

The Seed of Eternity Rebels against Death: Homily at Mass Said for the Happy Repose of Pope John Paul II

Dominican Priory, Ibadan, Nigeria, April 6, 2005

ANTHONY A. AKINWALE, OP
Dominican Institute
Ibadan, Nigeria

IN THE MIDST of life, we are faced with the mystery of death, with its certainty and with its uncertainty. That we shall die is certain. What is uncertain is when and how we shall die. But faith, hope, and love are indomitable in the face of the painful reality, the awesome mystery that death is. So even though we live and walk in the valley of death, we believe in the words of Zechariah, which the Church chants every morning, that in the tender compassion of our God, the rising Sun, Christ Jesus, continually shines upon us. He comes from on high to visit us, to give light to us who live and walk in darkness and the shadow dark as death, to guide our feet into the way of peace.

Pope John Paul II knew in a deeply personal way what it meant to live, to labor, and to walk in the valley of death. He faced the mystery of death and personal tragedy so early and so often in his life. His only sister died before he was born. His mother died when he was nine. His only brother died when he was thirteen. His father died when he was twenty-two. So at a tender age he had lost all his closest relatives. At the age of eighteen, he began his studies at the Faculty of Philosophy at the Jagielionian University. He was able to complete only one year. The Second World War broke out on September 1, 1939, and the new academic year did not last longer than November 6, 1939, the day the Germans who had invaded Poland rounded up all the professors in the University and deported them to the Sachsenhausen concentration camp. The young

Karol wanted to avoid being deported to do forced labor in Germany so he began to work as a laborer in a stone quarry. He was present when dynamite was being detonated, and some rocks fell on a co-worker and killed him. In his book, *Gift and Mystery,* written on the fiftieth anniversary of his priestly ordination, he wrote: "The experience left a profound impression on me."[1] He put his impressions from that occasion into a poem in which he said:

> They took his body, and walked in a silent line.
> Toil still lingered about him, a sense of wrong.[2]

And how can one ever forget the attempt on his life at St. Peter's Square on May 13, 1981?

As one who lived, labored, and walked in the valley of death, Pope John Paul II knew how to reflect on the reality of death. And in those reflections he left the world precious lessons. He taught the world from the parishes of the Church in Krakow, from the Episcopal chair of Krakow, from the chair of Peter in Rome, even on his deathbed. He proclaimed the Good News of hope in the resurrection in the final moments of his earthly life by asking that the narrative of the last three stations of the cross be read to him. By so doing, he taught us that life is a way of the cross, that death is the culmination of the way of the cross, and that the last station is in fact beyond the tomb. It is the resurrection.

In 1976, when Pope Paul VI invited Karol Cardinal Wojtyla to preach at the retreat of the Papal Household, Paul VI was himself at the twilight of his life. He would die two years later.[3] Perhaps because Paul VI was close to death, Karol the retreat preacher offered, among other reflections, a reflection on death. In it he said:

> Every dying man has in him the biological reality of death, the "dissolution of the body," and also the human experience of dying, in which "the seed of eternity . . . rebels against death," and this seed "is inherent in every man, who cannot be reduced to mere matter"; finally every man has inherent in him the mystery of a new life which Christ has brought and which he has grafted on to humanity. . . .
>
> Even though a man does not choose his own death, nonetheless by choosing his own way of life he does, in a way, choose his own death

[1] Pope John Paul II, *Gift and Mystery* (New York: Doubleday, 1996), 9.

[2] Pope John Paul, II, "The Quarry, IV, In memory of a fellow worker," 3–3, quoted in *Gift and Mystery*, 9.

[3] Those retreat conferences are found in the book *Sign of Contradiction* by Karol Wojtyla (London: Geoffrey Chapman, 1979).

> too. Thus his death becomes the perfect ratification of his life and of the choice he made.[4]

What the future pope said in that reflection came from the personalistic philosophy of the time. But that stance of personalistic philosophy—that we choose our death by the kind of life we choose to live—was anticipated by the writer of the second letter to Timothy when he wrote the words we used as the first reading of this Mass (2 Timothy 2:8–13). I had said some moments ago that when we shall die and how we die are uncertain. Yes. We may be lacking in mathematical certitude concerning the date and manner of death. But the way we choose to live our lives is indicative of the kind of death we have chosen. For this reason, it is very much true that, like Timothy, we too can rely on this saying: If we have died with him, then we shall live with him.

The one who chooses to live a life dedicated to the service of Christ and humanity chooses to die with Christ, and the one who chooses to die with Christ chooses to enter into glory with Christ. The one who chooses to live in union with Christ chooses a death that is a Passover from life to Life, from an earthly life lived in friendship with Christ to eternal life. So the saying is true: If we endure [with the Lord] then we shall reign with him.

Karol Wojtyla chose to labor through his life for the service of humanity, and for the service of the Gospel of Christ. When he chose to become a priest, he had his priestly formation in secret, in very difficult conditions. Concerning this, he wrote:

> During the time of the [German] occupation the Metropolitan Archbishop set up the seminary, clandestinely, at his residence. This could have led at any moment to severe repression directed against the superiors and the seminarians by the German authorities.[5]

What strikes me most about his priestly formation was the fact that he had to work as a laborer even while studying for the priesthood. And he suffered a lot for that reason. George Hunston Williams captured this vividly in his book, *The Mind of John Paul II,* as he wrote about the most difficult book the young seminarian Karol read:

> Wojtyla . . . remembers that the most difficult book for the future Pope, and perhaps the one that started him out on a career in philosophy, was one given him to study by Father Klosaka. It was entitled *Ontology or*

[4] Ibid., 160–61.

[5] *Gift and Mystery,* 12–13.

> *Metaphysics* and was written by Rev. Prof. Kazimierz Wais (1865–1934) of Lwow. . . . Workers saw Wojtyla puzzling over it while he awaited the periodic purification of water used in the boiler room he tended in Solvay. Fellow seminarian Mieczyslaw Malinski remembers Wojtyla, in his blue-grey overalls and clogs without socks, carrying the book on his way to the Solvay chemical factory and responding to an enquiry about the *Metaphysics* of Wais thus: "Yes, it's hard going. I sit by the boiler and try to understand it—I feel it ought to be very important to me." That was in September 1942. . . . Years later, in his pontifical garb, he would say to his priestly friend of so many years something more: "For a long time I couldn't cope with the book and I actually wept over it. It was not until two months later, in December and January (1942–43), that I began to make something of it, but in the end it opened up a whole new world to me. It showed me a new approach to reality, and made me aware of questions I had only dimly perceived. . . .[6]

Reading the chapter of his life on his priestly formation drives home a profound lesson that no priest or candidate for the priesthood must overlook. The story of his formation for the priesthood shows with extraordinary clarity that priestly formation is no bloodless myth. You become a great priest when you freely submit to the pedagogy of suffering. All that he learned from the school of suffering prepared him for the wonderful work he did as a parish priest, as a university professor, as Archbishop of Krakow, and as Bishop of Rome. As a seminarian, as a candidate for the priesthood, he learned to be led, and by so doing, he learned to lead. And he led us well. He led us very well.

Just as he loomed large in his earthly life, the person and work of Karol Jozef Wojtyla, all the noble values and ideals that John Paul II stood for, will remain conspicuous in the vast palaces of human memory. They will remain indelible in the minds of innumerable members of the human family. For us in Nigeria, we must not fail to remember the wise words he spoke to us in 1982 and in 1998. When he visited Nigeria for the first time in 1982, he referred to our country as "a credit to Africa." When he came a second time, we were in the grips of a mindlessly brutal military dictatorship. He did not fail to plead with the dictator "to let my people go." But for his intervention, current President Olusegun Obasanjo would have been executed. By the time of his second visit to Nigeria, things were so bad that the country that John Paul II had referred to as a credit to Africa in 1982 was described in 1998 as "a disgrace to Africa"

---

[6] George Hunston Williams, *The Mind of John Paul II* (New York: Seabury Press, 1981), pp. 86-88, quoted in Richard M. Liddy, *Transforming Light: Intellectual Conversion in the Early Lonergan* (Collegeville, MN: Liturgical Press/Glazer Books, 1993).

by the elder African statesman, Nelson Mandela. Now that it can be said that we are taking tentative steps in the direction of respect for the rule of law and holistic development, we would do well to reread the pope's speeches in Nigeria in 1982 and 1998.

As we come face to face with the mystery of death, of our death, and of the death of Pope John Paul II, Christ our rising Sun uses his words in the Gospel of this Mass to provide us with light, with meaning, with strength and consolation: "Come to me, all you who labor and are overburdened, and I will give you rest." He addressed those words to his disciples who had just returned from their preaching mission. And just as those disciples went back to Christ to give him a report of their preaching mission, John Paul II has gone back to the Lord to give an account of his stewardship as Chief Shepherd of the people of God.

May Christ our Lord say the same words to him: Come to me, you who labored so much for the Gospel; come, you who lived and worked in the shadow of death; come, and I will give you rest. *Amen.*

John Paul II and the Renewal of Thomism

AVERY CARDINAL DULLES, SJ
Fordham University
Bronx, New York

A DECADE AGO, my colleague Gerald A. McCool published a book on the internal evolution of neo-Thomism in which he contended that the revival initiated by Leo XIII had exploded in different directions and self-destructed. Convinced that a posteriori Thomism was unable to sustain the Kantian critique, Joseph Maréchal and his disciples constructed an aprioristic transcendental Thomism, which eventually became a separate system—a system severely criticized or rejected by the majority of Thomists. McCool's book concludes with the judgment: "The history of the neo-Thomist movement, whose *magna charta* was *Aeterni Patris*, reached its end at the Second Vatican Council."[1]

A glance at the contemporary philosophical and theological literature, however, indicates that Father McCool's obituary was at least premature. Aidan Nichols, in his *Discovering Aquinas*, admits that for various reasons Thomism experienced a period of decline after the middle of the twentieth century. "Only in the pontificate of John Paul II," he writes, "did it bounce back to the point that some now speak of a Fourth Scholasticism, a new Thomistic renaissance."[2] Comprehensive surveys of contemporary Thomism by authors such as Brian J. Shanley,[3] Fergus Kerr,[4] and John F. X. Knasas,[5] all published within the past year, indicate that it is

---

1 Gerald A. McCool, *From Unity to Pluralism: The Internal Evolution of Thomism* (New York: Fordham University Press, 1992), 230.

2 Aidan Nichols, *Discovering Aquinas: An Introduction to His Life, Work, and Influence* (Grand Rapids, MI: Eerdmans, 2003), 142.

3 Brian J. Shanley, *The Thomist Tradition* (Dordrecht, Holland: Kluwer, 2002).

4 Fergus Kerr, *After Aquinas: Versions of Thomism* (Oxford: Blackwell, 2002).

5 John F. X. Knasas, *Being and Some Twentieth-Century Thomists* (New York: Fordham University Press, 2003).

very much alive. The Aristotelian Thomism associated with the River Forest School of Dominicans in Chicago and the faculty of Fribourg in Switzerland still has its proponents.[6] Jacques Maritain and Étienne Gilson, the founders of existential Thomism, have fathered a generation of able disciples. But many other schools of Thomism must be taken into account: for example, the neo-Platonizing participation metaphysics of Cornelio Fabro and Louis Geiger, the actualist Thomism of Joseph de Finance, the personalist Thomism of W. Norris Clarke, the ethical intuitionism of John Finnis, the existential phenomenology of Edward Schillebeeckx, the virtue-ethics of Alasdair MacIntyre, and the postmodernist Thomism of radical orthodoxy being disseminated by John Milbank and Catherine Pickstock.

A number of voices are admonishing us not to forget that St. Thomas was, as Thomas O'Meara puts it, "first and always a theologian."[7] Nichols speaks of the need to integrate the philosophy of Aquinas "more thoroughly within an essentially theological vision."[8] Gilles Emery has presented a thorough analysis of St. Thomas's doctrine of the Trinity; Rudi Te Velde has studied his metaphysics of creation; Matthew Levering has expounded the Angelic Doctor's Christology with a strong emphasis on his biblical sources. Servais Pinckaers has shown the biblical and patristic grounding of his moral theology. Jean-Pierre Torrell presents him primarily as a spiritual master, whose spirituality was richly Trinitarian.[9]

Many recent interpreters of St. Thomas place him in conversation with later thinkers. The transcendental Thomists reinterpreted him in the light of Kant; Gustav Siewerth, Bernhard Welte, and more recently Jean-Luc Marion, seek to show that St. Thomas overcame the weaknesses of what Martin Heidegger called western ontotheology. Still others, like Elizabeth Anscombe, Peter Geach, Victor Preller, and John Haldane relate St. Thomas to Anglo-American analytic philosophy, thereby launching a new movement called "analytic Thomism."

It is not uncommon to expound the Angelic Doctor in the context of contemporary ecumenical and interreligious currents. Otto Hermann Pesch and Eugene Rogers place him in conversation, respectively, with

---

[6] For example, Georges Cottier, *Le Désir de Dieu: Sur les traces de saint Thomas* (Paris: Parole et Silence, 2002).

[7] Thomas F. O'Meara, *Thomas Aquinas Theologian* (Notre Dame, IN: University of Notre Dame Press, 1997), xi.

[8] Nichols, *Discovering Aquinas,* 142.

[9] Jean-Pierre Torrell, *Saint Thomas Aquinas,* vol. 2, *Spiritual Master* (Washington, DC: Catholic University of America Press, 2003).

Luther and Barth. David Burrell and Joseph DiNoia read him as a precursor of the contemporary dialogue among world religions.

However many be its varieties, and whatever be the labels attached to them, there can be no doubt about the vibrancy of Thomism in the world today. Thomas Aquinas continues to inspire countless philosophers and theologians, whether as their chief mentor or as one of the major influences on their thought. Although each school may tend to look upon itself as the true or superior Thomism, a rigid cult of Thomistic orthodoxy is undesirable. We may concede, of course, that some philosophers adhere more closely to the explicit teaching of St. Thomas, whereas others, drawing on a variety of sources, deliberately modify his thought in order to address questions that he himself neglected or did not solve to their satisfaction. Bold experiments should be encouraged, but their results must be critically appraised lest the tradition become unraveled and its patrimony squandered.

Our question relates to our Holy Father, Pope John Paul II. Can he be classified as a Thomist, and if so, to what school or variety of Thomism does he belong? Did he encourage the revival of Thomism, and if so, what initiatives did he recommend? To find answers to these questions it will be helpful, I believe, to distinguish three phases in his career: the student, the professor, and the pastor.

The Student

After studying in an underground seminary in Poland, the young Father Wojtyla was sent for his doctoral studies to the Athenaeum of St. Thomas Aquinas in Rome, known as the Angelicum. There he wrote his doctoral dissertation under the direction of a great pillar of Thomist orthodoxy, Réginald Garrigou-Lagrange. In his dissertation he indulged his attachment to Carmelite spirituality by writing on the theology of faith according to St. John of the Cross.[10] He agreed with the Spanish mystic that faith was not capable of effecting the union of the soul with God unless perfected by charity and the gifts of the Holy Spirit.

In an appendix Father Wojtyla sought to demonstrate that this position of the great Carmelite was in conformity with the doctrine of St. Thomas. He was able to find quotations that amply supported his thesis. But in comparison with Wojtyla's writings after Vatican II, which I shall mention later, the treatment of faith in this book is narrowly intellectualist. The object of faith, he says, is divine truth mediated through propositions. In this perspective it is not difficult to demonstrate that faith alone

---

[10] Karol Wojtyla, *Faith according to St. John of the Cross* (San Francisco: Ignatius, 1981).

is unable to unite the soul to God and that it must be supplemented by charity. One may suspect, however, that Wojtyla could have affirmed a closer relationship between faith and charity if he had drawn on what St. Thomas had to say about *credere in Deum*. In these texts Aquinas depicts faith as a dynamic, grace-filled movement toward union with God.

Perhaps Wojtyla, working under the supervision of Garrigou-Lagrange, was not yet familiar with the ground-breaking research of Pierre Rousselot and others into St. Thomas's views on the manner in which the act of faith is illuminated by divine grace and charity, which give faith the eyes it needs to discern its object.[11] However that may be, it is only fair to recognize that St. Thomas was not the primary object of the dissertation, which focuses directly on John of the Cross.

Back in Poland, Wojtyla soon composed a second dissertation (his *Habilitationsschrift*) on the ethical phenomenology of Max Scheler.[12] Again, as in the prior dissertation, St. Thomas is present, providing standards by which to judge the adequacy of Scheler's system. Scheler, he concluded, erred in describing values as mere objects of emotional experience and in denying them any foundation in reality. Recourse to classical philosophy could remedy this defect and supply a more adequate account of actual ethical experience. Meaningful choices, according to Wojtyla, have to be grounded in epistemological realism. The truth of things in the real order should be the basis for judging whether our choices are right or wrong. This realism of the moral judgment will be a pillar of his teaching as pope.

It would be wrong to minimize Wojtyla's debt to Scheler. Scheler taught him the importance of moral sentiments and, above all, the irreducible distinctiveness of the personal subject. In his thesis and in several articles growing out of it, Wojtyla began to mediate between Thomism and contemporary systems of thought, as he did thereafter.

The Professor

When Wojtyla became a professor at the University of Lublin in 1954, he joined a faculty with a strong orientation to Thomistic personalism—a school of thought that differed notably from that of Garrigou-Lagrange

11 Pierre Rousselot, *The Eyes of Faith* (New York: Fordham University Press, 1990); a translation of two essays first published in 1910 and some additional materials published in 1914 and 1920.

12 For discussion of this work, see Rocco Buttiglione, *Karol Wojtyla: The Thought of the Man Who Became Pope John Paul II* (Grand Rapids, MI: Eerdmans, 1997), 54–82; Jaroslaw Kupchak, *Destined for Liberty: The Human Person in the Philosophy of Karol Wojtyla/John Paul II* (Washington, DC: The Catholic University of America Press, 2000), 10–24.

and showed the influence of French Catholic personalists, including Maurice Blondel, Emmanuel Mounier, and Gabriel Marcel.[13]

As a professor at Lublin, Wojtyla delivered a series of "Lublin Lectures" in which he explicitly compared the systems of Aquinas, Kant, and Scheler.[14] Like Aquinas, and unlike the other two, Wojtyla found it impossible to account for experience of moral responsibility without reference to the intellectually perceived good as the object of the will. In these Lublin Lectures, "he clearly follows the existential Thomism of Gilson."[15] He contended that perfection consists primarily in actual existence, and only secondarily in that which satisfies the natural aspirations of a particular agent. In an essay from this period he declares: "The Aristotelian concept of the good, which placed the primary emphasis on teleology underwent a reconstruction in Thomas' view, which gave priority to the aspect of existence, such that Thomas' concept of the good may properly be called existential."[16]

In the articles on ethics that Karol Wojtyla wrote as a professor he clearly identifies himself as a Thomist and a personalist. He accepts from St. Thomas the idea that the human person, as a free and rational subject, is responsible to make decisions with reference to truth, which is the measure of the human mind. But from contemporary personalism he derives a phenomenology of experience that received little emphasis in the writings of St. Thomas. In one of his few critical remarks about St. Thomas, Wojtyla distances himself from the objectivism of the master:

> [W]hen it comes to analyzing consciousness and self-consciousness—there seems to be no place for it in St. Thomas' objectivistic view of reality. In any case, that in which the person's subjectivity is most apparent is presented by St. Thomas in an exclusively—or almost exclusively—objective way. He shows us the particular faculties, both spiritual and sensory, thanks to which the whole of human consciousness and

---

13 For information on the philosophical faculty at Lublin, see George Huntston Williams, *The Mind of John Paul* (New York: Seabury, 1981), 144–51; also Kupczak, *Destined for Liberty,* 27–28.

14 These lectures, consisting of notes and synopses intended for class, were not originally intended for publication, but they have appeared both in German and in Polish since Wojtyla became pope.

15 Kupczak, *Destined for Liberty,* 51.

16 Karol Wojtyla, *Person & Community: Selected Essays* (New York: Peter Lange, 1993), 74. A similar point is made by W. Norris Clarke in his "Two Perspectives on the Meaning of 'Good'" in Stephen Schwartz and Fritz Wenisch, eds., *Values and Human Experience: Essays in Honor of Balduin Schwartz* (New York: Peter Lange, 1999), 121–26, esp. 125.

> self-consciousness—the human personality in the psychological and moral sense—takes shape, but that is also where he stops. Thus St. Thomas gives us an excellent view of the objective existence and activity of the person, but it would be difficult to speak in his view of the lived experiences of the person.[17]

This enrichment of Thomism by closer attention to the experiential and subjective dimensions bears abundant fruits in Wojtyla's early book, *Love and Responsibility*.[18] Here he gives an analysis of sexual desire based on the account of the passions of the soul and concupiscence in St. Thomas as well as on conversations with young married couples. From Aquinas he takes over the idea that love is ordered to that which is objectively true and good. He formulates a personalistic norm to the effect that one may never use other persons simply as means to an end. This principle sounds very much like Immanuel Kant's categorical imperative, but whereas Kant argued formalistically from a postulate of practical reason, Wojtyla grounds this principle in the metaphysical insight that the person has inviolable intrinsic dignity.

Wojtyla's ethical norm stands in some tension with the eudaemonism commonly attributed to Aristotle and St. Thomas, that is to say, the idea that morality consists in a movement toward the happiness that we were made to seek.[19] Wojtyla does not deny that human beings have a divinely given desire for happiness, but he cautions against using this desire as an excuse for treating other persons as mere means to our own self-perfection. He propounds what he calls "the law of *ecstasis*" or "the law of the gift": that human beings cannot fulfill themselves except in giving themselves generously to others.[20]

In both *Love and Responsibility* and his next work, *The Acting Person,* Wojtyla attempts to build a philosophy of the human person by analyzing

---

17 Wojtyla, *Person and Community,* 170–71. See also Wojtyla's critique of the Boethian definition of the person in his article "Subjectivity and the Irreducible in the Human Being," ibid., 209–17.

18 Karol Wojtyla (John Paul II), *Love and Responsibility* (New York: Farrar, Straus and Giroux, 1981).

19 Seifert attributes to Wojtyla and Wojtyla's disciple Tadeusz Styczen a fundamental disagreement with the eudaemonistic ethical systems of Aristotle and Thomas Aquinas. Josef Seifert, "Karol Cardinal Wojtyla (Pope John Paul II) as Philosopher and the Cracow/Lublin School of Philosophy," *Aletheia* 2 (1981): 130–99, at 184–85.

20 On the "law of the gift," see George Weigel, *Witness to Hope: The Biography of John Paul II* (New York: Harper/Collins, 1999), 136–37 and the other pages indicated in Weigel's index.

the phenomenon of human agency.[21] Holding fast to the objective realism of Thomistic metaphysics, he enriches it with a phenomenology of emotion and affectivity that owes something to authors such as Scheler.

In *The Acting Person* Wojtyla brings the Angelic Doctor into dialogue with Marxism—a system that he considered flawed in its understanding of the human person. Against the materialist determinism of the Marxists he affirms the freedom, transcendence, and creativity of the person. Like St. Thomas, he contends that society should promote the common good without overriding the individual rights of its citizens. To reconcile the good of the whole community with that of its members, he argues that individual persons fulfill themselves as free and voluntary agents by participation in the life and benefits of the wider community. The community may indeed require sacrifices, but in so doing it may still be serving the true good of its individual members. In this way Wojtyla is able to mount a critique not only of socialist totalitarianism, but also of free-market individualism and anarchist alienation. Personal participation should be a safeguard against all three of these deviations. Already at this stage, we may conclude, his reliance on St. Thomas was by no means exclusive.

The Pastor

The Second Vatican Council initiated a new phase in the thinking of Bishop Wojtyla. He became deeply involved in the life of the Church and in the relationship between the Church and modern culture. The Council compelled him to deal with a multitude of characteristically modern questions. As a pastor he had to speak to the Catholic faithful and to the world in rather general terms without employing the technical language of the philosopher. His tasks as a bishop, and later as pope, have limited his opportunities for engaging in the kind of research and speculation associated with academic philosophy.

The profound mark that Vatican II made on the thought of Bishop Wojtyla is evident in *Sources of Renewal*, a commentary on the Council documents written for the archdiocesan synod of Cracow in 1971.[22] This work gives few evidences of the author's Thomistic background. He develops a theology of faith in which intellectual assent is still essential, but the emphasis is primarily on personal commitment. The Council, he contends, calls upon the faithful to enrich their faith by a more personal and responsible engagement in living as Christians in the contemporary world.

---

21 Karol Wojtyla/Pope John Paul II, *The Acting Person* (Dordrecht, Holland: D. Reidel, 1979).

22 Karol Wojtyla/John Paul II, *Sources of Renewal: the Implementation of Vatican II* (San Francisco: Harper & Row, 1980).

Shortly before becoming pope, Cardinal Wojtyla preached a Lenten retreat to the papal household and the Roman curia. At one point in these sermons he discusses what he calls the metaphysical key to the understanding and interpretation of reality. Not surprisingly, he finds it in the character of God as absolute and necessary being—*Ipsum Esse Subsistens.* But he adds that in contemporary thinking the Absolute has lost its appeal. Phenomenology and existentialism prefer to show that the God of philosophy is first and foremost a Person, a divine Thou.[23] He thus seeks to enrich existential Thomism with insights from modern personalism.

Since becoming pope, Wojtyla has written one work that directly records his personal thinking on a wide range of philosophical and religious topics. This work, *Crossing the Threshold of Hope,* contains two chapters on the existence of God that may be seen as a test case for the author's Thomism.[24] In the first of these chapters he adverts to the Angelic Doctor's discussion of the question *An Deus sit*? at the beginning of the *Summa theologiae*, and says that it is unfortunate that this masterpiece has been somewhat neglected in our time. But in the following chapter, where he discusses the proofs for God, he takes a very different line from the "five ways" of the master. He argues not from movement and causality, or from contingency or degrees of perfection, or from design and finality in nature, but from the human person's search for the meaning and purpose of his own existence. Man recognizes himself, says John Paul, as an ethical and religious being. For philosophers of dialogue such as Buber and Lévinas, he notes, the path to God lies through the experience of coexistence in community. He does not develop the proof, but he says enough to show that his personalist and communitarian approach diverges from traditional Thomism. The metaphysics of being becomes in his thought a metaphysics of persons in community.

A stronger case for the Thomism of the present pope can be made from the address he gave in 1979, just after the beginning of his pontificate, commemorating the centenary of Leo XIII's encyclical *Aeterni Patris.* Here he firmly espouses an "existential" Thomism. The philosophy of St. Thomas, he writes, "is a philosophy of being, that is, of the 'act of existing' *(actus essendi)* whose transcendental value paves the most direct way to rise to the knowledge of subsisting Being and pure Act, namely to God. On account of this we can even call this philosophy: the philosophy of the proclama-

---

[23] Karol Wojtyla/Pope John Paul II, *Sign of Contradiction* (New York: Seabury, 1979), 14.

[24] John Paul II, *Crossing the Threshold of Hope* (New York: A. A. Knopf, 1994), 27–36.

tion of being, a chant in praise of what exists."[25] The pope then recalls that according to St. Thomas the name "person" designates that which is most perfect in the whole of nature.[26] Later in the article he describes metaphysics as a distinct branch of knowledge that studies the whole of reality under the aspect of being *(sub ratione entis)*. Precisely because of this transcendental openness, he says, the follower of St. Thomas is open to the truth of all philosophical systems, and can enter into dialogue with them. St. Thomas himself, he recalls, taught that the philosopher ought to look at what is said, not at the person who said it.

In the concluding section of his address at the Angelicum John Paul II spoke of Thomas the theologian. For Aquinas as for himself, Christ is the way for all men. In his sojourn among men and in his return to the Father, Christ sets the path for humanity and the Church. In this connection the pope alludes to the doctrine of his first encyclical, *Redemptor Hominis*, regarding the need for man and the Church to follow the route traced by the Lord himself (14).

Once again, in addressing an International Thomistic Congress in 1990, the pope manifested his personalist and anthropological appropriation of St. Thomas, whom he describes as *"doctor humanitatis."* Surveying the principal points of the treatise *"De homine"* in the *Summa theologiae*, he finds the key to the Angelic Doctor's anthropology and ethics in the theocentrism whereby human life is understood as a movement of the rational creature back to God. He took the occasion, also, to extol the moderation and charity of St. Thomas as a model for those engaged in the evangelization of cultures today.[27]

The majority of Pope John Paul's speeches and official documents dealt with practical questions never addressed, at least in depth, by St. Thomas. Perhaps for this reason they contain relatively few references to the Angelic Doctor, and even those few references often cite him a representative of the general teaching of the Church. John Paul evidently felt that in writing as pope he could not appropriately enter into questions disputed within the Schools. As his preferred authorities he cited Holy Scripture, the Fathers of the Church, the Councils, and earlier popes.

But several notable exceptions must be mentioned. John Paul II spoke very personally in the set of General Audience talks later collected as the

---

25 John Paul II, "Perennial Philosophy of St. Thomas for the Youth of Our Times," *Angelicum* 57 (1980): 133–46; quotation from 140.

26 Ibid., 141, referring to the text: "Persona significat id quod est perfectissimum in tota natura, scilicet subsistens in rationali natura," *ST* I, q. 29, a. 3.

27 John Paul II, Allocution to Thomistic Congress of September 29, 1990, *AAS* 83 (1991): 404–10.

book *The Theology of the Body: Human Love in the Divine Plan*. The book is, in essence, a development of the nuptial theology of the body already sketched in *Love and Responsibility*, amplifying it with far greater attention to the scriptural foundations. Here, for instance, he grounds human dignity in the teaching of Genesis that man was created in the image and likeness of God (Gen 1:27).[28] St. Thomas is not a major source but is cited here and there. The pope mentions both him and Scheler in his treatment of the passions of the soul, such as sensual desire and shame.[29] He also argues that the hylomorphic anthropology of St. Thomas supports the Christian doctrine of the resurrection of the body in a way that Platonist dualism fails to do.[30]

Among the fourteen encyclicals of John Paul II, two stand out, in my opinion, for the prominence they give to the thinking of St. Thomas. I shall accordingly focus my remarks on these two, *Veritatis Splendor* and *Fides et Ratio*.

In *Veritatis Splendor* John Paul II reaffirms the line of ethical thought established in his articles as professor. He explicitly invokes the authority of St. Thomas in maintaining that natural law is a participation in the eternal law of God (§§41–44). Although he speaks of natural law and divine law, he avoids all legalism. He accepts from St. Thomas the idea of natural law as the light of natural reason imprinted upon our minds by God.[31] This law, he teaches, has divine providence as its source and beatitude as its goal. It must be gratefully received as a help for participating in the divine life through the mediation of Jesus Christ.

The "new law" of the gospel, for the pope as for St. Thomas, consists primarily of interior acts empowered by the Holy Spirit (§24). The encyclical quotes St. Thomas on the subjective obligation to follow even an erroneous conscience (§63) and follows his teaching on the moral evaluation of acts in terms of intention, object, and circumstances (§78). On the ground that the morality of the human act depends primarily on the object chosen, he uses St. Thomas to refute modern errors such as utilitarianism, proportionalism, and theories that unduly emphasize the fundamental option.

The encyclical *Fides et Ratio* is at root an appeal to philosophers to take up with courage their original sapiential task. The very name "philosophy," he recalls, signifies love of wisdom. Like St. Thomas, the pope recognizes that both philosophy and theology are concerned with wisdom, but

[28] John Paul II, *Theology of the Body* (Boston: Pauline Books & Media, 1997), 448–53.
[29] Ibid., 97, 200.
[30] Ibid., 240.
[31] John Paul II, Encyclical *Veritatis Splendor*, §42, quoting *ST* I–II, q. 91, a. 2.

they are distinct, inasmuch as philosophy proceeds by natural reason whereas theology seeks wisdom with the help of God's word, accepted in faith. The pope's position is in the end more dialectical than that usually attributed to the Angelic Doctor. He sees reason as oriented to a wisdom that surpasses its grasp and therefore as naturally ordered to receive guidance from beyond itself. Faith, consequently, is not a burden imposed upon reason but is reason itself perfected by the higher light of revelation. The pope goes so far as to say that faith and reason are interior to each other (§17) and that the relationship between them is circular (§73).

The conclusion seems to be more in line with Henri de Lubac's position than with those of Maritain, Gilson, and other well-known Thomists.[32] Like de Lubac, Wojtyla picks up the Augustinian theme of the soul driven by a hunger for the divine. This hunger, he sometimes suggests, is due to the workings of grace and gives rise to a kind of implicit faith that may, under some conditions, suffice for salvation.[33] In an earlier work he alluded to "anonymous Christians"—a term that had been popularized by Karl Rahner.[34]

In the course of *Fides et Ratio* the pope praises St. Thomas as a "guide and model" for theological studies and as "an authentic model for all who seek the truth" (§78). But he also recalls that "the Church has no philosophy of her own nor does she canonize any one particular philosophy in preference to others" (§49). Rather than insisting on Thomas alone as the master, he is content to depict him as one of the great triad of medieval doctors, the other two being Anselm and Bonaventure (§74).

Readers familiar with the previous writings of the pope will find an interesting confirmation of his existential Thomism in the following paragraph:

> If the *intellectus fidei* is to integrate all the wealth of the theological tradition, it must turn to the philosophy of being, which should be able to propose anew the problem of being—and this in harmony with the

[32] I have worked out this comparison in greater detail in my article "Can Philosophy Be Christian?" in D. R. Foster and J. Koterski, eds., *The Two Wings of Catholic Thought Essays on "Fides et Ratio"* (Washington, DC: The Catholic University of America Press, 2003), 3–21.

[33] In *Crossing the Threshold of Hope*, John Paul II says that in the ethical and religious systems of Asia and Australia there are many who have implicit faith in Christ and are reached by Christ's redemptive action (83).

[34] In *Sources of Renewal*, 130–31, while discussing *Lumen gentium* §16, Cardinal Wojtyla asks whether those who strive by God's grace to live a good life but do not explicitly believe in God might be "anonymous Christians"—a term commonly associated with Karl Rahner.

> demands and insights of the entire philosophical tradition. . . . Set within the Christian metaphysical tradition, the philosophy of being is a dynamic philosophy which views reality in its ontological, causal, and communicative structures. It is strong and enduring because it is based upon the very act of being itself, which allows a full and comprehensive openness to reality as a whole, surpassing every limit in order to reach the One who brings all things to fulfillment. [§97]

This paragraph of *Fides et Ratio* echoes and builds on the pope's remarks on the centenary of *Aeterni Patris*, mentioned above.[35]

In a longer essay it would be necessary to examine a number of other themes in the thought of John Paul II, and see to what extent they conform to the ideas of St. Thomas. His theology of work, set forth in *Laborem exercens* and in a number of his shorter speeches, made much of the Thomistic linkage between existence and action and the further distinction between immanent and transient action. As a personalist, the pope preferred to look on work as an action capable of perfecting the agent precisely as subject. Thomistic themes could be likewise detected in the pope's reflections on culture, leisure, and art.

In his ecclesiology John Paul II made sparing use of St. Thomas, as might be expected because St. Thomas has no formal treatise on the Church. But the pope's vision of the Church was generally in line with that of St. Thomas, who saw it as the assembly of the faithful *(congregatio fidelium)* brought about by the grace of Christ and hence as a mystical communion.[36] John Paul, however, combined this perspective with the Vatican II vision of the Church not simply as communion but rather as the sacrament of communion.[37]

In his teaching on the Eucharist John Paul II followed St. Thomas by strongly emphasizing the real presence of Christ in the consecrated elements and by defining the ordained priest primarily in terms of the power to consecrate in the person of Christ, the head of the Church.[38] For him, as for the Angelic Doctor, the Eucharist was the summit of the

---

35 A footnote in *Fides et Ratio* here refers to the pope's 1979 allocution on the centenary of *Aeterni Patris*, discussed above. I agree with the remark of Knasas: "No doubt should exist that *Fides et Ratio* is referring to Aquinas' central metaphysical notion of *actus essendi*"; *Being and Some Twentieth-Century Thomists*, xix–xx.

36 Avery Dulles, *Models of the Church* (New York: Doubleday, 2002), 43–44; idem, "The Church according to Thomas Aquinas," in *A Church to Believe In* (New York: Crossroad, 1983), 149–69.

37 See Avery Dulles, "The Ecclesiology of John Paul II," an appendix to the latest edition of *Models of the Church* (New York: Doubleday, 2002), 219–41.

38 The views of Pope John Paul II on the Eucharist are most conveniently accessible in his encyclical *Ecclesia de Eucharistia* (2003).

spiritual life and the goal of all the sacraments. Like St. Thomas, he regarded the Eucharist as the effective sign of the unity of the Church; he also followed St. Thomas in his deep devotion to the Blessed Sacrament and the practice of Eucharistic adoration, even outside of Holy Mass. But the pope by no means limited himself to reproducing the ideas of St. Thomas on the Eucharist. Warning against contemporary tendencies to reduce the Eucharist to a communal meal, he emphasized the sacrificial dimension of the Eucharist in terms that probably owe more to the Council of Trent than to St. Thomas.

Conclusion

John Paul II in his years as a student and professor became deeply attached to St. Thomas as his master in theology and philosophy alike. As pope he retained this preference but refrained from imposing Thomism as a requirement for all Catholic philosophers. He was content to exact from Catholic philosophers a metaphysical realism that acknowledged antecedent reality as the norm of truth and one validity of transempirical or metaphysical judgments.

The pope's own Thomism was not, for the most part, an academician's exposition of the texts of St. Thomas and still less a historian's review of past and current interpretations of the master. As a pastor John Paul used St. Thomas among other sources for evaluating and criticizing contemporary movements that are favorable or harmful to the spiritual life of Catholics. In particular, he criticized the shortcomings of phenomenology, Marxism, utilitarianism, and libertarian theories of freedom with the help of the Angelic Doctor.

What kind of Thomism should we attribute to this pope? It is, like all Thomism, a metaphysical realism; it upholds the capacity of the human mind to know reality in its full range, ascending even to the highest peaks of transcendence through the ways of causality, negation, and eminence. Unlike certain essentialist versions, Wojtyla's Thomism was existential insofar as it put the accent on actuality, as did Gilson, for example. More than this, it was a personalist Thomism, securely grounded in the Thomist principle that being at its most perfect is necessarily personal.

In his writings since Vatican II, our author came close to transcendental Thomism at certain points, for example, in holding that all men and women, even without explicit belief in God or Christ, can have implicit faith, which manifests itself in a sincere search for ultimate truth and goodness. This view is consonant with his acute sense of the universal presence of the Holy Spirit, who inspires authentic prayer and worship among people of many different religions.

John Paul II's potential contribution to the renewal of Thomism may be summarized under seven recommendations, which recapitulate points already made in this essay.

1. The student should be at home in the tradition of *philosophia perennis*, the broad stream of metaphysical inquiry launched by Plato and Aristotle, perfected by the Church Fathers with the light of biblical revelation, and continued by the great Scholastics of the Middle Ages and their followers in recent centuries.

2. Acceptance of this tradition will lead to metaphysical realism, which consists in recognizing the openness of the mind to reality as a whole, including the transcendent and the divine.

3. The primacy of the act of existing is a precious insight from St. Thomas that must not be lost. By focusing on existence as the root of all perfection, transcending all particular participations or essences, the mind finds liberation from the limitations of finite being and the capacity to rise to the Pure Act of subsistent being that is none other than God.

4. Following St. Thomas, we are able to acknowledge the person as that which is most perfect in all reality—free, rational, self-determining, and responsible. The person is incommunicably individual. Subjectivity, perceived from within through living experience, cannot be reduced to the objective knowability of things or natures.

5. The contemporary Thomist must not be enslaved to the letter of the Master, but must be ready to go beyond him in profiting from modern insights and addressing contemporary questions.

6. The Thomist of our time should be prepared to enter into non-polemical dialogue with other systems of thought, including even those which, like Marxism, are deterministic and atheistic. But authentic Thomism will always be on guard against a false conciliatory approach or a syncretism that would corrupt its own proper principles.

7. The Thomist should not hesitate to look to divine revelation as an indispensable help for achieving the full and coherent wisdom to which the human mind is naturally oriented. Wojtyla, like St. Thomas, recognizes the distinction between the disciplines of philosophy and theology. But they and their disciples will not

allow themselves to be imprisoned by methodological frontiers. They will seek integral wisdom, supplementing natural knowledge with revealed truth, and assimilating revelation with the aid of philosophical wisdom.

Incarnation, Redemption, and the Character of God

FREDERICK CHRISTIAN BAUERSCHMIDT
Loyola College
Baltimore, Maryland

IF ONE FOLLOWS the standard accounts of the matter, the kind that appear in theological textbooks, there are in Catholic theology two positions regarding the answer to the question, "Whether, if human beings had not sinned, God would have become incarnate?" Thomas and Thomists answer in the negative, Scotus and Scotists answer in the positive. Thomas sees the Incarnation as a remedy for sin, and therefore Christ's predestination was conditional: no sin, no Incarnation. Scotus, on the other hand, sees the Incarnation as the perfection of creation, something that would have occurred even if sin had never entered the world, and therefore Christ's predestination was absolute or unconditional.[1] Further, in the last century theology seems to be tilting in Scotus's direction; there seems to be a growing agreement that one ought to think of the Incarnation first in terms of perfecting creation for the glory of God rather than repairing it. Perhaps the most prominent proponent of this view among twentieth-century Catholic theologians was Karl Rahner, who identified his own

---

[1] This account can be found especially in any number of theological handbooks or textbooks in the last century. See, for example, Adolphe Tanquerey, *A Manual of Dogmatic Theology*, trans. John J. Byrnes, (New York: Desclee, 1959), vol 2, 92–93; Ludwig Ott, *Fundamentals of Catholic Dogma,* ed. James Canon Bastible, trans. Patrick Lynch (Cork: The Mercier Press, Ltd., 1958), 175–76; Albert Schlitzer, CSC, *Redemptive Incarnation: Sources and Their Theological Development in the Study of Christ* (Notre Dame, IN: University of Notre Dame Press, 1956), 317–29; John P. Galvin, "Jesus Christ," in *Systematic Theology: Roman Catholic Perspectives*, ed. Francis Schüssler Fiorenza and John P. Galvin (Minneapolis: Fortress Press, 1991), vol. 1, 280; Gerhard Ludwig Müller, "Incarnation," in *Handbook of Catholic Theology*, ed. Wolfgang Beinert and Francis Schüssler Fiorenza (New York: Crossroad, 1995), 378.

view with that of "the 'Scotist' school" that "the first and most basic motive for the Incarnation was not the blotting out of sin but . . . [rather] the Incarnation was already the goal of divine freedom even apart from any divine foreknowledge of freely incurred guilt."[2]

I think that this turn to the purportedly "Scotist" view on the Incarnation is related to a more general shift in Catholic theology toward a closer integration between the order of nature and the order of grace. Just as grace is no longer seen as an extrinsic and theoretically optional addition to human nature, so too the Incarnation of the Word is no longer seen as an extrinsic and theoretically optional addition to God's work in creation. Just as grace perfects nature, so too Incarnation perfects creation. The fundamental purpose of the Incarnation, therefore, is not to repair and, perhaps, "add-on" to human nature, but to elevate human nature to participation in the divine nature, something that would have occurred even if Adam and Eve had managed to resist the allurements of the serpent. In this view, were the Word never to become incarnate, creation would be incomplete, human nature would be frustrated, and God would be deprived of his proper glory.

We find this view not only in the writings of theologians like Rahner, but also in Church documents, most notably in *Gaudium et Spes*. As *Gaudium et Spes* §22 puts it: "[I]t is only in the mystery of the Word incarnate that light is shed on the mystery of humankind. For Adam, the first human being, was a representation of the future, namely, of Christ the lord. It is Christ, the last Adam, who fully discloses humankind to itself and unfolds its noble calling by revealing the mystery of the Father and the Father's love."[3] Here we see the view that it is only in the light cast by the Word-made-flesh that the human person becomes intelligible; therefore, unless we would be willing to embrace the possibility that God could create the universe without willing its completion and perfection, we seem to find endorsed here the view of Scotus that God wills the Incarnation primarily and absolutely for the crowning of creation, and only secondarily and contingently as a remedy for sin.

The text just quoted, *Gaudium et Spes* §22, runs like a red thread through the writings of John Paul II. Indeed, begining with his first, programmatic encyclical, *Redemptor Hominis,* John Paul returned again and again to what he called "this stupendous text from the Council's teaching" (§9) in order to underline his conviction that "through the Incarnation God gave human life the dimension that he intended man to have from his first

---

[2] *Theological Investigations Vol. V: Later Writings,* trans. Karl-H. Kruger (New York: Crossroad, 1983), 184–85.

[3] In *Decrees of the Ecumenical Councils*, ed. Norman P. Tanner (London: Sheed and Ward, 1990), vol. 2, 1081.

beginning" (§1). So, it would seem, on the question of the motive of the Incarnation, the Holy Father too was a Scotist in that he believed that the fundamental purpose of the Incarnation is the completion and crowning of God's creative work.

But things are not always as they would seem. In what follows, I propose that the question of what God would have done had humanity not sinned is not really of interest to either Aquinas or John Paul II. Rather, their shared concern is to stress the redemptive nature of the Incarnation, without ignoring its other purposes, in order to render for us the character of God as rich in mercy. Further, John Paul enriches Thomas's account of the redemptive purpose of the Incarnation by seeing it not only as a revelation of the divine nature, but also of human nature.

Cur Deus Homo?

It is remarkable how long it took Christian theologians to get around to asking explicitly the question of whether Christ would have become incarnate apart from human sin. Despite the reputation that the Greek Fathers have of holding a view of Christ that is more "cosmic" than later western theologians,[4] they do not really raise the question.[5] Anselm, of course, raises the famous question *Cur Deus homo*? though he does not consider the counterfactual situation of an unfallen world.

It is only when we get to Rupert of Deutz in the early twelfth century that we find an explicit formulation of the question, to which he answers that the Incarnation was part of God's original intention for creation and thus would have occurred even if humanity had not sinned. Rupert's contemporary, Honorius of Autun, raised the speculative stakes somewhat, arguing that God would have become incarnate in an impassible form had there been no sin for which to atone.[6] In the thirteenth century similar views were put forward by Robert Grosseteste, Alexander of Hales, and

---

4 See, for example, George A. Moloney, SJ, *The Cosmic Christ: From Paul to Teilhard* (New York: Sheed and Ward, 1968) and, recently, Ilia Delio, OSF, "Revisiting the Franciscan Doctrine of Christ," *Theological Studies* 64 (2003).

5 In fact, they presume a close link between the Incarnation and human redemption, and indeed make arguments for the divine identity of the incarnate one on the basis of his role as redeemer. See Georges Florovsky, "*Cur Deus Homo*? The Motive of the Incarnation" in *Creation and Redemption* (Belmont, MA: Nordland Publishing Company, 1976), 163–70. Florovsky's essay provides a succinct summary of the history of the question.

6 On Rupert and Honorius, see Florovsky, "*Cur Deus Homo*?," 165, as well as J. McEvoy, "The Absolute Predestination of Christ in the Theology of Robert Grosseteste," *Sapientia Doctrina,* ed. H. Bascour et al. (Leuven: Peeters, 1980), 212–30, at 220–21.

Albert the Great. The great champion of this view, as already noted, was John Duns Scotus, after whom the position becomes associated with the Franciscan order, though it is also held by such non-Franciscans as Denis the Carthusian, Gabriel Biel, as well as Francis de Sales and Malebranche.[7]

The first to pose the question and give a negative answer was the early Dominican Master at Paris, Guerric of St. Quentin, in the thirteenth century.[8] Bonaventure and Aquinas also answer in the negative and subsequent Dominican theologians tended to side with Aquinas, as well as such non-Dominicans as Bellarmine. Suarez attempted to reconcile the two approaches, arguing for a twofold, coordinated purpose for the Incarnation. From the mid-nineteenth century to the mid-twentieth century, interest in the issue revived, with theologians tending to identify themselves as "Thomist" or "Scotist" in inclination.[9]

Yet before we happily line up these figures on opposing sides (with Suarez, perhaps, in the middle) we ought to actually attempt to gain a bit more clarity regarding the theological point at issue. It is not immediately clear that there is a single point at issue in the question *cur Deus homo*? An indication of this is the variety of labels that are used to describe what is being argued. Is it a question about the motive of the Incarnation or are we considering an alternative, hypothetical universe without sin? Are we discussing the predestination of Christ or his primacy? We are confronted here with a tangle of issues, and it is not at all clear how they are related. What is clear is that the theological world does not clearly divide into Thomists and Scotists.

For example, the hypothetical question "What if humanity had not sinned?" is certainly one way of approaching the question of the motive of the Incarnation, if we presume that the Incarnation would have the same motive no matter what the contingencies were—indeed, presuming that speaking of "motivations" in regard to divine actions makes any sense at all. But if we do not make such presumptions, then the question looks like idle speculation. Likewise, we might be concerned with understanding the relationships among God's various "decrees" (i.e., the election of Christ, the election of individual human beings, etc.) without having any particular concern to see Christ as the "crown" of creation, and vice versa. Disputants

---

7 See Florovsky, "*Cur Deus Homo*?," 166–67, for citations and illustrative texts.

8 Quodlibet 7.1 *(Utrum Filius fuisset incarnatus si homo non peccasset)* in Guerric of Saint-Quentin, *Quaestiones de quolibet,* ed. Walter H. Principe, rev. Jonathan Black (Toronto: Pontifical Institute of Mediaeval Studies, 2002).

9 For a brief overview of some of these figures, see Jean-François Bonnefoy, OFM, *Christ and the Cosmos,* ed. and trans. Michael D. Meilach, OFM (Paterson, NJ: St. Anthony Guild Press, 1965), 3–6.

on all sides seem to quote the *Exultet: "O felix culpa, quae talem ac tantum meruit habere Redemptorem"* with the view that it supports their own view.[10]

Thomas on Fittingness

We cannot sort this tangle out here. But we should at least be led to wonder if Thomas himself held a "Thomist" position. Gilbert Narcisse has recently written that on the question of the motive of the Incarnation we can discern three positions: that of Scotus and his followers, that of the Thomists, and that of Thomas himself.[11] I am inclined to think that Narcisse oversimplifies here and that there are actually more than three positions in play; in particular, I am not convinced that Scotus's position is "Scotist."[12] Yet Narcisse's basic point is an extremely important one: In answer to the question of whether Christ would have become incarnate if human beings had never sinned, Thomas's answer is not the flatfooted "no" that some have identified as the "Thomist" position.

In looking at what Thomas has to say on this question, it is striking how *little* he in fact says. The texts that deal with the question constitute but a handful. It is only in his *Sentences* Commentary (lib. 3, d. 1, q. 1, a. 3) and in the *Summa theologiae* (3.1.3) that we find anything approaching a systematic treatment of the hypothetical question of whether or not Christ would have become incarnate apart from sin, and in both these cases Thomas devotes only a single article to the question. He also mentions it very much in passing in *De veritate* (29.4) and discusses it briefly in his commentary on 1 Timothy (1.4), where he says "this question is not of great importance, because God ordained things to be done in the way that they were to be done, and we are ignorant of what would have been ordained if he had not foreseen sin."[13]

---

[10] Thomas quotes this in support of his position in *Summa theologiae* III, q. 1, a. 3, as does Robert Jenson, who apparently believes himself to be in disagreement with Thomas. See Robert Jenson, "For Us . . . He Was Made Man," in *Nicene Christianity*, ed. Christopher R. Seitz (Grand Rapids, MI: Brazos Press, 2001), 76.

[11] Gilbert Narcisse, *Les raisons de Dieu: Arguments de convenance et Esthétique théologique selon saint Thomas d'Aquin et Hans Urs von Balthasar* (Fribourg: Éditions Universitaires, 1997), xxii.

[12] It is noteworthy that in outlining Scotus's position on the question, Richard Cross comments that "the whole argument has to be gleaned from several passages" (*Duns Scotus* [Oxford: Oxford University Press, 1999], 128); in other words, the "Scotist" argument is not something that is actually found in Scotus. Of course Cross and others are fully justified in connecting the dots that they find in Scotus, but it is possible that those same dots might be connected in a way somewhat different from traditional Scotism.

[13] *[H]aec quaestio non est magnae auctoritatis, quia Deus ordinavit fienda secundum quod res fiendae erant. Et nescimus quid ordinasset, si non praescivisset peccatum.*

Thomas's essential argument in both the *Sentences* Commentary and in the *Summa theologiae* is that the hypothetical question is really a question about the divine will, and as such is beyond our capacity to answer. This approach should come as no surprise to any careful reader of Aquinas. Despite the image that some have of him as one who believes that human reason can prove quite a number of things about God, Thomas in fact thinks that unaided reason not only cannot grasp what God is, neither can it deduce a priori what God wills to do. These two things are related, since in God being and doing are the same thing. Thus God's acting is always in conformity with God's nature, but since we cannot grasp God's nature, our thinking about God's actions must always be, as it were, after the fact. To put it in modern terms, there can be no deduction of salvation history. Though each and every event of that history is enfolded within the divine decree, we have no access to that decree except as it unfolds before us in time. So hypothetical questions about what *would* have happened if history had unfolded in some other way are for Thomas simply veiled attempts to grasp what is ungraspable: the divine essence. At the same time, to say that events *had* to unfold in precisely the way that they did is equally a reduction of God's essence to the graspable, as if the infinite mystery of God were exhausted in those events.

While Thomas always seeks to affirm God's freedom, at the same time he is careful not to make that freedom arbitrary. Though God's nature is not graspable by created intellect, God's actions are still an expression of that nature, and through those actions we can gain some inkling of the character of God. God's freedom is not contentlessness willing, and in God's actions the human reason is able to discern patterns that shape our understanding of who God is.

Thomas's chief tool for inquiring into God's character while still respecting divine freedom and incomprehensibility is the category of *convenientia* or "the fitting." Gilbert Narcisse writes that "fittingness is a realized possibility."[14] To inquire into the fittingness of something is first of all to acknowledge that it is contingent and not a matter of strict necessity: We wouldn't say that it is "fitting" for a circle to be round or for 2 plus 2 to equal 5, since these are matters of logical necessity. However, fittingness carries with it its own kind of necessity—one that is a matter of the relationship of means to ends.[15] Thus we might say that it is "necessary" for parents to feed their child or for citizens to pay taxes, not in the sense of a logical necessity (as if "child feeder" were part of the definition

---

[14] *Le raisons de Dieu,* 109.

[15] See *ST* III, q. 1, a. 1.

of "parent" or "taxpayer" were part of the definition of "citizen"), but rather in the sense that these are the most fitting means of achieving certain ends. While the result could be achieved in a number of possible ways (the child could be hooked up to an IV in order to nourish it; the government could employ privateers in order to raise revenue), a certain path toward that result is the most fitting one.

However, reasoning about fittingness is a matter of *realized* possibility, which is why it is largely a retrospective activity. It is only when presented with a certain way of proceeding that we can discern the way in which various factors come together *(con-venire)* to make that way the most fitting one. At the same time that judgments of fittingness are largely retrospective, there *is* a certain prospective element to them, which is related to the notion of "character." When we say that it is characteristic of a parent to feed their child or of a citizen to pay taxes, we are not saying that these sorts of things are definitive of parenthood or citizenship, but rather that these are the sorts of things that we could expect a good parent or citizen to do. We are making a claim not so much about the definition or nature of a parent or citizen, as we are about the "second-nature" that is character. Our discernment of the fittingness of a certain type of action is a discernment of the character of the agent. And while discernments of character, as a "second-nature," do not bring the kind of knowledge that accompanies discernments of essence or "first-nature," they can give us a reasonable hope that someone will act in a certain way in the future.

Of course in speaking of God's "character" we are speaking analogously. As a "habit," a human being's character is an accident, and the radical simplicity of God allows for no accidental properties. But my fundamental point is that the category of *convenientia* or "fittingness" provides Aquinas—and us—a way of "reasoning from revelation" in order to discern the character of the God whose nature reason cannot comprehend. In thinking about how the divine acts converge so as to fit into a decorous pattern, we do not grasp God's essence, but we receive the revelation of God's character in a way appropriate to intellectual creatures, in a way that allows our hope not to be irrational.

Thomas on Incarnation

In the specific case of the Incarnation, we can see how Thomas is clear that there is nothing external or internal that necessitates the Incarnation in the strict sense of logical necessity.[16] Nothing in the divine nature, or in the nature of creation, compels God to enter into personal union with

---

[16] See *ST* III, q. 1, a. 2.

creatures. As an uncompelled act of divine love toward humanity and all creation, the Incarnation cannot be deduced a priori, but can only be revealed to us. As Aquinas writes in his *Sentences* commentary, "Only he who was born and was offered up can know the truth concerning this question, because he willed it."[17] However, once we accept that God *did* will to become flesh, we can reason from this revealed truth in order to gain insight into God's character, in order to deepen our grasp of how the truth that God took flesh fits with other things we believe about God, and what this tells us about God's character.[18] In other words, the hypothetical question of whether Christ would have become incarnate apart from sin is located within a larger context of seeking to discern the fittingness of the Incarnation in order to hope appropriately in God. It is not an inquiry into possible worlds, but a jumping-off place for a deeper understanding of what God's taking flesh says about who God is for humanity and the cosmos.

Thomas thinks that, on the whole, the witness of revelation is that, as 1 Timothy 1:15 says, "Christ Jesus came into the world to save sinners." At the same time, he is somewhat tentative in his voicing of this view: In the *Sentences* commentary he notes that this is "said probably" *(probabiliter dicunt)*, and in his commentary on 1 Timothy he says that the view that God would not have become incarnate apart from sin is "the view to which I am more inclined" *(in quam partem ego magis declino)*. In the *Summa*, having said that, in light of Scripture, it was "more fitting to say" *(convenientius dicitur)* that the Incarnation was ordained by God as a remedy for sin, he then adds, "And yet the power of God is not limited to this;—even if sin had not existed, God could have become incarnate."

---

[17] *Super Sententia* lib. 3, d. 1, q. 1, a. 3, corpus.

[18] Note that seeing the fittingness is not the same thing as seeing the "necessary reasons" for the Incarnation. Thomas's view can be distinguished from two other possible views of how reason might be used in relation to the Incarnation. One view would be to say that unaided human reason can arrive at the truth that God must become incarnate apart from divine revelation. I cannot think of any medieval who held such a view, but this might well describe the view of Hegel. Another view, which is found in medieval writers such as Anselm, would be to say that unaided human reason cannot arrive at the Incarnation, but once one holds the truth of the Incarnation on the basis of faith, one can use reason to grasp the "necessary reason" for the Incarnation. Thomas's view can also be distinguished from the fideistic view that reason is of no use whatsoever in grasping the truth of the Incarnation. For this delineation of possible positions I am indebted to the discussion (with reference to the Trinity, not the Incarnation) of Gilles Emery, "The Threeness and Oneness of God in Twelfth- to Fourteenth-Century Scholasticism," *Trinity in Aquinas,* trans. Matthew Levering et al. (Ypsilanti, MI: Sapientia Press, 2003), 1–32.

Thomas's seeming hesitation, and even equivocation, is not a matter of him being unable to make up his mind; rather, it is the precisely appropriate rhetorical stance to take when speaking of the fittingness of realized divine possibilities. Thomas is unwilling to adopt the apodictic tone that one finds in some later Thomists when they speak on this issue because, as noted earlier, he wishes to guard the incomprehensibility of God from those who are sure they can deduce what God's nature must entail in a given possible order of things. Of course God could become incarnate even if sin had not existed; there is no logical contradiction involved in the idea. But we have no way of knowing if God *would* have become incarnate, and equally we have no way of knowing that God *would not* have become incarnate.

In the *Sentences* commentary, Thomas goes so far as to say that "others say truly" that, in addition to freeing humanity from sin, the Incarnation of the Son of God exalts human nature and consummates the whole universe, and that it is possible to sustain this as a probable cause of the Incarnation.[19] Such a comment might at first surprise us, since Thomas seems to take his firm stand on the biblical datum that "Christ Jesus came into the world"—this actually existing order of things—"to save sinners." But Thomas in no way restricts the purpose of the Incarnation to the remedying of original sin. It is a serious distortion of his view to say, as one recent author does, that Aquinas—and "Western Christology" in general—"maintains a strict correlation between the Incarnation, sin, and redemption"[20] or to accuse him of "hamartiocentrism." Thomas repeatedly makes the point that the Incarnation, and the sacramental economy flowing from it, has the twofold purpose of freeing us from sin and advancing us in goodness,[21] and in his discussions he seems sometimes to highlight the first purpose and sometimes the second.

If we look at the brief discussion in the *Compendium theologiae* we get some sense of the richness of Thomas's understanding of the purpose of the Incarnation. He first sketches the way in which the Incarnation liberates us from sin by making satisfaction to God, recalling us to the spiritual life, and freeing us from the power of demons by showing us the dignity of our human nature. He then goes on to speak, in Abelardian fashion, of

---

19 *Alii vero dicunt, quod cum per Incarnationem filii Dei non solum liberatio a peccato, sed etiam humanae naturae exaltatio, et totius universi consummatio facta sit; etiam peccato non existente, propter has causas incarnatio fuisset: et hoc etiam probabiliter sustineri potest.*

20 Delio, "Revisiting the Franciscan Doctrine of Christ," 23.

21 For example, *Summa contra Gentiles* III, ch. 54; *ST* III, q. 1, aa. 2, 5; III, q. 53, a. 1; III, q. 63, a. 1; III, q. 65, a. 1; *De rationibus fidei,* ch. 5; *Compendium theologiae,* §199–201.

how the Incarnation displays the greatness of God's love for humanity, inciting a mirroring love in us. In addition, in the union of humanity and divinity in the person of Christ we catch a glimpse of our union with God in glory, a glimpse that helps us to have faith. Finally, sounding what some might think a "Scotist" note, Thomas says that God's whole work in creation is "perfected" *(perficitur)* or brought to fulfillment by the Incarnation, which brings human beings—the last of God's creatures to be made—back into union with the creator from whom they came forth.

Even in this brief treatment, Thomas offers us an example of how reflection on the realized possibility that is God's free action in our history yields a rich picture of God's character, a picture that grounds Christian hope. Thomas is in fact little concerned with how God's character might have been manifested in a hypothetical world without sin. Instead, he wishes to direct our eyes to God's character as both just and merciful, a God who invites his creatures into communion with himself, and who never ceases to work to bring creation to perfection. This character of God cannot be deduced by human reason, but can only be shown to us in the event of Incarnation itself. Yet our reason *can* see how the character of this incarnate God, who loves us freely in drawing us to himself, is not incompatible with the God who creates the world. The dim knowledge that we have from creation of God as self-diffusive goodness itself is entirely consonant with the God who shares himself with us by becoming incarnate. Thus revealed knowledge of God perfects and does not destroy natural knowledge of God.

John Paul II and Human Redemption

Though John Paul II spoke warmly of Duns Scotus, "with his splendid doctrine on the primacy of Christ,"[22] I know of no text where he weighs in on the hypothetical question of whether Christ would have become incarnate if humanity had never sinned. One can certainly find statements by John Paul that present the Incarnation of Christ as the completion and crowning of God's creative activity. "Paul pointed out that the goal of history lies in the Father's plan to 'unite all things in him [Christ], things in heaven and things on earth' (Eph 1:10). Christ is the centre of the universe, who draws all people to himself to grant them an abundance of grace and eternal life."[23] In particular, John Paul presents the

[22] Meeting with the Duns Scotus Commission of the Order of Friars Minor, February 16, 2002. Text at: www.vatican.va/holy_father/john_paul_ii/speeches/2002/february/documents/hf_jp-ii_spe_20020216_frati-minori_en.html.

[23] General Audience, April 22, 1998, §4. Text at: http://www.vatican.va/holy_father/john_paul_ii/audiences/1998/documents/hf_jp-ii_aud_22041998_en.html.

Incarnation as a uniting of time and eternity: "By becoming man, the Son of God embraced human time with his humanity, to guide man through all the measures of this time towards eternity and to lead him to participation in the divine life, the true inheritance of the Father, the Son and the Holy Spirit."[24] In his first encyclical, *Redemptor Hominis,* he writes, "Through the Incarnation God gave human life the dimension that he intended man to have from his first beginning" (§1).

Such purposes seem to have no necessary connection to liberation from sin, and thus such texts can give the impression that John Paul would answer our hypothetical question with a clear "yes"—the Incarnation serves the eternal intention of God to unite creation with himself, and would have occurred even if we had not fallen into sin. But if we continue reading *Redemptor Hominis*, we find John Paul saying that God fulfilled his eternal intention for humanity,

> in the way that is peculiar to him alone, in keeping with his eternal love and mercy, with the full freedom of God—and he has granted it also with the bounty that enables us, in considering the original sin and the whole history of the sins of humanity, and in considering the errors of the human intellect, will and heart, to repeat with amazement the words of the Sacred Liturgy: "O happy fault . . . which gained us so great a Redeemer!" (§1)

Here the picture gets a bit more complex. John Paul shares some of the same concerns as Aquinas in trying to hold together God's freedom with God's nature. God's freedom is of a sort that is "peculiar to him alone" because it is not constrained by contingencies, nor is it contentless willing, but is entirely oriented toward love and mercy. Also, like Aquinas, John Paul is not speaking of some hypothetical world order, but of the concrete order in which we find ourselves, the order marred by human sin.

For John Paul, no less than Thomas, the Incarnation is a redemptive Incarnation.[25] Yes, Christ is the new Adam, but he is the one who comes to "cancel the work of devastation, the horrible idolatries, violence and every sin that rebellious Adam sowed in the age-old history of humanity and in the created realm."[26] The approach John Paul employs is not

---

[24] Homily, November 30, 1996. Text at: www.ewtn.com/library/PAPALDOC/JP961130.HTM. See also John Paul II, *Fides et Ratio,* §12.

[25] See John Paul II, *Crossing the Threshold of Hope,* ed. Vittorio Messoria, trans. Jenny McPhee and Martha McPhee (New York: Alfred A. Knopf, 1994), 68: "Christianity is a religion of salvation."

[26] General Audience, February 14, 2001 §3. Text at: www.vatican.va/holy_father/john_paul_ii/audiences/2001/documents/hf_jp-ii_aud_20010214_en.html.

unlike Thomas's way of *convenientia*. It is a reasoning from God's actions in history toward God's character, through the discerning of patterns of fittingness, which takes reason outside of itself so as to see the typological structure of human history. As he puts it in *Fides et Ratio*,

> The fundamental conviction of the "philosophy" found in the Bible is that the world and human life do have a meaning and look towards their fulfillment, which comes in Jesus Christ. The mystery of the Incarnation will always remain the central point of reference for an understanding of the enigma of human existence, the created world and God himself. The challenge of this mystery pushes philosophy to its limits, as reason is summoned to make its own a logic which brings down the walls within which it risks being confined.[27]

For John Paul, the "philosophy" of Scripture is oriented toward the love of Wisdom incarnate, and in the light of that Wisdom, human reason is, as it were, "colonized" by the light of glory. It is not that this light replaces human wisdom, but it elevates it and transforms it so as to allow us to discern the character of the God who is always beyond reason's grasp. Or, as John Paul puts it at the beginning of the encyclical *Dives in Misericordia*, "it is 'God who is rich in mercy' whom Jesus Christ has revealed to us as Father."[28]

This emphasis on divine mercy is fundamental to John Paul's understanding of how the Incarnation leads us to characterize God. Mercy is "love's second name and, at the same time, the specific manner in which love is revealed and effected vis-à-vis the reality of the evil that is in the world."[29] In the cross and resurrection we experience the love that is God, pouring itself out without counting the cost, so that we may be freed from evil and share in the goodness of God's own life. An Incarnation in a hypothetical world without sin (perhaps, as Scotus speculates, by a Christ with an impassible body)[30] would not offer us the same characterization of God. This is not, of course, to say that sin is necessary; such a claim would require that we somehow could characterize God apart from how God has acted in our present world order. But it is to say that in our actual world we cannot fully understand God's character apart from the cross, and it is the divine character as revealed in the cross that grounds our hope.

So we see a very similar approach in Aquinas and John Paul to Incarnation, redemption, and the discerning of God's character. However, John

27 *Fides et Ratio,* §80.

28 *Dives in Misericordia,* §1.

29 Ibid., §7.

30 See *Ordinatio* III, d. 7, q. 3.

Paul is distinctively modern in comparison with Thomas in the role that theological anthropology plays in his thought. Like much modern theology, John Paul adopts an anthropological approach—seeing in the mystery of the human person the starting point for theological inquiry—that is quite alien to Aquinas.[31] Yet John Paul's specific anthropological approach is in some ways equally alien to much modern theology, not least because it remains a thoroughly Christocentric anthropology. Most striking is his emphasis, inspired by *Gaudium et Spes,* §22, on people as mysteries to themselves, mysteries that only become clear in the light cast by the Incarnation. In a sense, as fully divine and fully human, Christ accomplishes at the same time the revelation of God and the revelation of true humanity.

Here I think we see an insight that renews and genuinely enriches Thomas's thinking about the Incarnation. Though I think Thomas's account of the human person is theological through and through, and casts light on his Christology, that light is not reflected back so that Christology illumines anthropology. While Thomas discerns in the Incarnation certain truths about human beings, such as their dignity and their destiny, one does not find in him the strong emphasis on the Incarnation as a revelation of the character of humanity as well as of the character of God. At times, one gets the impression that Thomas thinks that it is pretty obvious what a human being is and is supposed to be. Because of this, Thomas seems to have been insufficiently critical in his thinking about what was and was not "natural" for human beings (slavery and the subordination of women come to mind as obvious examples). What John Paul offers is the insight that human nature cannot simply be "read off" of conventional social or cultural patterns, not only because our nature has been distorted by sin, but also because our nature is itself paradoxical: We are the "thinking reed," created in time but destined for eternity. Therefore, our understanding of what authentic human existence is must be clarified and purified by our discernment of the human character of Christ. As John Paul writes in *Redemptor Hominis*:

---

[31] It is difficult to imagine Aquinas making a statement like: "Man in the full truth of his existence, of his personal being and also of his community and social being—in the sphere of his own family, in the sphere of society and very diverse contexts, in the sphere of his own nation or people (perhaps still only that of his clan or tribe), and in the sphere of the whole of mankind—this man is the primary route that the Church must travel in fulfilling her mission: he is the primary and fundamental way for the Church, the way traced out by Christ himself, the way that leads invariably through the mystery of the Incarnation and the Redemption" (*Redemptor Hominis,* §14).

> The man who wishes to understand himself thoroughly—and not just in accordance with immediate, partial, often superficial, and even illusory standards and measures of his being—he must with his unrest, uncertainty and even his weakness and sinfulness, with his life and death, draw near to Christ. He must, so to speak, enter into him with all his own self, he must "appropriate" and assimilate the whole of the reality of the Incarnation and Redemption in order to find himself. (§10)

John Paul indicates that in our thinking about human beings, no less than in our thinking about God, we ought to accept the fragmentariness of our knowledge. In seeking to discern what is "fitting" for human beings, we ought to look to Christ. For if we need Christ to know what we should hope for from God, no less do we need Christ to know what we should hope for as human beings. For only Christ can give us the "realism of hope," the realism that, as John Paul put it, "knows that the world, in spite of everything, is instilled with that paschal grace which sustains and redeems it."[32]

---

[32] General Audience, November 8, 1995, §10. Text at: www.ewtn.com/library/PAPALDOC/JP95118b.HTM.

John Paul II's Ecclesiology and St. Thomas Aquinas

CHARLES MOREROD, OP
The Angelicum
Rome, Italy

What Will Be Compared in Both Ecclesiologies

TO COMPARE John Paul II's ecclesiology to Aquinas's is not an easy task, and requires some choices. Some of the difficulties in comparing the two arise from St. Thomas. Like all theologians of his time, Thomas never published a specifically ecclesiological text; his ecclesiology is present implicitly, diffused in all his works.[1] Some difficulties also came from John Paul II. His texts have different levels of authority, and although all of them are canonically "his" texts, his direct involvement in them is not always the

[1] See Yves M.-J. Congar, "Vision de l'Eglise chez Thomas d'Aquin," *Revue des Sciences Philosophiques et Théologiques* 62 (1978): 523–24: "Il n'y aura de traité spécial ou séparé de l'Eglise que sous l'action de deux conjonctures qui n'étaient pas encore à l'oeuvre au moment où Thomas rédigeait: d'abord quand la société temporelle, au moins dans l'action de ses chefs, affirmera son autonomie à l'égard de la 'sainte Eglise': et ce seront, à partir de 1300, d'abord à l'occasion du conflit entre Philippe le Bel et Boniface VIII, puis jusque vers 1360, une bonne trentaine de traités sur le pouvoir ou la juridiction du Pape et des souverains. Deuxièmement, quand des éléments importants de l'institution ecclésiastique seront mis en question: lors du schisme d'Occident et du conciliarisme, puis du gallicanisme; par les Réformes protestantes du XVIe siècle. L'écrit de S. Thomas édité sous le titre trompeur de *Contra errores Graecorum* ne rente pas encore dans cette seconde vague: il n'est qu'une consultation demandée par le Pape touchant un libellus ou recueil de textes, hélas, en partie inauthentiques. Il semble difficile de penser que Thomas ne se soit pas posé la question de l'Eglise. Il aura estimé en avoir suffisamment exposé tous les éléments dans la synthèse malheureusement inachevée de la Somme. De fait, quand on les recherche on les trouve et l'on peut en dresser une liste. S. Thomas a dû penser avoir traité en leur lieu propre des réalités qui intègrent la réalité complexe de qu'est l'Eglise et qui n'est autre que le retour à Dieu de l'humanité par les voies et moyens aptes à le procurer. Ces mots évoquent le plan même de la Somme, et donc la conception de la théologique que Thomas a pratiquée."

same. When we speak about compared theologies, such a direct involvement matters. Therefore, I will limit myself to those texts that possess such great authority that we can assume that the pope looked closely at them (encyclicals, Apostolic Constitutions, *Motu proprio*).

The main difficulty is to choose the subjects to compare. Both authors have addressed many ecclesiological topics, and what they say is often what any Catholic would or should say. It also happens that their positions differ: They have different positions (e.g., on the difference between priest and bishop,[2] or on the focus on the Church as Communion)[3] not

[2] Vatican II (cf. *Lumen Gentium,* §21) teaches that the episcopate is sacramental, being the fullness of the sacrament of Orders, and not only jurisdictional. This was not clear in medieval theology. For Thomas the main point is that the priest can consecrate the Eucharist, which is the highest priestly act, and therefore the distinction between the bishop and the priest is only a distinction of jurisdiction (cf. *Summa theologiae* III, q. 67, a. 2; *Summa contra Gentiles* IV, ch.76). He deals with some notions coming from the ancient Church which confuse him somewhat: He knows that the vocabulary has not always been most clear, but that there was some distinction in reality (cf. *ST* II–II, q. 184, a. 6, ad 1). Of course he maintains that the successors of the apostles are the bishops (cf. *ST* III, q. 72, a. 11; *De perfectione vitae spiritualis*, cap. 16). Some authors would insist more than I do on the significance of Thomas's texts about the distinction between bishop and priest (most notably Joseph Lécuyer, "Les étapes de l'enseignement thomiste sur l'épiscopat," *Revue Thomiste* 57 [1957]: 29–52; Cardinal Walter Kasper followed a similar line in an unpublished conference at the Angelicum in 2000). I agree with Fr. Gy's questions to Fr. Lécuyer: "Le P. Lécuyer a étudié la théologie de l'épiscopat de saint Thomas, en particulier dans un article très important de la *Revue Thomiste* où il rassemble tous les textes susceptibles d'être interprétés dans le sens de la sacramentalité de l'épiscopat. Le P. Lécuyer examine de façon détaillée les écrits de saint Thomas, mais pas ceux des théologiens contemporains ni ceux des canonistes de la même époque. Il montre à juste titre que la pensée de Thomas sur l'épiscopat est nuancée, mais à mon avis il la force un peu dans le sens de la sacramentalité et il l'isole par rapport à son contexte historique. De plus, il ne tient pas assez compte de deux données: à savoir, d'une part, l'importance croissante, depuis la fin du XIIe siècle, de la distinction entre ordre et juridiction et, d'autre part, l'insistance de Thomas sur le ministère sacerdotal de l'eucharistie" (Pierre-Marie Gy, OP, "Evolution de saint Thomas sur la théologie du sacrement de l'ordre," *Revue Thomiste* 99 [1999]: 186); in the same issue of the *Revue Thomiste*, I tried to show Cajetan's theology on the difference between priest and bishop, following the line of St. Thomas, dealing with historical questions, and concluding that the best approach was to follow the custom of the Church (cf. "Le prêtre chez Cajetan," *Revue Thomiste* 99 [1999]: 260–63). On this point the main line of the whole Thomistic tradition has not been followed by Vatican II: The Council followed an older tradition, which Thomas partly knew without fully following it.

[3] One of the first theologians (perhaps the first one among Roman Catholics) to develop this notion did so in connection to his master Thomas: Jean-Jérôme Hamer, OP, *L'Eglise est une communion* (Paris: Cerf, 1962). For John Paul II the ecclesiology

so much because of their own systems, but because of the prevalent theology of their time.

Some typical topics must be identified if both ecclesiologies are to be compared on a specific way. As it seems that John Paul II has to be compared with Thomas rather than vice versa (since Thomas came first and we can examine his influence on the pope), I have selected three topics in Aquinas's texts which demonstrate his understanding of the Church within his whole theology, and to which I shall compare some of the pope's texts:

1. the cooperation of the Church with God,
2. Church unity and Church membership, and
3. the possibility of the proclamation of faith and Church authority.

The Cooperation of the Church with God

Thomas: God Speaks a Human Language with Human Beings

One of the main questions in ecclesiology asks whether the Church's role in bringing out to the world the salvation obtained once and for all by Christ is an active role, or whether she is purely passive. For Thomas, there is no doubt that the Church is active; for instance, he holds that the sacraments really give grace and do not only declare it to have been given.[4] The global efficiency of the Church appears best–but not only–in the sacraments, and in the sacramental ministry.

Thomas's theology of the efficiency of the Church depends first on the fact that for him Christ's humanity is the instrument of his divinity: "To give grace or the Holy Ghost belongs to Christ as He is God, authoritatively; but instrumentally it belongs also to Him as man, inasmuch as His manhood is the instrument of His Godhead *[eius humanitas fuit instrumentum divinitatis eius]*."[5] The ministers of the Church are then human instruments in a way that derives from and depends on the instrumentality of Christ's humanity.[6]

---

of communion is certainly much more important than for Thomas, but he attributes this ecclesiology to Vatican II: "The Extraordinary Assembly of the Synod of Bishops in 1985 saw in the concept of an 'ecclesiology of communion' the central and fundamental idea of the documents of the Second Vatican Council."

4 Cf. *ST* III, q. 62, a. 1.

5 *ST* III, q. 8, a. 1, ad 1. Cf. *ST* III, q. 22, a. 2: "[T]hese effects [the remission of sin, the preservation in a state of grace, our unity to God] were conferred on us by [through] the humanity of Christ *[Haec autem per humanitatem christi nobis provenerunt]*."

6 Cf. *ST* III, q. 64, a. 3.

Most important is that God uses the visible, material, sense-oriented aspects of the life of the Church to communicate with us. There are several reasons for God's use of material elements in the sacraments, which provide spiritual health. The *Summa contra Gentiles* mentions three of them:

> These remedies had to be administered with certain visible signs: first, because God provides for man, as for other beings, according to his condition; and it is the condition of man's nature to be led through sensible things to things spiritual and intelligible:[7] secondly, because instruments must be proportioned to the prime cause; and the prime and universal cause of man's salvation is the Word Incarnate: it was convenient therefore that the remedies, through which that universal cause reaches men, should resemble the cause in this, that divine power works invisibly through visible signs. Third, because man fell into sin by clinging unduly to visible things. Therefore, that one might not believe visible things evil of their nature, and that for this reason those clinging to them had sinned, it was fitting that through the visible things themselves the remedies of salvation be applied to men. Consequently, it would appear that visible things are good of their nature—as created by God—but they become damaging to men so far as one clings to them in a disordered way, and saving so far as one uses them in an ordered way.[8]

The *Summa theologiae* adds a slightly different reason: "[M]an is prone to direct his activity chiefly towards material things. Lest, therefore, it should be too hard for man to be drawn away entirely from bodily actions, bodily exercise was offered to him in the sacraments, by which he might be trained to avoid superstitious practices."[9] The *Summa theologiae* concludes that "through the institution of the sacraments man, in a manner consistent with his nature, is instructed through sensible things; he is humbled,

---

[7] There is a clear parallel between this and Thomas's epistemology: cf. *ST* III, q. 60, a. 4: "Divine wisdom provides for each thing according to its mode; hence it is written (Wis 8:1) that 'she . . . orders all things sweetly': wherefore also we are told (Mt 25:15) that she 'gave to everyone according to his proper ability.' Now it is part of man's nature to acquire knowledge of the intelligible from the sensible. But a sign is that by means of which one attains to the knowledge of something else. Consequently, since the sacred things which are signified by the sacraments are the spiritual and intelligible goods by means of which man is sanctified, it follows that the sacramental signs consist in sensible things: just as in the Divine Scriptures spiritual things are set before us under the guise of things sensible. And hence it is that sensible things are required for the sacraments; as Dionysius also proves in his book on the heavenly hierarchy *(Coel. Hier. i)*."

[8] *SCG* IV, ch. 56. Cf. also the beautiful text of SCG IV, ch. 74 (for which the English translation is inadequate).

[9] *ST* III, q. 61, a. 1.

through confessing that he is subject to corporeal things, seeing that he receives assistance through them;"[10] we do not stop at the level of the sensible things, but "though we cannot reach God with the senses, our mind is urged by sensible signs to approach God."[11] The *Contra impugnantes* adds that God works through intermediate causes in his creation.[12]

The importance of these texts for Thomas's ecclesiology can hardly be emphasized enough, although they do not speak about the Church. The Church exists, with all its human and material elements, because God loves his creation, particularly his human creation, and communicates with us in our own language. We can see this primarily in the Incarnation: What is more typical of the divine communication in human language than the Divine Word made man? The Eucharistic presence affirms the same truth that God's love for us is expressed in our language: The Incarnation "belongs to Christ's love, out of which for our salvation He assumed a true body of our nature. And because it is the special feature of friendship to live together with friends, as the Philosopher says (Ethic. ix), He promises us His bodily presence as a reward."[13]

The material dimension of the Church is considered a scandal by many, and is at the center of the concerns of the Reformation, which considered human actions to diminish divine action.[14] Thomas's metaphysics solves this opposition: Divine action and human action produce both 100% of the same effect, at two different and subordinate levels.[15]

[10] *ST* III, q. 61, a. 1. The assistance of the sacraments is compared by Thomas to seven basic conditions of individual and common human life, cf. *ST* III, q. 65, a. 1.

[11] *ST* II–II, q. 84, a. 2, ad 3.

[12] Cf. *Contra impugnantes*, proeemium: "Quamvis autem ipse, cum sit omnipotens, per se ipsum posset gloriam suam ab hominibus, et salutem hominum procurare; disposuit tamen, ut ordo servaretur in rebus, ministros eligere, quorum ministerio perficeretur utrumque; unde recte tales Dei adiutores dicuntur, I Cor. III, 9." The text goes on explaining that the devil also has some human helpers.

[13] *ST* III, q. 75, a. 1.

[14] Cf. Martin Luther, *The Bondage of the Will* (*De servo arbitrio,* 1525), in Luther's *Works*, vol. 33 (Philadelphia: 1972), 35: "[T]he mercy of God alone does everything, and that your will does nothing, but rather is passive; otherwise, all is not ascribed to God"; John Calvin, *Institutes of the Christian Religion,* The Library of Christian Classics, vols. 20–21 (Philadelphia: The Westminster Press, 1967), L. II, III.9, 65–66: "It is, therefore, robbery from God to arrogate anything to ourselves, either in the will or the act"; L. III, XIII.2, 229: "The sum is, that man cannot claim a single particle of righteousness to himself, without at the same time detracting from the glory of the divine righteousness."

[15] Cf. *ST* III, q. 64, a. 1: "There are two ways of producing an effect; first, as a principal agent; secondly, as an instrument. In the former way the interior sacramental effect is the work of God alone: first, because God alone can enter the soul wherein the sacramental effect takes place; and no agent can operate immediately

Thomas does not want in any way to deny that God's action is sufficient: "God's grace is a sufficient cause of man's salvation. But God gives grace to man in a way which is suitable to him."[16] The fact that the means of salvation are given to the Church in no way shows any kind of divine insufficiency; it is divine love adapted to human nature. This divine way of acting is shown already in the Incarnation, in which God wants humanity to accept actively its gratuitous salvation, by Mary's "yes": "It was reasonable that it should be announced to the Blessed Virgin that she was to conceive Christ . . . in order to show that there is a certain spiritual wedlock between the Son of God and human nature *[quoddam spirituale matrimonium inter filium Dei et humanam naturam]*. Wherefore in the Annunciation the Virgin's consent was besought in lieu of that of the entire human nature."[17]

A last comment about the materiality of the Church: For Thomas, sin has made it "necessary" for God to introduce the material element into his relation to us. In the hypothetical but theologically useful "state of nature," says Thomas, relation to God was only interior: "Just as under the state of the Law of nature man was moved by inward instinct and without any outward law, to worship God, so also the sensible things to be employed in the worship of God were determined by inward instinct. But later on it became necessary for a law to be given (to man) from without: both because the Law of nature had become obscured by man's sins; and in order to signify more expressly the grace of Christ, by which the human race is sanctified. And hence the need for those things to be determinate, of which men have to make use in the sacraments."[18] To

where it is not: secondly, because grace which is an interior sacramental effect is from God alone, as we have established . . . ; while the character which is the interior effect of certain sacraments, is an instrumental power which flows from the principal agent, which is God. In the second way, however, the interior sacramental effect can be the work of man, in so far as he works as a minister. For a minister is of the nature of an instrument, since the action of both is applied to something extrinsic, while the interior effect is produced through the power of the principal agent, which is God." Cf. *SCG* III, ch. 70.

16 *ST* III, q. 61, a. 1, ad 2. The sacraments would be at the center of Protestant concerns: If they produce grace, Christ's Passion is not sufficient. For Thomas, Christ's Passion is a sufficient cause of our salvation, and the necessity of the sacraments depends on the sufficiency of the Passion (cf. *ST* III, q. 61, a. 1, ad 3).

17 *ST* III, q. 30, a. 1.

18 *ST* III, q. 60, a. 5, ad 3. Does this dependence on material things make salvation more difficult? No, since what is required can be obtained easily, says Thomas (cf. *ST* III, q. 60, a. 5, ad 3), who is somewhat limited by the geographical knowledge of his time. Actually, the material elements can be more accessible than the interior dispositions alone.

desire a purely spiritual relationship to God is to forget that we are human, and that as such, we are marked by original sin.

The Human Dimension of the Relationship with God in John Paul II

The Human Being at the Centre of John Paul II's Apostolate

One of the most obvious aspects of John Paul II's apostolate was his concern for the human being. He made his program clear in his first encyclical, which is in continuity with his previous philosophical and theological studies: "[Man] is the primary and fundamental way for the Church."[19] This very strong statement is in no way an anthropocentrism that would forget God, since "the Church's fundamental function in every age and particularly in ours is to direct man's gaze, to point the awareness and experience of the whole of humanity towards the mystery of God."[20] His theology's emphasis on man is due to the Incarnation, which appears in the context of the text just quoted: "[Man] is the primary and fundamental way for the Church, the way traced out by Christ himself."[21] The pope was inspired by *Gaudium et Spes*: "Christ the Lord indicated this way especially, when, as the Council teaches, 'by his Incarnation, he, the Son of God, in a certain way united himself with each man.' "[22] Christ's union to every human being implies a union also of the Church to every human being: "Every individual, precisely by reason of the mystery of the Word of God who was made flesh (cf. Jn 1:14), is entrusted to the maternal care of the Church."[23]

The human dimension is not only individual: The human being is understood completely only in community, and in a community related to God.[24] Quoting Vatican II again, the pope taught that "Christ's Eucharistic presence, his sacramental 'I am with you,' enables the Church to discover ever more deeply her own mystery, as shown by the whole ecclesiology of the Second Vatican Council, whereby 'the Church is in

---

19 *Redemptor Hominis,* §14.

20 Ibid., §10.

21 Ibid., §14.

22 Ibid., §13. Cf. also, §18.

23 *Evangelium Vitae,* §3.

24 Cf. *Centesimus Annus*, §24: "Man is understood in a more complete way when he is situated within the sphere of culture through his language, history, and the position he takes towards the fundamental events of life, such as birth, love, work and death. At the heart of every culture lies the attitude man takes to the greatest mystery: the mystery of God."

Christ as a sacrament or sign and instrument of the intimate union with God and of the unity of the whole human race.' "[25] In Christ a unity, which was the original purpose of creation,[26] and which therefore corresponds to the expectation of any human heart,[27] is reestablished at a higher level. There is a mark of unity in every aspect of the life of the Church. In her social actions, the Church promotes every human dimension: "The social concern of the Church, directed towards an authentic development of man and society which would respect and promote all the dimensions of the human person. . . ."[28] To care for the whole, for all dimensions, is to be "catholic."

Human Cooperation with God

We have seen that the Church is sacrament of the unity of humanity with God. The word "sacrament" is used here only analogically with respect to the seven sacraments,[29] and in a more basic way. In all these sacraments of different levels, there are some common elements, which are summarized by the pope: " 'By her relationship with Christ, the Church is a kind

---

[25] *Dominum et Vivificantem,* §63. Cf. also *Sollicitudo Rei Socialis*, §31.

[26] Cf. *Slavorum Apostoli*, §16: "And, among its statements on the subject of universality, the same Council included the following: 'All men are called to belong to the new People of God. Wherefore this People, while remaining one and unique, is to be spread throughout the whole world and must exist in all ages, so that the purpose of God's will may be fulfilled. In the beginning God made human nature one. After his children were scattered, he decreed that they should at length be unified again (cf. Jn 11:52). . . .' " Cf. *Dominum et Vivificantem* 64: "Vatican II adds that the Church is 'a sacrament . . . of the unity of all mankind'. . . . This unity has its roots in the mystery of creation and acquires a new dimension in the mystery of the Redemption, which is ordered to universal salvation."

[27] Cf. *Evangelium Vitae*, §2: "The Church knows that this Gospel of life, which she has received from her Lord, has a profound and persuasive echo in the heart of every person—believer and non-believer alike—because it marvellously fulfils all the heart's expectations while infinitely surpassing them. . . . For this reason, man—living man—represents the primary and fundamental way for the Church."

[28] *Sollicitudo Rei Socialis,* §1.

[29] Cf. *Dominum et Vivificantem*, §64: "When we use the word 'sacrament' in reference to the Church, we must bear in mind that in the texts of the Council the sacramentality of the Church appears as distinct from the sacramentality that is proper, in the strict sense, to the Sacraments. Thus we read: 'The Church is . . . in the nature of a sacrament—a sign and instrument of communion with God.' But what matters and what emerges from the analogical sense in which the word is used in the two cases is the relationship which the Church has with the power of the Holy Spirit, who alone gives life: the Church is the sign and instrument of the presence and action of the life-giving Spirit."

of sacrament or sign and means of intimate union with God, and of the unity of all mankind', and the source of this is he, he himself, he the Redeemer."[30] The three elements of this sacrament that is the Church are therefore the following:

1. sign of union with God,
2. means of union with God, and
3. the first sacrament, source of all other sacraments, is Christ himself.

When I described Thomas's view, I insisted that the actions of the Church are not only signs or declarations of God's action, but are themselves efficient, still always depending on divine action, especially the divine action in the Redemption. Similarly, the Church as sacrament is a sign, but not merely a sign. This sign is efficient, and depends on Christ. All elements that Aquinas underlines are also present, though expressed with another vocabulary.

Most important is that, far from detracting from Christ's action, the cooperation of the Church comes from him: "The first beneficiary of salvation is the Church. Christ won the Church for himself at the price of his own blood and made the Church his co-worker in the salvation of the world. Indeed, Christ dwells within the Church. She is his Bride. It is he who causes her to grow. He carries out his mission through her."[31] Already in creation, God had made the human being his co-worker.[32] Of course the human co-worker does not always work well; he sometimes wants to be the first ruler and disturbs the order of nature.[33] But that does not destroy God's desire for human cooperation. The key that we must remember is that in our action we depend on a higher ruler: "Man, as the living image of God, is willed by his Creator to be ruler and lord. . . . Man's

---

30 *Redemptor Hominis,* §7.

31 *Redemptoris Missio,* §9.

32 Cf. *Evangelium Vitae*, §43: "A certain sharing by man in God's lordship is also evident in the specific responsibility which he is given for human life as such. It is a responsibility which reaches its highest point in the giving of life through procreation by man and woman in marriage. As the Second Vatican Council teaches: 'God himself who said, 'It is not good for man to be alone' (Gen 2:18) and 'who made man from the beginning male and female' (Mt 19:4), wished to share with man a certain special participation in his own creative work. Thus he blessed male and female saying: 'Increase and multiply' (Gen 1:28).' " Cf. *Laborem Exercens*, §25.

33 Cf. *Centesimus Annus*, §37: "Instead of carrying out his role as a co-operator with God in the work of creation, man sets himself up in place of God and thus ends up provoking a rebellion on the part of nature, which is more tyrannized than governed by him."

lordship however is not absolute, but ministerial: it is a real reflection of the unique and infinite lordship of God."[34]

I have said that for Thomas human cooperation with God applies to the life of the whole Church, and in a specific way, to Mary. For John Paul II also, Mary cooperates in a specific way with God, because the "fiat of Mary—'let it be to me'—was decisive, on the human level, for the accomplishment of the divine mystery."[35] Her role is not only passive, but really active,[36] and her yes involves the whole Church.[37]

On this first topic—cooperation of the Church with God—there is a real convergence between Thomas's and the John Paul's theologies. Both see the Church as actively cooperating with divine action, because God wills it so. In Thomas, we can see that this basic Catholic understanding connects with his metaphysics, which the pope did not have to develop in his magisterial teaching.

Church Unity and Church Membership

According to St. Thomas Aquinas

In the Church the unity of the universe created by God, and above all the unity of the creatures who are God's image,[38] is restored. Significantly, Christ was born "while the world was governed by one ruler,"[39] and one of the reasons for the Incarnation is that Christ must be "the head of all human beings according to grace" *(caput omnium hominum quantum ad gratiam).*[40] This is Thomas's basic ecclesiological pattern.

---

[34] *Evangelium Vitae,* §52.

[35] *Redemptoris Mater,* §13.

[36] Cf. Ibid., §44: "And here Mary is not only the model and figure of the Church; she is much more. For, 'with maternal love she cooperates in the birth and development' of the sons and daughters of Mother Church. The Church's motherhood is accomplished not only according to the model and figure of the Mother of God but also with her 'cooperation.'"

[37] Cf. Ibid., §5: "The reality of the Incarnation finds a sort of extension in the mystery of the Church—the Body of Christ. And one cannot think of the reality of the Incarnation without referring to Mary, the Mother of the Incarnate Word."

[38] The other rational creatures, the angels, are also members of the Church: cf. *ST* III, q. 8, a. 4; q. 80, a. 2, ad 2. Christ is the head of the angels also according to his human nature: cf. *De veritate* q. 29, a. 4, ad 5.

[39] Cf. *ST* III, q. 35, a. 8, ad 1: "It was fitting that Christ should be born while the world was governed by one ruler, because 'He came to gather His own [Vulg.: 'the children of God'] together in one' (Jn 11:52), that there might be 'one fold and one shepherd' (Jn 10:16)." Of course this symbol must be taken as such. We know that parts of the world were not part of the Roman Empire.

[40] *ST* III, q. 19, a. 4, ad 1.

Christ Is the Head of the Church, His Body

It is well known that Thomas considers the Church first of all as Body of Christ. This does not mean that he ignores other names or images for the Church. He sees the Church as prefigured in the Old Testament;[41] and in the New Testament he sees her as Body of Christ,[42] but also as "Christian People,"[43] tabernacle of God,[44] Temple of God,[45] Spouse of Christ,[46] Kingdom of God,[47] and so forth.

To say that Christ is the Saviour of the whole world or to say that he is the Head of his Body are the same: "It is written (1 Tim 4:10): 'Who is the Saviour of all men, especially of the faithful,' and (1 Jn 2:2): 'He is the propitiation for our sins, and not for ours only, but also for those of the whole world.' Now to save men and to be a propitiation for their sins belongs to Christ as Head. Therefore Christ is the Head of all men."[48] As salvation is offered to all human beings, all belong to the Church: "[T]he body of the Church is made up of the men who have been from the beginning of the world until its end *[corpus Ecclesiae constituitur ex hominibus qui fuerunt a principio mundi usque ad finem ipsius]*."[49] But some belong to the Church in act, even unto the next world, and some belong to the Church only potentially.[50] Furthermore, people who lived before

---

41 Cf., for example, *ST* I–II, q. 102, aa. 2–6; II–II, q. 173, a. 3.

42 Cf. the texts quoted later, and also *ST* III, q. 49, a. 3, ad 3; III, q. 58, a. 4, ad 1.

43 Cf. *ST* II–II, q. 99, a. 1, ad 2 ("populus Christianus per fidem et sacramenta Christi sanctificatus est").

44 Cf. *ST* I–II, q. 102, a. 4, ad 9.

45 Cf. *In Psalm.* 17.7 (Busa 17.4).

46 Cf. Ibid., 44.10 (Busa 44.7): "[S]ponsa christi est ecclesia."

47 Cf. Ibid., 33.1 (Busa 33.1): "[R]egnum david est populus judaeorum, regnum dei est ecclesia"; In IV Sent., dist. 49, q. 1, quaest. 5; Busa: q.1, articulus 2E ; *SCG* IV, ch. 83. I have discussed this topic in more detail in "Eglise et Royaume I: le débat théologique," *Nova et Vetera* 74 (1999): 5–36; "Eglise et Royaume II: Vatican II," *Nova et Vetera* 75 (2000): 39–61. I had missed an important article with which I fully agree: Christoph Schönborn, OP, "L'Eglise de la terre, le Royaume de Dieu et l'Eglise du Ciel," *Esprit et Vie* 96 (1986): 689–97.

48 *ST* III, q. 8, a. 3, sed contra. Congar summarized well this teaching: See Yves Marie-Joseph Congar, OP, *Esquisses du mystère de l'Eglise* (Paris: Cerf, 1952), 66: "[D]éfinir l'Eglise comme un corps se trouvant avec Dieu dans un rapport de vie, c'est la considérer comme étant l'humanité lorsqu'elle oriente sa vie vers Dieu, par les vertus théologales. . . . Et donc, dans la Somme théologique, toute la IIa Pars est ecclésiologique."

49 *ST* III, q. 8, a. 3.

50 Cf. *ST* III, q. 8, a. 3: "We must therefore consider the members of the mystical body not only as they are in act, but as they are in potentiality. Nevertheless, some are in potentiality who will never be reduced to act, and some are reduced

Christ can belong to the Church by anticipation: "[T]he ancient Fathers, by observing the legal sacraments, were borne to Christ by the same faith and love whereby we also are borne to Him, and hence the ancient Fathers belong to the same Church as we;"[51] in their case as in all cases, salvation is given by Christ.[52]

The Holy Spirit and the Church

To belong to the Church, to the Body of Christ, means to be under the salvific influence of the Head of the Body. Since the Holy Spirit is given by Christ and communicates the salvation obtained by Christ, the one mediator, the Spirit is not given outside the Body of Christ, outside the Church.[53]

The Spirit is the soul of the Church,[54] who communicates to her by charity a participation in divine unity;[55] he "unites the Church together, and communicates the goods of one member to another"[56] (this is the

---

at some time to act; and this according to the triple class, of which the first is by faith, the second by the charity of this life, the third by the fruition of the life to come. Hence we must say that if we take the whole time of the world in general, Christ is the Head of all men, but diversely *[Christus est caput omnium hominum, sed secundum diversos gradus]*. For, first and principally, He is the Head of such as are united to Him by glory; secondly, of those who are actually united to Him by charity; thirdly, of those who are actually united to Him by faith; fourthly, of those who are united to Him merely in potentiality, which is not yet reduced to act, yet will be reduced to act according to Divine predestination; fifthly, of those who are united to Him in potentiality, which will never be reduced to act; such are those men existing in the world, who are not predestined, who, however, on their departure from this world, wholly cease to be members of Christ, as being no longer in potentiality to be united to Christ."

51 *ST* III, q. 8, a. 3, ad 3.

52 Cf. *ST* III, q. 27, a. 3: "[I]t does not seem fitting that any one should be freed from that condemnation, according to the flesh, except after His Incarnation."

53 Cf. *ST* II–II, q. 176, a. 1, ad 3: "As Augustine says (Tract. xxxii in Joan.), '(. . .) whoever is not in the Church, receives not the Holy Ghost.' "

54 Cf. *Expositio in Symbolum Apostolorum*, a. 9: "Sicut videmus quod in uno homine est una anima et unum corpus, et tamen sunt diversa membra ipsius; ita Ecclesia Catholica est unum corpus, et habet diversa membra. Anima autem quae hoc corpus vivificat, est spiritus sanctus."

55 Cf. *ST* II–II, q. 24, a. 2: "[C]harity can be in us neither naturally, nor through acquisition by the natural powers, but by the infusion of the Holy Ghost, Who is the love of the Father and the Son, and the participation of Whom in us is created charity, as stated above." Cf. *In Ioan.*, cap. 7, lect. 5: "Quia iam universalis ecclesia linguis gentium loquitur, quia per spiritum sanctum datur caritas; Rom. V,V. 5: caritas dei diffusa est in cordibus nostris, et haec, faciens omnia communia, facit quemlibet cuilibet loqui."

56 *ST* III, q. 68, a. 9, ad 2.

Communion of the saints[57] or the communion within the one mystical person who is the Church)[58] and preserves the peace among the members of the Church.[59] To be a member of the Church and to have the Spirit are one and the same thing: "If somebody does not have the Spirit of Christ, he does not belong to Christ [i.e., to the Body of Christ]. Because the unity of the Holy Spirit makes the unity in the Church."[60]

The presence of the Spirit outside of the Body of Christ would contradict St. Thomas's anthropology: For him, unlike all authors before him and most after him, the human person is one substance composed of body and soul, and not two substances, much less one substance that only comprises either the soul or (oddly enough) the body.[61] Furthermore, as I have already said, God acts in his relation to all creatures according to

---

57 Cf. *Expositio in Symbolum Apostolorum*, 10: "Sicut in corpore naturali operatio unius membri cedit in bonum totius corporis, ita in corpore spirituali, scilicet Ecclesia. Et quia omnes fideles sunt unum corpus, bonum unius alteri communicatur. Apostolus, Rom. XII, 5: singuli autem alter alterius membra. Unde et inter alia credenda quae tradiderunt apostoli, est quod communio bonorum sit in Ecclesia; et hoc est quod dicitur, sanctorum communionem. Inter alia vero membra Ecclesiae, principale membrum est Christus, quia est caput. Ephes. I, 22–23: ipsum dedit caput super omnem Ecclesiam, quae est corpus ipsius. Bonum ergo Christi communicatur omnibus Christianis, sicut virtus capitis omnibus membris; et haec communicatio fit per sacramenta Ecclesiae, in quibus operatur virtus passionis Christi, quae operatur ad conferendam gratiam in remissionem peccatorum. . . . Sic ergo per hanc communionem consequimur duo: unum scilicet quod meritum Christi communicatur omnibus; aliud quod bonum unius communicatur alteri."

58 Cf. *ST* III, q. 48, a. 2, ad 1: "The head and members are as one mystic person [caput et membra sunt quasi una persona mystica]; and therefore Christ's satisfaction belongs to all the faithful as being his members. Also, in so far as any two men are one in charity, the one can atone for the other as shall be shown later." Cf. *ST* III, q. 15, a. 1, ad 1; q. 19, a. 4.

59 Cf. *ST* II–II, q. 183, a. 2, ad 3: "Just as in the natural body the various members are held together in unity by the power of the quickening spirit, and are dissociated from one another as soon as that spirit departs, so too in the Church's body the peace of the various members is preserved by the power of the Holy Spirit, Who quickens the body of the Church [in corpore Ecclesiae conservatur pax diversorum membrorum virtute spiritus sancti, qui corpus Ecclesiae vivificat], as stated in Jn. 6:64. . . ."

60 "[S]i quis spiritum christi non habet, hic non est eius. Nam unitas spiritus sancti facit in ecclesia unitatem" (*In Ioan.,* cap. 1, lect. 10).

61 Cf. *SCG* II, ch. 69. Even when—after death—the soul is separated from the body, it keeps a natural inclination to the union with the body, cf. *ST* I, q. 76, a. 1, ad 6. Thomas is isolated in this position; cf. A. Capizzi, "Anima e corpo nel XIII secolo," *Giornale Critico della Filosofia Italiana* (1951), 24–42, 205–27.

their nature: He does not act in his relation to the human community in a way that would contradict the nature of all human individuals.

Cardinal Journet, whose ecclesiology Fr. Congar described as the "application of St. Thomas's principles,"[62] sees in the Church two souls, one depending on the other. The Holy Spirit, "Uncreated Soul," gives to the Church a created soul, which is its charity; in its full state, this charity is "oriented" by the teaching of the Church and made "conformed to Christ" by the sacraments.[63] He strictly maintains that "where the created soul of the Church is, there is her body; conversely, where the body of the Church is, there is her soul."[64] This is his principle of the "coextensivity" of body and soul that, in my view, shows the link between Thomas's anthropology and ecclesiology, precisely because God relates to human beings according to their nature.[65] The key to that unity between

---

62 Journet's ecclesiology "apparaît comme la mise en œuvre même de la synthèse de saint Thomas" (Yves M.-J. Congar, *Esquisses du mystère de l'Eglise* [Paris: Cerf, 1953], 7).

63 Cf. Charles Journet, *L'Eglise du Verbe Incarné,* vol. 3 (Saint-Maurice: Saint-Augustin, 2000), 1434 (ed. 1951, vol.2, 872): "Si la Trinité veut se faire une demeure vivante au milieu de ses créatures, si l'Esprit saint veut devenir le principe, plus encore l'hôte et la forme incréée de l'Eglise, bref son Ame incréée, il faudra qu'il revête les hommes, pour les préparer à de si hautes destinées, de dons spirituels qui seront comme un épanchement de la grâce capitale déposée dans la sainte âme du Christ, tête de l'Eglise, à savoir de sa puissance sacerdotale, de sa grâce, de sa vérité, et qui deviendront les éléments, soit présupposés, soit constitutifs, de l'âme créée de l'Eglise; ce sont, nous l'avons dit, les caractères sacramentels, les grâces sacramentelles, et enfin la droite orientation juridictionnelle en tant qu'émanant des pouvoirs juridictionnels et en tant que reçue dans le cœur des fidèles. Bref, pour tout résumer en un mot, il faudra que l'Esprit saint revête les hommes de la charité en tant qu'elle est sacramentelle et orientée. Voilà, en effet, l'âme créée indivise de l'Eglise. Cette âme descend vers les hommes. Elle s'incarne en eux. Elle les transforme intérieurement. Les vertus permanentes et les pouvoirs secrets qu'elle leur confère seront pour eux le principe d'une nouvelle manière d'agir, d'œuvrer. Dès lors, un changement se produira jusque dans leur condition et leur comportement extérieurs. L'ensemble de ces manifestations extérieures, voilà le corps de l'Eglise."

64 "Où est l'âme créée de l'Eglise, là est son corps; inversement, où est le corps de l'Eglise, là est son âme" (Charles Journet, *L'Eglise du Verbe Incarné,* vol. 2 (Saint-Maurice: Saint Augustin, 1999), 43 (ed. 1951, vol. 2, xxxiv).

65 I have presented the topic in "La coexistence de l'âme et du corps en philosophie et en ecclésiologie," *Nova et Vetera* 73 (1998): 23–33. Some interpreters of St. Thomas think that the Head of the Church has some action that does not strictly build the Body; cf. Yves M.-J. Congar, OP, "Vision de l'Eglise chez Thomas d'Aquin," *Revue des Sciences Philosophiques et Théologiques* 62 (1978): 539: "La vérité du Christ-Tête dépasse les limites de l'Eglise. Ce ne sont pas des énoncés d'ecclésiologie, mais de christologie." I agree with Jean-Pierre Torrell, OP, when he

the body and soul of the Church is that any action of the Spirit, any act of charity, even by non-baptized, must have some visibility: "[I]t is impossible, either that the soul of the Church, as received in men . . . does not work to reveal outside the body of the Church, or that the body of the Church can appear where is not her soul."[66] Perhaps most or all us, because of our insufficient holiness, will not be able to discern this visibility, which will be for us a kind of "invisible visibility."[67]

Who Does Belong to the Church?

Contemporary Christians will wonder: Does this ecclesiology mean that only people who are clearly Christians, or even Catholics, can be saved? At least since the time of Pius IX,[68] this is not the teaching of the Church. Neither is it Thomas's teaching, since for him all human beings belong, in a way, to the Church. The understanding of the Church, which derives from St. Robert Bellarmine, that "the Church is an assembly of men, as visible and palpable as the assembly of the Roman people, or the Kingdom of France, or the Republic of the Venetians,"[69] popularized by the Counter-Reformation, leads to a deep misunderstanding of what Church membership could mean.

On first glance Thomas and Bellarmine seem to have similar views, because of the fundamental importance of the sacraments in Thomas's

---

comments on Congar's opinion: "Cette affirmation est pour le moins étonnante, et je doute que S. Thomas l'eût reprise à son compte" ("Yves Congar et l'ecclésiologie de saint Thomas d'Aquin," *Revue des Sciences Philosophiques et Théologiques* 82 [1998]: 218–19).

66 "[I]l est impossible, ou bien que l'âme de l'Eglise, en tant que reçue dans les hommes . . . ne travaille pas à faire apparaître au-dehors le corps de l'Eglise, ou bien que le corps de l'Eglise puisse apparaître là où n'est pas son âme" (Charles Journet, *L'Eglise du Verbe Incarné,* vol. 3 [Saint-Maurice: Saint Augustin, 2000], 1553; ed. 1951, vol. 2, 950).

67 Cf. Charles Journet, *L'Eglise du Verbe Incarné,* vol. 3, 1557–58; ed. 1951, vol. 2, 953: "Où paraît quelque chose de l'âme de l'Eglise, paraît quelque chose du corps de l'Eglise. Les justes qui appartiennent à L'Eglise par le désir de leur charité, voto, mentaliter, sans encore lui appartenir de manière complète, *re, corporaliter,* tendent, même sans le remarquer, à extérioriser leur désir. Toutefois le sens véritable de ce désir demeurant souvent caché aux yeux et inaperçu d'eux-mêmes, on pourra parler, à propos de ces justes, d'appartenance invisible à l'Eglise visible."

68 Cf. Pius IX, Allocution *Singulari Quadam,* in Consistorio Secreto, 9.12.1854; Encyclical *Quanto conficiamur moerere,* 10th August 1863, Denz. 2865–66.

69 "Ecclesia enim est coetus hominum ita visibilis et palpabilis, ut est coetus populi romani, vel regnum Galliae, aut respublica Venetorum" (St. Robert Bellarmine, SJ, *De controversiis christianae fidei adversus hujus temporis haereticos,* II, lib. 3, *De Ecclesia militante,* caput II [Naples: Josephum Giuliano, 1857], tomus II, 75).

ecclesiology, based on the fact that "through the sacraments of the New Law man is incorporated with Christ."[70] A logical conclusion follows: "[I]t is clear that no one can obtain salvation but through Christ. . . . Consequently it is clear that all are bound to be baptized: and that without Baptism there is no salvation for men."[71] The similarity between Thomas's ecclesiology and the so-called "Bellarminian" ecclesiology (which is rather unfair to Bellarmine), however, is limited by Thomas's broader understanding of the Church: Despite the importance of the sacraments, "God did not so limit His power to the law of the sacraments."[72] God can give by other means the grace that is "normally" given by the actual sacraments. Someone can receive the grace of baptism by desire, without receiving it actually: "Those who are unbaptized, though not actually in the Church, are in the Church potentially. And this potentiality is rooted in two things—first and principally, in the power of Christ, which is sufficient for the salvation of the whole human race; secondly, in free-will."[73] The salvation obtained for all is not unrelated to baptism, since this is a baptism that can be obtained by the right orientation of the free will: "He who is not baptized, though he belongs not to the Church either in reality or sacramentally, can nevertheless belong to her in intention and by similarity of action *[potest tamen ad eam pertinere intentione et similitudine actus]*, namely, in so far as he intends to do what the Church does, and in baptizing observes the Church's form, and thus acts as the minister of Christ, Who did not confine His power to those that are baptized, as neither did He to the sacraments."[74] The same applies to confirmation[75]

70 *ST* III, q. 62, a. 1.

71 *ST* III, q. 68, a. 1. Cf. III, q. 69, a. 5: "By Baptism man is born again unto the spiritual life, which is proper to the faithful of Christ, as the Apostle says (Gal 2:20): 'And that I live now in the flesh; I live in the faith of the Son of God.' Now life is only in those members that are united to the head, from which they derive sense and movement. And therefore it follows of necessity that by Baptism man is incorporated in Christ, as one of His members." About the Church and sacraments according to Aquinas, cf. Matthew Levering, *Christ's Fulfillment of Torah and Temple: Salvation according to Thomas Aquinas* (Notre Dame, IN: University of Notre Dame Press, 2002), 121–25.

72 *ST* III, q. 27, a. 1, ad 2.

73 *ST* III, q. 8, a. 3, ad 1.

74 *ST* III, q. 67, a. 5, ad 2.

75 Cf. *ST* III, q. 72, a. 6, ad 1: "The Divine power is not confined to the sacraments. Hence man can receive spiritual strength to confess the Faith of Christ publicly, without receiving the sacrament of Confirmation: just as he can also receive remission of sins without Baptism. Yet, just as none receive the effect of Baptism without the desire of Baptism; so none receive the effect of Confirmation, without the desire of Confirmation. And man can have this even before receiving Baptism."

and penance.[76] To be complete, one must add that for Thomas only adults, and not children, can receive the sacrament by desire[77] (some will later suggest that the desire of the parents can obtain the grace of baptism). The case of the Eucharist is more complex, although in the same line, but I do not need to develop it here.[78]

For Thomas, then, the idea of salvation outside the Church, or the idea of the Spirit working outside the Body of Christ would contradict the basic principles of his ecclesiology, of his Christology (Christ is the only

---

[76] Cf. *ST* III, q. 86, a. 2: "It is impossible for a mortal actual sin to be pardoned without penance, if we speak of penance as a virtue. . . . But the sacrament of Penance . . . is perfected by the priestly office of binding and loosing, without which God can forgive sins, even as Christ pardoned the adulterous woman, as related in Jn 8, and the woman that was a sinner, as related in Luke vii, whose sins, however, He did not forgive without the virtue of penance: for as Gregory states (Hom. xxxiii in Evang.), 'He drew inwardly by grace,' i.e,. by penance, 'her whom He received outwardly by His mercy.' "

[77] Cf. *ST* III, q. 73, a. 3: "[B]y Baptism a man is ordained to the eucharist, and therefore from the fact of children being baptized, they are destined by the Church to the eucharist; and just as they believe through the Church's faith, so they desire the eucharist through the Church's intention, and, as a result, receive its reality. But they are not disposed for Baptism by any previous sacrament, and consequently before receiving Baptism, in no way have they Baptism in desire; but adults alone have: consequently, they cannot have the reality of the sacrament without receiving the sacrament itself."

[78] The basic element is that "the reality of the sacrament is the unity of the mystical body, without which there can be no salvation; for there is no entering into salvation outside the Church *[res sacramenti est unitas corporis mystici, sine qua non potest esse salus, nulli enim patet aditus salutis extra Ecclesiam]*, just as in the time of the deluge there was none outside the Ark, which denotes the Church, according to 1 Pt 3:20,21. And it has been said above, that before receiving a sacrament, the reality of the sacrament can be had through the very desire of receiving the sacrament. Accordingly, before actual reception of this sacrament, a man can obtain salvation through the desire of receiving it, just as he can before Baptism through the desire of Baptism" (*ST* III, q. 73, a. 3). But in fact the desire for the Eucharist comes from baptism (cf. III, q. 73, a. 3), and for that reason it does not seem that for Thomas a non-baptized person can normally have the real desire for the eucharist, although he does not exclude it completely: although "the non-baptized are not to be allowed even to see this sacrament" (III, q. 80, a. 4, ad 4), if it were to happen that an unbeliever receives the eucharist, he could "perchance" have a sufficient intention to receive it sacramentally (cf. III, q. 80, a. 3, ad 2). The reception—actual or by desire—of the Eucharist does not seem to be indispensable for salvation, because "Baptism is the beginning of the spiritual life, and the door of the sacraments; whereas the eucharist is, as it were, the consummation of the spiritual life, and the end of all the sacraments. . . . Consequently, the reception of Baptism is necessary for starting the spiritual life, while the receiving of the eucharist is requisite for its consummation" (III, q. 73, a. 3).

mediator), and of his theology of the Trinity (the Spirit proceeds from the Father and the Son eternally and temporally). Yet, one risks misunderstanding his texts if one reads them with the restricted ecclesiological vocabulary inherited from the Counter-Reformation.

Church Unity and Church Membership According to John Paul II

John Paul II's teaching on the Body of Christ focused on the sacraments: "Incorporation into Christ, which is brought about by Baptism, is constantly renewed and consolidated by sharing in the Eucharistic Sacrifice."[79] He normally understood the sacraments in the light of their actual reception. John Pauls basic understanding of the Body of Christ thus focused on what Thomas would consider a more or less full membership to the Body of Christ, although the pope also said that all human beings belong to or are somehow ordained to the Church,[80] which echoes Aquinas. Without being a "Bellarminian,"[81] John Paul II usually spoke about the Church in her "normal" sacramental fullness. In these terms, it is not easy to address the question of the salvation of non-baptized people.

The encyclical *Redemptoris Missio* deals with this question. It affirms first of all that Christ is the only Saviour, which is also the key to Thomas's

---

79 *Ecclesia de Eucharistia,* §22. Cf. *Dominum et Vivificantem*, §61: "This new coming of Christ by the power of the Holy Spirit, and his constant presence and action in the spiritual life are accomplished in the sacramental reality. In this reality, Christ, who has gone away in his visible humanity, comes, is present and acts in the Church in such an intimate way as to make it his own Body. As such, the Church lives, works and grows 'to the close of the age.' All this happens through the power of the Holy Spirit"; *Veritatis Splendor,* §21: "Having become one with Christ, the Christian *becomes a member of his Body, which is the Church* (cf. Cor 12:13, 27). By the work of the Spirit, Baptism radically configures the faithful to Christ in the Paschal Mystery of death and resurrection; it 'clothes him' in Christ (cf. Gal 3:27): 'Let us rejoice and give thanks', exclaims Saint Augustine speaking to the baptized, 'for we have become not only Christians, but Christ. . . . Marvel and rejoice: we have become Christ!' (In *Iohannis Evangelium Tractatus*, 21, 8: CCL 36, 216)."

80 Cf. *Redemptoris Missio*, §9 (which quotes *Lumen Gentium*, §13): "To this catholic unity of the people of God, therefore, . . . all are called, and they belong to it or are ordered to it in various ways, whether they be Catholic faithful or others who believe in Christ or finally all people everywhere who by the grace of God are called to salvation."

81 He reacts against a contemporary equivalent of it, a reduction of the Church to a human society, which human sciences could fully study (cf. *Redemptor Hominis*, §21), and he insists on the necessary unity of body and soul in the human person (cf. *Veritatis Splendor*, §49), without connecting that to ecclesiology.

ecclesiology.[82] It does not affirm, however, that only those who are explicitly Christians can be saved, since salvation is offered to all. Thus we are confronted with what seems to be a paradox: "It is necessary to keep these two truths together, namely, the real possibility of salvation in Christ for all mankind and the necessity of the Church for salvation."[83] To solve the paradox John Paul distinguished between explicit and implicit membership to the Church:

> The universality of salvation means that it is granted not only to those who explicitly believe in Christ and have entered the Church. Since salvation is offered to all, it must be made concretely available to all. But it is clear that today, as in the past, many people do not have an opportunity to come to know or accept the gospel revelation or to enter the Church. . . . For such people salvation in Christ is accessible by virtue of a grace which, while having a mysterious relationship to the Church, does not make them formally part of the Church but enlightens them in a way which is accommodated to their spiritual and material situation. This grace comes from Christ; it is the result of his Sacrifice and is communicated by the Holy Spirit. It enables each person to attain salvation through his or her free cooperation.[84]

All elements of this passage are important: Non-explicit Christians, who had no real opportunity to meet or understand the Gospel, can be saved, but always under two conditions: (1) salvation occurs through a grace that comes from Christ, is communicated by the Spirit, and is related to the Church, and (2) this process involves some free cooperation on their part.

What I just called an "implicit" membership to the Church could also be expressed in terms of visibility, as John Paul did, quoting Vatican II: "The same Dogmatic Constitution listed at length 'the elements of sanctification and truth' which in various ways are present and operative beyond the visible boundaries of the Catholic Church."[85] Knowing as we do the painful divisions among the baptized, that were not so present in the reality and

---

[82] Cf. *Redemptoris Missio*, §5: " '[T]here is no other name under heaven given among men by which we must be saved' (Acts 4:10, 12). . . . No one, therefore, can enter into communion with God except through Christ, by the working of the Holy Spirit. Christ's one, universal mediation, far from being an obstacle on the journey toward God, is the way established by God himself, a fact of which Christ is fully aware. Although participated forms of mediation of different kinds and degrees are not excluded, they acquire meaning and value *only* from Christ's own mediation, and they cannot be understood as parallel or complementary to his."

[83] *Redemptoris Missio,* §9.

[84] Ibid., §10.

[85] *Ut Unum Sint,* §12.

in the consciousness of the thirteenth century, we accept that the "visible boundaries" of the Roman Catholic Church are not equivalent to the visibility of the Church.[86] This leads to more delicate questions.

The relationship between the Holy Spirit and the Church is especially delicate. The first principle is the link between Christ and the Spirit: "[I]n the Holy Spirit-Paraclete, who in the mystery and action of the Church unceasingly continues the historical presence on earth of the Redeemer and his saving work, the glory of Christ shines forth."[87] The Spirit acts in Christ's life and then in continuity with him: "This is the same Spirit who was at work in the Incarnation and in the life, death and resurrection of Jesus, and who is at work in the Church. He is therefore not an alternative to Christ, nor does he fill a sort of void which is sometimes suggested as existing between Christ and the Logos. Whatever the Spirit brings about in human hearts and in the history of peoples, in cultures and religions serves as a preparation for the Gospel and can only be understood in reference to Christ."[88] The fact that the Spirit's action is always in continuity with Christ's action does not prevent it from being universal: He can reach every heart,[89] including the hearts of those who are not Christians: In them he prepares and "begins" the mission.[90]

This indispensable link between Christ and the Holy Spirit is the basis for any understanding of the relationship between the Spirit and the Church: He unifies her in love,[91] renews her,[92] helps her deepen Reve-

[86] Cf. *Ut Unum Sint,* §13: "[I]t is not that beyond the boundaries of the Catholic community there is an ecclesial vacuum." This is especially true of the Eastern Churches, in which the Catholic Church acknowledges all sacraments; cf. *Ut Unum Sint,* §50.

[87] *Dominum et Vivificantem,* §7.

[88] *Redemptoris Missio,* §29.

[89] Cf. Ibid., §28: "The Spirit manifests himself in a special way in the Church and in her members. Nevertheless, his presence and activity are universal, limited neither by space nor time. The Second Vatican Council recalls that the Spirit is at work in the heart of every person, through the 'seeds of the Word,' to be found in human initiatives—including religious ones—and in mankind's efforts to attain truth, goodness and God himself."

[90] Cf. Ibid., §45: "In proclaiming Christ to non-Christians, the missionary is convinced that, through the working of the Spirit, there already exists in individuals and peoples an expectation, even if an unconscious one, of knowing the truth about God, about man, and about how we are to be set free from sin and death."

[91] Cf. *Evangelium Vitae,* §76: "[T]he Spirit . . . builds up communion in love creates between us a new fraternity and solidarity, a true reflection of the mystery of mutual self-giving and receiving proper to the Most Holy Trinity."

[92] Cf. *Fidei Depositum,* §4: "May it *[Catechism of the Catholic Church]* serve the renewal to which the Holy Spirit ceaselessly calls the Church of God, the Body of Christ, on her pilgrimage to the undiminished light of the kingdom!"

lation,[93] and gives her the missionary impulse.[94] It also helps interpret some sentences where John Paul spoke—quoting Vatican II—about "the Holy Spirit's activity also 'outside the visible body of the Church' "[95] or about "not excluding the action of Christ and the Spirit outside the Church's visible boundaries."[96] These statements are not meant to deny the necessary link between any action of the Spirit and the Church,[97] because that would undermine the link between the Spirit and Christ.

Still, on this point it would be difficult not to see a dissimilarity between Aquinas and some—few—texts by John Paul II: To speak about the Spirit acting outside the Church in any way, even taking into consideration the distinction between visible and invisible Church, cannot be expressed in Thomas's ecclesiology, because for him it would contradict both the link between the Head and Body of the Church and his conviction of a link between anthropology and divine action with human beings. Certainly John Paul II agreed with these two principles, and there is no real difference between him and Aquinas in this regard. The differences are on two levels:

1. The vocabulary: The pope must use a vocabulary that contemporary readers understand, and most contemporary readers still understand by "Church" simply some kind of visible society. To teach to them a broader understanding of the Church remains a task that has been well begun since Vatican II.

2. The consciousness of the fact that many do not belong to the Catholic Church as such, among whom many are baptized. This fact requires some distinctions between different levels of influence of Christ and of the Spirit.

---

93 Cf. *Fides et Ratio*, §11: "[B]y the unceasing action of the Holy Spirit (cf. Jn 16:13) the contents of revealed truth may find their full expression."

94 Cf. *Redemptoris Missio*, §21: *"The Holy Spirit is indeed the principal agent of the whole of the Church's mission."* The same encyclical says that "love, which has been and remains the driving force of mission . . ." (*Redemptoris Missio*, §60). There is therefore at least a real parallel between the action of the Spirit and love.

95 *Dominum et Vivificantem*, §53.

96 *Redemptoris Missio*, §18.

97 Cf. one of the quoted sentences in its context: "The result is a unique and special relationship which, while not excluding the action of Christ and the Spirit outside the Church's visible boundaries, confers upon her a specific and necessary role" (*Redemptoris Missio*, §18). Cf. *Redemptoris Missio*, §29: "[T]he universal activity of the Spirit is not to be separated from his particular activity within the body of Christ, which is the Church."

Church Authority and the Possibility of the Proclamation of the Faith

Structure of Faith and Infallibility in the Thomistic School

All Christians should agree that the Church must preach the faith. But how is it to be done? And above all: What is the role of the Church and of her authority in preaching the faith? This issue is at the heart of ecumenical dialogue. I think that Thomas and the Thomistic school can give an important contribution to theology in this field.

One important element of the question of preaching faith is the authority of the pope. I think that Thomas's contribution to that particular question is due to his systematic approach to the logic of Christian faith.

Several theologians involved in the dialogue about the ministry of the successor of Peter have noticed that the solution cannot be found in historical studies. The Orthodox Metropolitan of Pergamon, John Zizioulas, is especially clear: "If there is a necessity for the primacy of the Bishop of Rome this could not be because history demands it, for even if history demanded it (which is in my view doubtful, to say the least) it would not make a necessary thing for the Church's *esse*. The same thing would have to be said if the reasons offered for such a primacy were to be practical and utilitarian. . . . The primacy of the Bishop of Rome has to be theologically justified or else be ignored altogether."[98] Eminent theologians such as John Henry Newman,[99] Charles Journet,[100] and Joseph Ratzinger[101] have insisted on the fact that history cannot provide

---

[98] Metropolitan John of Pergamon (Zizioulas), "Primacy in the Church: An Orthodox Approach," in James F. Puglisi, SA, ed., *Petrine Ministry and the Unity of the Church. Toward a Patient and Fraternal Dialogue* (Collegeville, MN: The Liturgical Press, 1999), 123.

[99] Cf. John Henry Newman, *Certain Difficulties Felt by Anglicans in Catholic Teaching,* In a Letter addressed to the Rev. E. B. Pusey, DD, on occasion of his Eirenicon of 1864; and in a Letter addressed to the Duke of Norfolk, on occasion of Mr. Gladstone's Expostulation of 1874, Vol. II. (London: Longman, Green, and Co., 1900), 312: "For myself, I would simply confess that no doctrine of the Church can be rigorously proved by historical evidence: but at the same time that no doctrine can be simply disproved by it."

[100] Cf. Charles Journet, *What is dogma?* (London: Burns & Oates, 1964), 57: "God helps us, and to suppose that we can rediscover, by means of purely human disciplines: archaeology, philology, exegesis, history of religions, contemporary philosophies, the meaning of 'things no eye has seen, no ear has heard, no human heart conceived, the welcome God has prepared for those who love him' (1 Cor 2:9)."

[101] Cf. Joseph Ratzinger, "Discorso in apertura del Simposio," in *Il primato del successore di Pietro* (Rome: Libreria Editrice Vaticana, 1998), 17: "Indubbiamente è vero che la storia come tale non può fornire una certezza apodittica della verità di

the necessary certitude.[102] That makes a systematic approach at least a necessary complement to historical research.

Thomas studies systematically the conditions for faith, in a passage that summarizes the method of proclaiming the faith that is demonstrated in the New Testament:

> Two things are requisite for faith. First, that the things which are of faith should be proposed to man: this is necessary in order that man believe anything explicitly. The second thing requisite for faith is the assent of the believer to the things which are proposed to him. Accordingly, as regards the first of these, faith must needs be from God. Because those things which are of faith surpass human reason, hence they do not come to man's knowledge, unless God reveal them. To some, indeed, they are revealed by God immediately, as those things which were revealed to the apostles and prophets, while to some they are proposed by God in sending preachers of the faith.[103]

In the "normal" Christian economy the proposal of faith arrives to individuals through some disciples of Christ, through the Church. This intervention of the disciples also comes from the fact that the Church must always explain faith with new words, throughout the centuries.[104] And human intervention in the process of faith can pose a problem, which is well described by one of the most important commentators of Thomas, Cardinal Cajetan:[105]

> Two things interact in faith . . . namely [first] the assent and [second] the proposition and explanation of the things which must be believed; on the point of view of the assent, faith depends only on God as agent, object end and rule. But on the point of view of the proposition of the

---

fede"; 18: "[T]ale collaborazione [tra storia e teologia] esige che la questione della valutazione dottrinale dei dati storici sia fatta alla luce della Tradizione, come luogo e criterio della coscienza veritativa della fede ecclesiale."

102 At least history should be read theologically; cf. Hermann J. Pottmeyer, article "Bischof," *Lexikon für Theologie und Kirche*, Vol. 2 (Freiburg im Breslau: Herder, 1994 [3rd ed.]), col. 484–85: "Die Ursachen, die zur Entwicklung und Durchsetzung des Monepiskopats führten, werden von der historischen Forschung unterschiedlich gewichtet. Übereinstimmung besteht darüber, daß es sich um ein Bündel von Ursachen handelt. . . . Während die Historiker die vielfältige Bedingtheit der Entwicklung sieht, erblickt der Glaube im historischen Verlauf das Ergebnis der Führung Gottes."

103 *ST* II–II, q. 6, a. 1.

104 Cf., *ST* I, q. 29, a. 3, ad 1.

105 Thomas De Vio, 1469–1534, Master of the Order of Preachers (1508–1518), Cardinal in 1517, met Luther in 1518.

> things to be believed, it can depend on angels and human beings, through whom God proposes this or that to be believed; on this point of view, "faith comes from hearing the word of God," as Rom. 10 says. And so that no error might appear in the proposal or explanation of things to believe, the Holy Spirit provided a created rule, which is the sense and the doctrine of the Church, so that the authority of the Church is the infallible rule of the proposition and explanation of things which must be believed by faith. Therefore, two infallible rules concur to faith, namely divine revelation and the authority of the Church; there is between them this difference: divine revelation is the formal reason of the object of faith, and the authority of the Church is the minister of the object of faith.[106]

John of St. Thomas adds that there are always controversies on the meaning of Scripture, which sometimes have an impact on faith, and that in such cases the authority to decide on the correct interpretation cannot be given to all: The contoversy would just go on and faith would be uncertain.[107] He adds that to give the power of judging infallibly to more than one person (e.g., some important bishops in different parts of the world) would leave intact the question of who can judge if they disagree.[108] John of St. Thomas is perfectly in line with St. Thomas, who argues for the

106 "Constat autem quod, cum ad fidem concurrant duo, ut infra patet, scilicet assensus et propositio atque explicatio credendorum, fides ex parte assensus a solo Deo dependet ut agente, obiecto, fine et regula. Ex parte autem propositionis credendorum potest dependere ab angelis et hominibus, mediantibus quibus Deus proponit haec vel illa esse credenda: ex hac enim parte 'fides ex auditu est verbi Dei', ut dicitur ad Rom. X. Et propterea quoad proponendum et explicandum credenda, ne possit accidere error, providit Spiritus Sanctus de infallibili regula creata, sensu scilicet et doctrina Ecclesiae: ita quod auctoritas Ecclesiae est infallibilis regula proponendi et explicandi ea quae sunt fide tenenda. Unde, duabus concurrentibus ad fidem infallibilibus regulis, scilicet revelatione divina et auctoritate Ecclesiae, inter eas tanta est differentia quod revelatio divina est ratio formalis obiecti fidei, auctoritas autem Ecclesiae est ministra obiecti fidei" (Cajetan, In *ST.,* II–II, q. 1, a. 1, no. X; my translation).

107 Cf. John of St. Thomas, *In Iam,* q. 1, disp. I, a. 3; in Ioannes a Santo Thomas, *Cursus theologicus,* In Summam theologicam D. Thomae, Nova editio, Tomus primus, in Primae Partis Quaestiones I–VII (Paris:Vivès, 1883), 433: "Non potest autem quilibet hoc declarare resolutorie determinando, et infallibiliter, cum de hoc ipso sit tota controversia, an contineatur in Scriptura id quod Ecclesia sic proponit et declarat, et quidam negent, alii affirment, unde si quilibet posset hoc declarare, quilibet pro sua parte pronuntiaret, et manerent omnes in eadem confusione; ergo oportet, quod ipsa declaratio, et propositio Ecclesiae careat omni suspicione, et fallibilitate, alias semper dubitaremus, an ita contineatur in Scriptura." My translation.

108 Cf. *In Iiam–IIae*, qq. 1–7, disp. I, a. 3 , in *Cursus theologicus,* Tomus septimus, in Secundam Secundae (1886), 185: "XVIII . . . si autem in his quae sunt de substantia

supreme authority of one in the Church of the earth as in the Church of Heaven, for the sake of the common good and of peace.[109] Still, Thomas views the power of the pope within the context of the infallibility of the whole Church,[110] and as limited by the nature of some objects.[111] Even though for Thomas the pope has a universal immediate jurisdiction, he should not use it in a way that would destroy the authority of the local bishops.[112] Of course the ministry of the pope should not be considered only as a way of solving problems in the Church. Infallibility is only one aspect of his ministry, but it is a very contentious one among Christians, and such an issue cannot be fully resolved with historical or even biblical arguments. The systematic approach of the Thomistic School, founded on the New Testament, is an important contribution.[113]

To summarize the approach of Thomas and his school:

1. because God wants it, faith normally requires human preachers;
2. this preaching requires new expressions of the same faith through the centuries;
3. these human preachers have different interpretations of Scripture;
4. therefore God has given to the Church an infallible authority, so that faith remains certain;

---

religionis omnes illae supremae potestates deberent eodem modo convenire, et eodem modo regere, alias si unus aliter se haberet quam alter, periret unitas fidei, et religionis Ecclesiae, multo melius id efficitur per unum."

109 Cf. *SCG*, IV, ch. 76.

110 Cf. *ST* III, q. 72, a. 12, which speaks about the infallibility of the Church as such.

111 Above all, "nec Papa nec aliquis mortalium potest ecclesiasticam hierarchiam divinitus ordinatam immutare aut eversare" (*Contra impugnantes,* cap. 4, §4, ed. Leon. vol. 41, A 72, l. 311–313; cf. *ST* III, q. 62, aa. 2 and 4); for Thomas, the argument is more theological than juridical, cf. *ST* II–II, q. 88, a. 11: "[T]he Pope cannot make a man who has made his religious profession cease to be a religious, although certain jurists have ignorantly held the contrary."

112 Cf. *Contra impugnantes*, cap. 4, §13, ed. Leon. vol. 41, l.1242–1249: "Quod autem Papa universalem pontificem se prohibet nominari, non hoc ideo est quia ipse non habeat auctoritatem immediatam et plenam in qualibet ecclesia; sed quia non praeficitur cuilibet particulari ecclesiae ut proprius et specialis illius ecclesiae rector, sic enim cessarent omnium aliorum pontificum potestates."

113 About this topic cf. Yves M.-J. Congar, OP, "Saint Thomas Aquinas and the Infallibility of the Papal Magisterium (*ST* II–II, q. 1, a. 10)," *The Thomist* 38 (1974): 81–105; Serge-Thomas Bonino, OP, "La place du pape dans l'Eglise selon saint Thomas d'Aquin," *Revue Thomiste* 86 (1986): 392–422; idem, "Le rôle des apôtres dans la communication de la Révélation selon la Lectura super Ioannem de saint Thomas d'Aquin," *Bulletin de Littérature Ecclésiastique* 103 (2002): 317–50; Ulrich Horst, OP, *Papst-Konzil—Unfehlbarkeit. Die Ekklesiologie der Summenkommentare von Cajetan bis Billuart* (Mainz: Matthias-Grünewald, 1978).

5. this authority, at the supreme level, is suitably given to one only, since otherwise the risk of division would remain.

The argument provides at least some theological probability for the ministry of the pope as the Catholic Church professes it, whereas any exegetical or historical argument could not reach such a level of probability. Beyond this point, only faith gives the ultimate answer.

The Teaching Authority of the Church According to John Paul II

When John Paul II spoke about the ministry of the person called "to occupy the episcopal see that once belonged to Peter in this city of Rome,"[114] he did not limit himself—nor did Thomas—to discussing the teaching authority exercised on controversial points of doctrine. He also sometimes added a personal touch due to the fact that he was the one then actively exercising this ministry.[115] Clearly he insisted more on collegiality than Thomas did, due to the relative rediscovery sanctioned by Vatican II.[116] He also spoke of his ministry in the context of ecumenical dialogue,[117] which was also new, compared to the thirteenth century. Beyond such differences, can we find in the theology of John Paul II the basic lines of Thomistic theology that I have just explained? Instead of developing the whole teaching of John Paul II on this question, I shall merely show that the five main arguments used by the Thomistic School in favor of the papal ministry were also present in John Paul II.

1. First of all, to preach faith is the duty of Christians: "No believer in Christ, no institution of the Church can avoid this supreme duty: to proclaim Christ to all peoples."[118]

---

114 *Slavorum Apostoli,* §28.

115 Cf. *Ut Unum Sint,* §4: "This is a specific duty of the Bishop of Rome as the Successor of the Apostle Peter. I carry out this duty with the profound conviction that I am obeying the Lord, and with a clear sense of my own human frailty"; *Ut Unum Sint,* §91: "It is important to note how the weakness of Peter and of Paul clearly shows that the Church is founded upon the infinite power of grace (cf. Mt 16:17; 2 Cor 12:7–10). Peter, immediately after receiving his mission, is rebuked with unusual severity by Christ, who tells him: 'You are a hindrance to me' (Mt 16:23)."

116 Cf. *Redemptor Hominis*, §5; *Apostolos suos,* §§1–2, 9–10; *Evangelium Vitae,* §5; *Ut Unum Sint,* §94.

117 Cf. *Ut Unum Sint,* §4: "In our ecumenical age, marked by the Second Vatican Council, the mission of the Bishop of Rome is particularly directed to recalling the need for full communion among Christ's disciples."

118 *Redemptoris Missio,* §3; cf. *Evangelium Vitae*, §101: " 'We are writing you this that our joy may be complete' (1 Jn 1:4). The revelation of the Gospel of life is given

2. The Church must guard the deposit of faith,[119] and such a proclamation always requires a "deeper investigation into the truths of faith and morals,"[120] "a deeper insight into Revelation and of an understanding in the light of faith of new historical and cultural situations,"[121] new theological explanations[122] (with the help of reason),[123] and the interpretation of the signs of the times.[124] This has always applied to the necessities of inculturation.[125]

---

to us as a good to be shared with all people: so that all men and women may have fellowship with us and with the Trinity (cf. 1 Jn 1:3). Our own joy would not be complete if we failed to share this Gospel with others but kept it only for ourselves."

119 Cf. *Fidei Depositum*, Introduction: "Guarding the deposit of faith is the mission which the Lord has entrusted to his Church and which she fulfils in every age."

120 *Ad tuendam fidem,* §1.

121 *Veritatis Splendor,* §27.

122 Cf. *Sapientia Christiana*, §III: "From this assiduous contact with reality, theologians are also encouraged to seek a more suitable way of communicating doctrine to their contemporaries working in other various fields of knowledge, for 'the deposit of faith, or the truths contained in our venerable doctrine, is one thing; quite another is the way in which these truths are formulated, while preserving the same sense and meaning.' "

123 Cf. *Fides et Ratio*, §42: "Faith asks that its object be understood with the help of reason"; *Fides et Ratio,* §65: "Philosophy contributes specifically to theology in preparing for a correct auditus fidei with its study of the structure of knowledge and personal communication, especially the various forms and functions of language. No less important is philosophy's contribution to a more coherent understanding of Church Tradition, the pronouncements of the Magisterium and the teaching of the great masters of theology, who often adopt concepts and thought-forms drawn from a particular philosophical tradition. In this case, the theologian is summoned not only to explain the concepts and terms used by the Church in her thinking and the development of her teaching, but also to know in depth the philosophical systems which may have influenced those concepts and terms, in order to formulate correct and consistent interpretations of them."

124 Cf. *Veritatis Splendor*, §2: "The Church remains deeply conscious of her 'duty in every age of examining the signs of the times and interpreting them in the light of the Gospel, so that she can offer in a manner appropriate to each generation replies to the continual human questionings on the meaning of this life and the life to come and on how they are related.' "

125 Cf. *Slavorum Apostoli*, §10: "[T]hey always succeeded in maintaining perfect orthodoxy and consistent attention both to the deposit of tradition and to the new elements in the lives of the peoples being evangelised"; *Slavorum Apostoli,* §11: "In order to translate the truths of the Gospel into a new language, they had to make an effort to gain a good grasp of the interior world of those to whom they intended to proclaim the word of God in images and concepts that would sound familiar to them. They realized that an essential condition of the success of their missionary activity was to transpose correctly Biblical notions and Greek theological concepts into a very different context of thought and historical experience."

3. There are some errors, against which the pope has the duty of protecting the faithful: "To protect the faith of the Catholic Church against errors arising from certain members of the Christian faithful, especially from among those dedicated to the various disciplines of sacred theology, we, whose principal duty is to confirm the brethren in the faith (Lk 22:32). . . ."[126]

4. In such a situation, the ministry of the successor of Peter is the necessary means for keeping communion in faith: "It is impossible to remain faithful to the Tradition while breaking the ecclesial bond with him to whom, in the person of the Apostle Peter, Christ himself entrusted the ministry of unity in his Church."[127]

5. Within a theology of episcopal collegiality, the ministry of one is necessary to unity: "full communion, of which the Eucharist is the highest sacramental manifestation, needs to be visibly expressed in a ministry in which all the Bishops recognize that they are united in Christ and all the faithful find confirmation for their faith."[128]

All the steps from faith as such to the ministry required for its permanent unity were present in the teaching of John Paul II as in the Thomistic School. Of course I have selected short texts, which in the original were not as systematically ordered as I have arranged them for our present purpose. To organize the arguments is a matter more of theology than of magisterial teaching, and here Thomistic theology can really help to explain some magisterial texts, which it assisted in bringing to light in the first place.

Conclusion

I have spoken about three topics which I consider keys to St. Thomas's ecclesiology:

1. The Church is God's co-worker. This implies a whole understanding of divine and human causality, at different levels of being, without which the existence of the Church is at least "relativized."

2. To belong to the Church means to receive grace from Christ, Head of the Church, through the Holy Spirit. Church member-

---

126 *Ad tuendam fidem,* §1.
127 *Ecclesia Dei,* §4.
128 *Ut Unum Sint,* §97.

ship and salvation are synonyms. Thomas's understanding of "Church" is far broader than what post-Counter-Reformation Christians usually mean.

3. The Thomistic School analyses systematically the preaching of faith, from the fact that God has decided to communicate his revelation through human preachers to the authority necessary to protect faith from human errors. That gives at least a probability to the constant Petrine ministry in the Church.

All these elements are also present in the writings of John Paul II. Especially striking is his insistence on the human element (human rights), whose connection to more typically religious aspects is not always well understood. In the basic understanding of these three very Thomistic theological developments, there is a deep continuity between Thomas and Pope John Paul II. The vocabulary, linked to the historical context, is probably the main reason for some differences on the second point. Finally, other apparent dissimilarities can be explained by the difference normally existing between the works of a theologian, who must explain his arguments and their mutual links, and those of a pastor who cannot and should not reduce magisterial teaching to the level of theological speculation. Both works are therefore complementary.

Mercy "Twice Blest"

GUY MANSINI, OSB
Saint Meinrad Seminary
Saint Meinrad, Indiana

DIVES IN MISERICORDIA (1980) is John Paul II's second encyclical. He explains in the introduction that *Redemptor Hominis* (1979), his first, leads from man to Christ, where alone the complete truth about man is to be found. This encyclical, *Dives in Misericordia,* leads from Christ to the Father, where the truth about Christ is to be found.[1] We will know ourselves, and the Church will know herself, only in this final context of divine paternity, beyond which there is no further horizon. This Fatherhood is the final horizon of our understanding only under a definite description, however. God is our Father only as Father of mercy, whose mercy is incarnate in Christ.[2] Mercy is the greatest attribute of God and the Redeemer, the Holy Father tells us, and God just is infinite mercy.[3] The truth about us in Christ is therefore a truth about a sinful, but mercifully redeemed, humanity. Moreover, just as the Holy Father found warrant for *Redemptor Hominis* in the programmatic §22 of *Gaudium et Spes*—"Christ the new Adam fully reveals man to himself and brings to light his lofty calling"—so also does he find warrant for *Dives in Misericordia* in this same place. For the passage goes on to explain that this revelation of man occurs "in the very revelation of the mystery of the Father and his love."[4] And

---

1 *Dives in Misericordia* (Rich in Mercy), §1.

2 Ibid., §2; cf. §13.

3 Ibid., §13.

4 It is worth noting that in 1965, in an intervention preparatory to the Second Vatican Council's Decree *Presbyterorum ordinis*, Karol Wojtyla, as Archbishop of Cracow, had expressed the desire to see priests in the light of the ministry of mercy: "Est enim sacerdos quasi praeco misericordiae divinae: praedicatio autem misericordiae eiusque ministerium in mundo hodierno maximi est momenti. . . ." (*Acta Synodalia Sacrosancti Concilii Vaticani II* [Rome: Typis Polyglottis Vaticanis, 1970–], IV/5, 519.)

mercy, John Paul will explain later, is love's "second name," the form it takes when directed to sinful and suffering humanity.[5]

At the outset of the letter, the Holy Father notes a "problem of major importance," that of "the meaning of terms and the content of concepts."[6] What does mercy mean? One of the goals of the letter is in fact nothing more than to address this problem of meaning, and rescue "mercy" from several false understandings. That is the focus of this essay.

He proposes to find the meaning of mercy primarily by a reading of Sacred Scripture. As we have learned to be typical of the Holy Father's proceeding, rather than simply piling up individual citations, he finds some exemplary, emblematic passage of Scripture, a patient and "thick" reading of which will reveal to us the matter at hand. For *Dives in Misericordia*, this is the parable of the Prodigal Son. First, however, he directs us to Christ in the synagogue at Nazareth in Luke 4 and the Baptist's deputation in Luke 8, in order to point out that mercy may justly be said to be the content of the mission of Christ, and second, he makes a sort of canvass of the Old Testament. Most but not all of the work of clarifying the meaning of mercy is accomplished in the sections dealing with the Old Testament and the Prodigal Son (Parts III and IV, §§4–6). The delimitation of the meaning of mercy is finished only at the cross, by the Paschal Mystery, which is the heart of the letter. Thence the Holy Father proceeds to the special urgency of a deployment of mercy today, and last to the Church's mission in this deployment. The mercy that we deploy as Christians, it is important to observe, is very much a supernatural mercy: It is the mercy of God, revealed fully and exercised perfectly by Christ, commended to the Church, which we in our turn individually are called to practice.

In what follows, I first summarize some of the material of *Dives in Misericordia*. Next, after recalling Aristotle's description of pity, St. Thomas will help us appreciate by contrast the properly divine and supernatural character of Christian mercy. Last, Rousseau's reduction of mercy to a form of self-love, and Nietzsche's indictment of pity as the first movement of nihilism, will help us see how even human pity needs Christian mercy to survive in the modern world.

Mercy as Delimited in *Dives in Misericordia*

We begin with a summary of §§4–6, the paragraphs that deal with the Old Testament and the Prodigal Son. The Holy Father proceeds descriptively,

5 *Dives in misericordia,* §7.

6 Ibid., §3.

and *Dives in Misericordia* might almost be considered an essay in what Robert Sokolowski calls the "theology of disclosure"—phenomenological theology. The resources of this theology as practiced by John Paul are principally the economy of salvation as read off in Sacred Scripture,[7] and secondarily, and taking account of the dative to whom he wants to manifest the content of mercy, a description of the needs of the present moment in the light of that economy.[8]

From the Holy Father's Reading of the Old Testament, Five Points Emerge

1. First, divine mercy extends to all suffering and evil, both the suffering of physical evil and the guilt of moral evil. "Both physical and moral evil, namely sin, cause the sons and daughters of Israel to turn to the Lord and beseech his mercy."[9] Again, "The Old Testament encourages people suffering from misfortune, especially those weighed down by sin—as also the whole of Israel, which had entered into the covenant with God—to appeal for mercy, and enables them to count upon it."[10] Esther, Nehemiah, and Tobit are examples of the confident invocation of God's mercy, and David shows us that mercy is to be invoked even for sin, one's own sin and the misery it entails. This comprehensiveness of mercy, embracing both "evil suffered" and "evil done," in Herbert McCabe's words, is insisted on it throughout the letter.[11]

2. The revelation of mercy precisely upon the unfaithfulness of Israel to the covenant is especially revealing of the character or nature of God, and, in the second place, the Holy Father sees this in the very language the Old Testament typically uses to speak of God's mercy. *Hesed* names the covenant relation, and is grace, love, loving kindness, loyalty, and also mercy. In mercy as *hesed*, the Holy Father notes that in being merciful, the Lord is being true to the covenant established with Israel, and this means that in being faithful to

[7] That Scripture really is the primary source is evident from his citations: 5 to *Gaudium et Spes*; 2 to Paul VI; 2 to the liturgy; 1 to the Nicene-Constantinopolitan Creed; 133 to Sacred Scripture, including two extended remarks on the Old Testament vocabulary of mercy.

[8] See *Dives in Misericordia*, §§10 and 11 on the modern world in which the Church is situated.

[9] Ibid., §4.

[10] Ibid., §4.

[11] Ibid., §§3, 6, 8, 13.

Israel in mercy, he is being true to himself, faithful to his own self as good, faithful, to be counted on.[12] Of course the covenant is freely entered into, but in being freely adopted, and carried out, it shows something of the very being and nature of the Lord.

3. Third, also from the Old Testament vocabulary of mercy, mercy as *rahamim* suggests we see in the mercy of God a gratuity of love, like that of a mother for the child of her womb *(rehem)*.[13] God may be faithful to himself in being merciful, but radically, mercy is unowed, and is not something we merit.

4. Fourth, there is the relation of mercy to justice. From the Psalms, the Holy Father perceives that mercy is something "deeper" than justice. Mercy bespeaks the love that is more fundamental than justice, more original because resting in the mystery of creation.[14] The Holy Father quotes the book of Wisdom (11:24): " 'You hold nothing of what you have made in abhorrence," which points us to the mystery of creation as the first place to discern God's relation to what he has made, a relation more original than justice, the relation of love.

   Mercy, therefore, is not opposed to justice, but as he says toward the end of the letter, is rather "the most profound source of justice."[15] Justice can be said to be the goal of forgiveness.[16] On the other hand, "love . . . conditions justice and, in the final analysis, justice serves love."[17] Love comes before and goes after justice; if it is for it, the further *telos* of justice is once again love (mercy).

5. Fifth, love (mercy) goes deeper than justice, past things owed to the person who owes. "The equality brought by justice is limited to the realm of objective and extrinsic goods, while love and mercy bring it about that people meet one another in that value which is man himself, with the dignity proper to him."[18] Mercy is not an unjust relaxation of justice, but regards what the other person should be, a justice that is directed to what the person wants to be, what the person in good condition looks like.[19]

[12] Ibid., §4, note 52.
[13] Ibid.
[14] Ibid., §4.
[15] Ibid., §14.
[16] Ibid.
[17] Ibid., §4.
[18] Ibid., §14.
[19] Ibid.

Justice apart from love, and therefore from mercy, would be insufficient to foster human relationships and human society.[20]

The Parable of the Prodigal Son

Two more things are to be added from the Holy Father's reading of the parable of the Prodigal Son.

6. In the sixth place and developing the last point, there is the issue of the distance between the one who is merciful and the one on whom mercy is bestowed. The Holy Father thinks it a mistake to imagine the one who is merciful as high above and far removed from the one to whom mercy is given. Rather, the "relationship of mercy is based on the common experience of that good which is man, on the common experience of the dignity that is proper to him."[21] Moreover, he says toward the end of the letter that one who is merciful can imagine himself needing mercy.[22]

7. Seventh, also with respect to the same issue of dignity, mercy not only recognizes common dignity, but restores lost dignity. The Holy Father thinks it a mistake to suppose that mercy demeans, or denigrates, or belittles. Rather does mercy restore dignity, and this we see in a striking way in the parable, as the Holy Father points out to us the marks of dignity and respect with which the father receives his wayward son.[23] This is the case, it is to be noted, even when dignity has been lost by fault of the one to whom mercy is given. Mercy looks to the person as he could and should be. It is what justice is for.

Mercy and the Paschal Mystery

That substantially concludes the descriptive account of mercy the Holy Father offers in *Dives in Misericordia*. There is only one more thing, but an extraordinary thing, to mention. As we should expect him to say, the divine mercy is most notably displayed, in the Paschal Mystery. Here, we behold the one who was always merciful receiving no mercy from us; precisely in this, he becomes the way of God's mercy for us.[24] Moreover,

---

[20] Ibid. This does not mean that justice in the form of reparation is not a condition of asking for forgiveness; see the discussion of compensation and satisfaction.

[21] Ibid., §6.

[22] Ibid., §14.

[23] Ibid., §6.

[24] Ibid., §7.

the mercy of the cross fulfills, and does not oppose justice;[25] it shows us in a way not to be surpassed that mercy is love's "second name," since it is the revelation of love in a sinful and suffering world.[26] We learn that, eschatologically, mercy will be revealed as love; here, within the present aeon, love is revealed as mercy.[27] In sum, "The paschal Christ is the definitive incarnation of mercy."[28] All of this we might expect.

8. More remarkably, however, the Holy Father says that the one on whom Christ has mercy by his cross, has mercy on Christ in accepting it, in being restored to freedom and freely accepting his restored dignity in Christ.[29] I pick this out as an eighth mark of John Paul II's description of mercy: In being merciful, we not only restore the dignity of the one who has mercy shown him, but do ourselves grow in dignity. This is verified in a premier way in Christ. But the Holy Father also says it of us, too, quite explicitly: Mercy always redounds to the giver; and in giving mercy, we receive it from the one to whom we give it.[30] This is a function of the mutuality of love. It is a function of humility.[31] The Holy Father was not first to make this point.

> The quality of mercy is not strain'd,
> It droppeth as the gentle rain from heaven
> Upon the place beneath: it is twice blest;
> It blesseth him that gives and him that takes:
>
> —*The Merchant of Venice*, Act IV, scene 1

It blesses both giver and taker, also in the "instance" of Christ: so, "twice blest."

Pity in Aristotle

According as we live and move and have our being in the Church, it is hard for us to see how extraordinary this point is, indeed, the whole description of mercy that comes from the Holy Father, that comes from Scripture, that comes from God. Aristotle can help us see this.

---

[25] Ibid., §§7 and 8.
[26] Ibid., §7.
[27] Ibid., §8.
[28] Ibid.
[29] Ibid.
[30] Ibid., §14.
[31] Ibid.

In Book II of the *Rhetoric*, Aristotle teaches the speaker how to put his hearers in a frame of mind receptive to his argument. For this, the speaker must know the moral affections of his hearers—the moral affections of man. Chapter 8 discusses pity *(eleos)*:

> a feeling of pain
> caused by the sight of some evil, destructive or painful,
> which befalls one who does not deserve it,
> and which we might expect to befall ourselves or some friend of ours
> and moreover to befall us soon.[32]

Taking the elements in order: First, John Paul's mercy is not defined as a feeling, since it must be able to be thought of as an attribute of the God who cannot suffer alteration or decay. Second, yes, mercy and pity are caused by the knowledge of some destructive or painful evil befalling another. Third, for Aristotle, this evil is undeserved. This is contrary to the comprehensiveness of the divine mercy, which includes mercy for sinners (no.1, above). There is a contrast also with the gratuity of mercy: For Aristotle, the suffering of the one pitied must be undeserved; for John Paul, it is the unmerited character of mercy that is emphasized (no. 3). Aristotle's account seems to be of a pity that it is suitably given, as it were, something just and objectively befitting the undeserved suffering of the good man. Fourth, for Aristotle, the one who pities must be close to the one whom evil has befallen, and must be able to imagine himself in the same evil spot, and almost as it were anticipate it. This is similar to one of the elements of the Holy Father's position we have picked out: The merciful share a common dignity with the suffering (no. 6). But then, this gives occasion for thought. While this may be true of men who pity men, how can we think God to have a common dignity with us?

On the other hand, there are elements in John Paul's mercy not included by Aristotle. First, there is the assumption that mercy has hands, that as an affective response in men or the attribute it is in God, it is a ground of action for the alleviation of suffering. If this is in Aristotle, it is only touched on remotely, insofar as we can suppose the speaker, in a forensic setting, to be trying to move a jury to the redress of the undeserved suffering of his client. In this case, pity would be a font of justice just as is mercy according to the Holy Father. Second, Aristotle does not make explicit the issue of dignity, common dignity, or restoration of dignity. The common dignity of the pitied and the pitying seems to be

32 *Rhetoric*, trans. W. Rhys Roberts, in *The Basic Works of Aristotle*, ed. Richard McKeon (New York: Random House, 1941), II, 8, 1385b1214.

rather folded into the requirement of similarity of position and condition of life. Third, there is nothing in Aristotle to the effect that pity, if it moves to the alleviation of suffering, also ennobles the one who so acts.

Summing up, we can say that the most salient differences have to do, first, with the desert of the suffering that moves to pity, second, with the reciprocal issue of the unmerited quality of mercy, third, with the closeness or similarity of the pitied and the one who pities, if we are thinking of the divine mercy, and fourth, with the benefit that accrues to the one who is merciful.

About the first and third issues, Aristotle is quite clear. We feel pity only for the good, the innocent, especially for the noble innocent.[33] We must "believe in the goodness of at least some people; if you think nobody good, you will believe that everybody deserves evil fortune."[34] And in the *Poetics*, c. 13, speaking of a bad man falling into misfortune: "[S]uch a story may arouse the human feeling in us, but it will not move us to either pity or fear; pity is occasioned by undeserved misfortune, and fear by that of one like ourselves."[35] The opposite of pity, moreover, is indignation, which is pain at the unmerited good fortune of another.[36]

As to the common condition of the pitied and the pitying, there should be similarity of circumstance and position (age, character, social standing, birth).[37] Also, pity is not felt by ruined men or by the immensely fortunate: There must be the likeness both of having something to lose (unlike the ruined man) and of being able to lose it (unlike, in his own estimation, the very fortunate man).[38] On the other hand, the one whom we pity must not be too close to us, else we feel for the one who suffers as we do for ourselves, in which case we experience terror, not pity.[39]

Both of these differences can seem to make trouble for John Paul II's view. From Aristotle's perspective, it can seem as if the pope was countenancing a mercy that is indifferent to good and evil, a sort of evenhanded good will that makes the sun to shine on the good and the evil, and sends rain to both just and unjust (cf. Mt 5:45). Is such a mercy, and is therefore such a God, good? If God's mercy is unmerited, is it capricious? Just as Aristotle cannot imagine that there be friendship between gods and

---

[33] Ibid., II, 8, 1386b5–7.

[34] Ibid., II, 8, 1385b35–1386a1.

[35] *Poetics*, trans. Ingram Bywater, in *The Basic Works of Aristotle*, ed. Richard McKeon (New York: Random House, 1941), 13, 1453a4–5.

[36] *Rhetoric*, II, 9, 1386b9–10.

[37] Ibid, II, 8, 1386a25.

[38] Ibid., II, 8 ,1385b16–24.

[39] Ibid., II, 8, 1386a1822.

men, since friendship supposes some equality, and there is none between the divine and the human,[40] so and for the same reason it would be hard to imagine him conceiving it really possible for the gods to take pity on men: There is not sufficient commonality between them. A god could not imagine himself subject to the misfortunes that befall mortals. For Aristotle's metaphysical theology, remember, we cannot conceive that the gods even know the misfortune of men. Particularly inappropriate would be to think that a god is being faithful to himself, or even showing himself more godlike in pitying men in their misfortunes.

St. Thomas

Aristotle helps us appreciate the novelty of the Christian conception of divine mercy, the astonishing features of God's revelation of himself as the merciful God, "visiting the iniquity of the fathers upon the children to the third and the fourth generation" of those who hate him, "but showing steadfast love *[hesed]*" to thousands of generations of those who love him (Ex 20:5b–6). But Aristotle's account also raises awkward questions. If we wish to mediate between these two truths about mercy, the human and the divine, we shall need a metaphysical resource. The Holy Father invited us to this sort of mediation in *Fides et Ratio* (§83):

> A theology without a metaphysical horizon could not move beyond an analysis of religious experience, nor would it allow the *intellectus fidei* to give a coherent account of the universal and transcendent value of revealed truth.

Without a metaphysical horizon, human experience philosophically clarified and religious experience faithfully described do not know how to take the measure of each other, or—to stay more closely within the Holy Father's metaphor—how to locate themselves relative to one another. We turn to St. Thomas.

Mercy for Sinners

When St. Thomas takes up mercy as a virtue in the *Secunda secundae* of the great *Summa*, it can seem that he hoes pretty much in Aristotle's furrow. To be sure, although mercy is an interior effect of supernatural charity and so itself a supernatural virtue, it must be that Aristotle's nature helps us to understand supernature.[41] Even so, the very context of the Aristotelian texts

---

40 *Nicomachean Ethics*, trans. W. D. Ross, in *The Basic Works of Aristotle*, ed. Richard McKeon (New York: Random House, 1941), VIII, 7, 1158b35–36.

41 *ST* II–II, q. 28, introduction.

intimates to us the gulf there will be between human pity and divine mercy. St. Thomas must repair to the *Rhetoric* and not the *Ethics* to find the relevant material in Aristotle. There is no discussion of mercy in the *Ethics*.[42] Mercy seems no important part of the repertoire of the virtuous man for Aristotle, and the account of pity migrates toward a discussion of political and poetic things. It is noteworthy that the discussion of the *Rhetoric* is from the point of view of the legislator or lawyer, and not from the point of view of the one who is merciful. In the *Secunda secundae*, on the other hand, St. Thomas is assembling the arms of the soldier of Christ, mercy among them.

Article 1 of Question 30 asks whether evil is the proper motive of mercy. In the corpus of the article, St. Thomas lists three desires corresponding to three motives of mercy. There is the desire to be and to live; there is the desire pertaining to deliberated choice; and there is the desire for a thing, not in itself, but in its cause. These are correlated with material from Aristotle's *Rhetoric*, rather more systematically than we might expect from Aristotle's text, and according to which we have: mercy for evils corruptive of what we desire naturally, such as to be and to live;[43] mercy for the more pitiable evils that befall us accidentally and contrary to what we had expected of our choice; and mercy for the most pitiable evils, undeserved evils that are entirely contrary to the will. To the first and second desires, notice, there correspond two kinds of evil when the desires are thwarted. The third kind of evil, however, is correlated with the absence of the third desire, desire for something in its cause: The innocent man does not desire evil even in its cause.

The first desire is desire for things wanted naturally as ends; the second, elective desire is desire for something that pertains to an end. The third desire is the interesting one. It is an indirect desire for things. It desires them neither as ends nor as means—else it is not distinct from one of the first two; it is a desire for things neither naturally wanted nor deliberately chosen. It is a desire for things wanted in wanting their causes, as for instance in the example St. Thomas provides, we in fact want to be sick if we directly want to eat what is not good for us.

What St. Thomas does not do is answer the question whether or not the evil of punishment, deserved evil, can be a motive of mercy. He opens up a space for this question, however. We know that undeserved evil is a motive of mercy, and in that we stand with Aristotle. It is most pitiable. But what of punishment? Is it pitiable at all? That is, what of the sinner, who can be said to want the evil of punishment only in that he has

[42] There is a brief discussion of envy at II.7.1108a35–1108b6.

[43] And we could add such things also as to live in society and to know the truth about God—see *ST* I–II, q. 94, a. 2.

wanted its cause—his misdeed? Can we suitably feel mercy for a man who is miserable because justly punished?

St. Thomas addresses this question in the answer to the first objection by addressing the even more difficult question of whether the evil of guilt itself can be a motive of mercy. Here, he takes as implicit from the corpus that we can pity a man for his justly deserved stripes, since after all there is something contrary to the will in suffering them (they were not directly willed). On that basis, he answers the more difficult question whether we can pity a man for his guilt.

> Because guilt can sometimes be a punishment, insofar as it has something joined to it that is against the will of the sinner, in that way it enters into the idea of the miserable. And on this account we are sorry and have compassion for sinners: just as St. Gregory says in one of his homilies, that "true justice is not disdainful"—that is, of sinners, "but has compassion for them." And Matthew 9:36 says: "seeing the crowd, Jesus was sorry for them, because they were troubled and lay about like sheep without a shepherd."[44]

Now guilt *(culpa)* or sin can be said to be punishment for sin, and therefore contrary to the will, either because one sin causes another, or because the act of sin, interiorly and exteriorly, is painful.[45] A fortiori, we can be sorry for those who suffer the lesser punishment of the privation of the goods of the body or of exterior goods. We therefore do, and ought to do, what Aristotle does not have us do, namely, be sorry for sinners.

In using St. Gregory to blind-side Aristotle, St. Thomas does not tell us exactly what he is doing; in fact, he lets the truth of Aristotle remain, but only within the larger framework of the gospel. The suffering of the malefactor is found in some way to be contrary to his will, and so can be shoehorned into the category of the miserable—what can be sorrowed over, what can be pitied. Even so, he does not call it "undeserved."

The larger framework has been erected earlier in the *Summa*, in q. 21 of the *Prima pars*, on the justice and mercy of God. Article 3 argues that God is merciful not as feeling the passion of sorrow but as most powerfully remedying defect and alleviating suffering. For defects are not removed

---

44 *ST* II–II, q. 30, a. 1, ad 1: [Q]uia culpa potest esse aliquod modo poena, inquantum scilicet habet aliquid annexum quod est contra voluntatem peccantis, secundum hoc potest habere rationem miserabilis. Et secundum hoc miseremur et compatimur peccantibus: sicut Gregorius dicit, in quadam homilia, quod *vera iustitia non habet dedignationem*, scilicet ad peccatores, *sed compassionem*. Et Matth. 9 [36] dicitur: *videns Iesus turbas misertus est eis: quia erant vexati et iacentes sicut oves non habentes pastorem.*

45 *ST* I–II, q. 87, a. 2.

except by some perfection, and God is infinitely perfect.[46] The reply to the second objection addresses the question of mercy for sinners, and has it that mercy for sinners is not unjust, but goes beyond justice by way of a gift given: "qui enim aliquid remittit, quodammodo donat illud," just as Ephesians 4:32: "give to one another"—that is, "forgive one another"—"just as Christ as forgiven you." In this way, mercy is the fullness of justice, and as James 2:13 says, "mercy triumphs over *(superexaltat)* justice." Article 4, in turn, roots mercy as a gift most firmly in the fundamental relation of creature to God, that of creation. Divine justice, St. Thomas says, presupposes the divine mercy. That something be due to a creature in justice supposes something in the creature, as hands are due to the rational nature of man; but that the creature be at all cannot be something due: Prior to creation, there is no creature to owe anything to. Creation is purely an act of generosity and love, and in this sense, mercy—a form of love—always goes before justice. The Holy Father's thought at no. 4 of *Dives in Misericordia* finds here a more complete articulation.

The context of creation lets us appreciate the difference between pagan pity and Christian mercy. It is not just that the creator is powerful, all-powerful, and so can do things a pagan or even a pagan god cannot. There is also more basically a different sense of what sorts of things must be in the world, and a different sense of how things must end, a different sense of the necessity and so of the finality of evil. It is this difference that brings with it a different sense of what can and cannot be changed. We follow here in the path laid out by Robert Sokolowski.[47]

For the Greeks, evil, including moral evil, is something terminal; it is a part and a necessary part of the universe. It cannot be the case that all men become virtuous, just as it cannot be the case that all acorns become healthy oaks. Moreover, there cannot be the beautiful without the ugly, or the fine without the base. As to human things and human destinies, therefore, there is an aspect of the universe that is tragic. In the face of this tragedy, one can only behold, and tremble.[48] There is nothing to do, nothing no agent whatsoever can do, to change it. It must be that men suffer; and it must be that men suffer from their own actions. Moreover, while Aristotle is alive to evil influence on the production of character, still, he makes men responsible for their character.[49] The character of a man, settled and abiding, is not an object of manipulation by another man.

---

46 *ST* I, q. 6, a. 4.

47 Robert Sokolowski, *The God of Faith and Reason* (Notre Dame, IN: University of Notre Dame Press, 1982), 93–95.

48 Ibid., 86.

49 *Nicomachean Ethics* III, 5.

The Christian God, on the other hand, can pluck out the heart of stone and insert a heart of flesh. For Christians, it could have been that there was no evil of natural defect, had God not created the material universe. Even more thought provoking, it could have been that even in a world such as ours, where there does and must exist the evil of natural defect—it could have been that there was no sin, had God not permitted it. For Christians, the goodness of God surpasses all, and it is not necessarily bound up with evil and defect as are the goods of the world. He can be thought of, in undiminished splendor and goodness, without necessarily thinking in addition any blemish or evil. And since every perfection is found in him, there is a remedy for every defect, of the natural or voluntary order. As the *Catechism* says (§298):

> Since God could create everything out of nothing, he can also, through the Holy Spirit, give spiritual life to sinners by creating a pure heart in them and bodily life to the dead through the Resurrection.

Mercy is nothing but the original generosity whence the world proceeds in the first place reexpressed in a world where sin is permitted. It is a gift in keeping with the prior gift of creation.

Mercy Gratuitous

The question of the gratuity of divine mercy can now be met more directly. The reply to the first objection of question 21, article 4, directs us to the work of justification. As a work of justice, justification means God forgives sins because of the love the sinner has for him. As a work of mercy, justification, which includes the forgiveness of sins, supposes that the love of the sinner is God's unmerited gift to the sinner. Here we have the reason for the Holy Father's confidence, following the Old Testament, that our prayer for God's mercy is always answered.[50] We are sure to receive mercy, since the very prayer in which we ask for it is already his grace. In answering this prayer, God answers a request he has elicited. So to speak, he completes a motion he himself has started.

As the beginning, so the end of the motion is gratuitous. Divine mercy is unmerited because divine love is unmerited. By desert, the sinner merits punishment rather than mercy. In this way, Thomas has it, the work of justification is greater than the work of glorification, because of their differing points of departure.[51] Glory follows the harvest of grace, but the grace of conversion makes a garden out of wilderness. Further, mercy

---

[50] *Dives in Misericordia*, §§4 and 10.

[51] *ST* I–II, q. 113, a. 9.

restores us not to ourselves, but to God, and in that respect surpasses the work of creation. Creation brings a finite good from nothing, but grace and glory terminate in the divine goodness.

The key, therefore, is the divine love. If it is gratuitous, then mercy must be also. And it must be, for unlike our love, which responds to an existing good, God's love is creative of the good. This has been explained long before in question 20, article 2, of the *Prima pars*. God's love cannot be owed to what it creates, since apart from God it is nothing; so also it must be that his mercy, which is a love directed to remedy a defect, is gratuitous. This will be so for mercy directed to both kinds of evils. The good order of created things that produces the evil of natural defect is a greater good than that destroyed by such evil, and so the mercy that restores to an individual the good lost by natural defect is a gift beyond the gift establishing the greater good of the material universe as a whole. Much more is the restoration of lost innocence, the reparation of voluntary evil, gratuitous.

Therefore is the quality of mercy always "unstrained," and that is the meaning of the phrase. When Portia says: "[T]hen must the Jew be merciful," Shylock asks: "On what compulsion must I? Tell me that." He does not understand the necessity of gratuity. Hence, Portia: "[T]he quality of mercy is not strain'd; It droppeth as the gentle rain from heaven." Uncompelled, unmerited, unstrained.

We recall that Aristotle lists chance as one of the causes of the evil eliciting pity, the chance that makes a man friendless or mutilated or deformed.[52] For St. Thomas, on the contrary, every indirectly willed instance of bodily evil, every permitted sin, as also every production of every good, and every remedy of every defect, is owing to the originating love or the mercy of God, whose providence embraces all things, and for whom there is no chance. For those who love God, all things, including natural defect and past sin, work to the good (Rom 8:32). That is, God works them so.

In the question on mercy in the *Secunda*, article 4 hails mercy is as the chief of the virtues, taking precedence over every other, "for it belongs to mercy to pour out good on others and to take away their defects." This belongs to a superior, St. Thomas says, and most all therefore to God.

> 'Tis mightiest in the mightiest; it becomes
> The throned monarch better than his crown;
> . . .
> it is an attribute of God himself;

[52] Aristotle, *Rhetoric* II, 4, 13869–16.

As for those who are in Christ, charity is a greater thing for us than mercy insofar as it unites us to God, but as relating us to our neighbor, mercy is greatest. Therefore, we can say that while charity likens us to God in our affection, mercy likens us to God in our works[53] and is therefore "the sum total" of the Christian religion as to exterior works.[54] It is a sacrifice more acceptable to God than our worship of him, since in mercy we help others, while our worship does not profit him but rather us.[55]

> And earthly power doeth then show likest God's
> When mercy seasons justice.

Closeness, Similarity

On our closeness to the one in trouble, on the similarity of our position and circumstance, rests the possibility of imagining ourselves in same situation, and so being moved to compassion. For us to do or suffer evil, we must be both fallible and passible. God is neither. He cannot see himself suffering the evils we do. When St. Thomas picks up the issue of the commonality or likeness between the pitied and the one who pities in the second article of question 30, therefore, although he repeats the teaching of the *Rhetoric* to the effect that we pity those who are like us, he adds that we also pity those who are joined to us in love. Because God joins us to himself in love, and regards us as his own, he has mercy for us, notwithstanding the fact that it is impossible he suffer as the one whom he pities does.[56] This love is not the love of a creator, only, but the love of charity, whereby God gives us to have the same end as himself, namely himself.[57] He makes us like to him in giving us a real ordination to himself as our true last end possessed in the very way in knowledge and love that he possesses himself.

Therefore, while the questions of desert and gratuity are to be resolved in the metaphysics of creation and creative love, the question of the similarity between the pitied and the one who pities can be resolved in the likeness established by supernatural friendship with God. It is patient also of a Christological resolution. Moreover, we want someone whose mercy we can believe because we see that he is like us, identifies with us, as Christ, like us in all things but sin (Heb 4:15; cf. 2:17).

---

53 *ST* II–II, q. 30, a. 4, ad 3.
54 *ST* II–II, q. 30, a. 4, ad 2.
55 *ST* IIII, q. 30, a. 4, ad 1.
56 Love depends on likeness, *ST* I–II, q. 27, a. 3; but while creatures are like God, God is not like creatures, *SCG* I, ch. 29.
57 *ST* II–II, q. 23, a. 1.

In commenting on the Letter to the Hebrews, St. Thomas notes that temptation is threefold. First, there is sinful temptation, where the flesh desires against the spirit. "But there is another temptation proceeding from the enemy and the world. And this in two ways, either by enticing us with happy things or by terrifying us with adverse things. And in these two ways Christ was tempted."[58] He is tested in the first way by the temptations of the devil, touching on the desires of the flesh, the desire of the eyes, and the pride of life, and in the second way by the plots of the Pharisees.

> Therefore, he was tempted so that in all things both worldly and otherwise, sin only excepted, he might be like us. For if he had been without temptation, he would not have been tried by them, and so he would have been without compassion for them. On the other hand, had he sinned, he would not have been able to help us but would rather have been in need of help.[59]

In this way, Aristotle's condition is fulfilled and more than fulfilled. As it were, Christ is more like us in our temptations than we are, for sin obscures the mind.[60] Christ, however, is sinless. Therefore does he know more perfectly, more perfectly also experientially than we, what temptation is?[61] Had he sinned, he could neither have compassion for us as well nor offer us the example we need—not how to fall, but how to stand.

It is true that we have compassion for the sinner because we can, all of us, imagine ourselves being, because we remember ourselves to have been, sinners. But our compassion comes not from sin, but from the love that comes from the grace that has restored us to friendship with God. Just as such, sin closes, isolates, and makes pity and mercy impossible. Our Lord's greater compassion is a function of his greatest love, and of the greatest human knowledge of temptation and sin this love makes possible.

---

58 *Lectura in epist. ad* Hebraeo,s ch. 4, lect. 3, no. 236: "Alia est tentatio ab hoste et a mundo, et hoc dupliciter: Vel alliciendo per prospera, vel terrendo per adversa. Et his duobus modis fuit tentatus Christus."

59 Ibid., no. 237: "Ideo tentatus est, ut per omnia tam in temporalibus quam in omnibus aliis, nisi in solo peccato, similis esset nobis. Si enim fuisset sine tentationibus, not fuisset eas expertus, et sic not compateretur. Si vero habuisset peccatum, non potuisset nos iuvare, sed magis indiguisset adiutorio."

60 *Lectura super Epistolam ad Rom.,* ch. 1, lect. 7, no. 130 (at 1:21).

61 And not simply in virtue of his human mind's immediate vision of God, whence he would share in the perfect knowledge of evil God possesses in the divine nature; cf. *ST* I, q. 14, a. 10.

Rousseau

Our attention to Aristotle was introduced with the remark that, according as we live and think in the Church, it can be hard to us to appreciate the novelty of certain of the features of divine, revealed mercy. Of course, we do not live and think only in the Church, but in a post-Christian era, an era constructed quite self-consciously in opposition to Christianity and a Christian ethos. Aristotle helps us focus things Christian, and in part because he represents a sort of indeterminacy of reason relative to revelation, of knowledge to faith. Moderns, on the other hand, expressly deny what Christ taught and offer alternative accounts of things not only Christian but simply human. We may take Rousseau's account of pity to begin, and Nietzsche's to end, the modern period.

Allan Bloom summarizes "the psychic mechanism" of pity *(pitié)* according to Rousseau as follows.[62] First, once our imagination is developed enough to suppose ourselves in another's place, we naturally feel pain upon beholding the sufferings of others. This fact gives rise to the "first maxim" of compassion for Rousseau: "One pities in others only those ills from which one does not feel oneself exempt."[63] This is familiar enough territory. Rousseau also preserves the idea that it is only undeserved suffering that properly excites pity.[64] The second moment of the psychic mechanism, however, is not familiar to us, and it is this: Past the first pain, the reflection that it is, after all, the other and not myself that is in misery produces pleasure. As Rousseau says, "pity is sweet because, in putting ourselves in the place of one who suffers, we nevertheless feel the pleasure of not suffering as he does."[65] And again, "he shares the sufferings of his fellows; but this sharing is voluntary and sweet."[66] There is further enjoyment, in the third place, because, if he who pities knows he can help the suffering, there is satisfaction in one's strength and in showing one's strength.[67] Last, there is satisfaction, too, in knowing that one is a good fellow in feeling sorry for others and helping them.

What we had thought to be the most purely other-regarding sentiment proves to be no such thing. Our regard for the other is no more than a way station in returning to ourselves. We love to pity because we love ourselves, and it is pleasant to know ourselves as not suffering; it is

---

62 See Bloom's Introduction to Jean-Jacques Rousseau, *Emile or On Education*, trans. with notes by Allan Bloom (New York: Basic Books, 1979), 18.

63 Rousseau, *Emile,* 224.

64 Ibid., 225, 244, 253.

65 Ibid., 221.

66 Ibid., 229.

67 Ibid.

pleasant to know ourselves strong to help, if we choose, those who are suffering; and it is pleasant to contemplate ourselves as sensitive, beneficent, good-natured. Pity does regard others, but not, so to speak, terminally. It goes through the other to end in my own self-satisfaction.

For Rousseau, things must be so. It is not just that human pity is no longer charged with supernatural charity. In addition, the foundational passion and first appetite of man has been reconceived. True, he makes love the foundational passion underlying all others, and in this Rousseau sounds classical.[68] However, it is not love simply speaking, but love of self, *amour de soi*, that is at the bottom of all our passions, and this makes Rousseau modern. Now, *amour de soi* becomes *amour propre* upon comparing ourselves to other men. If we compare ourselves to those who are stronger, richer, happier, than we, our love of self will make us miserable. If we compare ourselves to those weaker and poorer than we, those who are miserable, we pity them and are pleased at our advantage. Jean-Jacques takes care that Emile's first comparison of himself with others is of the second kind.[69]

In this way, Rousseau thinks to make men who can come together into a stable and peaceful political community. For there is no natural linkage of one man to another; all our bonds to one another are artificial.[70] Sexuality binds us, it is true, but in itself, not permanently, and not as men but only as animals. For Rousseau, according to Bloom, compassion is the first sublimation of sexual desire, and (romantic) love the second. It is pity that is to be regularized and made into our first thought when thinking of other men. It serves as the glue that holds the modern egalitarian democratic state together, so much so that it is a requirement for high office.[71] In that it has to be instilled in Emile from the outside by Jean-Jacques, it is an artificial glue. On the other hand, its installation is a matter of shaping *amour de soi*. Since it involves comparison with other men, it is a form of *amour propre*. But it is a form that, in due amounts, redounds to the good of society and not to its demise, as would self-love become pride, arrogance, and the desire for domination.

The social utility of compassion, in fact, sets it off most strikingly from Christian charity. Charity regards the neighbor here, present, wounded, hungry, naked. Rousseau's compassion finds its privileged and wonted object, however, not in the neighbor, but in "mankind."

---

[68] Cf., e.g., *ST* I–II, q. 25, aa. 1 and 2.

[69] Bloom, Introduction to Rousseau, *Emile,* 17.

[70] Ibid., 15. And see Pierre Manent, "On Modern Individualism," in *Modern Liberty and Its Discontents*, ed. and trans. Daniel J. Mahoney and Paul Seaton (Lanham, MD: Rowman & Littlefield, 1998), 153.

[71] Bloom, Introduction to Rousseau, *Emile,* 15–16.

> To prevent pity from degenerating into weakness, it must therefore, be generalized and extended to the whole of mankind. Then one yields to it only insofar as it accords with justice, because of all the virtues justice is the one that contributes most to the common good of men. For the sake of reason, for the sake of love of ourselves, we must have pity for our species still more than for our neighbor, and pity for the wicked is a very great cruelty to men.[72]

This pity is evidently an instrument of my own good, and so is expressly distinguished from the Christian love of neighbor, of the actual living and breathing human being next to one in need. Is it an altogether different thing from charity? Not completely. It is hard to be exact here. Part of the contestation is over the first things, the first human things, the very data of our moral life. We might say that Rousseau is speaking of Aristotle's sadness for evil befalling another allied and necessarily so because of our fundamental *amour de soi* with the pleasure that evil is not befalling me. Christianity, on the other hand, speaks of Aristotle's sadness for the evil of another allied with both natural benevolence and supernatural charity. For Rousseau, benevolence cannot be anything real over and above what he calls pity.

The pleasure of pity, and so our continued practice of it, depends very much on our knowing of our own power and strength relative to one pitied. The height I occupy and from which I stoop to give aid is formal to the transaction of Rousseau's mercy. It is this in particular that the Holy Father wishes to reprove as a faulty idea of mercy. For the Holy Father, one imagines oneself the same as (close to) the man in misery in order to come close, first to realize a common dignity and second to restore it where it has been wounded. For Rousseau, one imagines oneself the same as (close to) the man in misery in order to enjoy a real difference (distance), and another's suffering is the occasion of my pleasure. On Rousseau's account, mercy is not twice blest. The one who suffers is an occasion of my beholding of myself and enjoyment of myself as high and mighty. But I do not truly receive from him. What Aristotle is silent about, mercy's twice blest character, Rousseau must deny. The miserable may be clothed and fed, and society may be preserved from too-great disparity of estate, but I am not really ennobled by mercy (though it be part of the plan of the one who constructs modern society that I think I am).

With Rousseau, we have not only forsaken divine pity, but evacuated human pity of its original meaning and force. Denying supernature, nature is deformed. This is, as it were, a description of the Fall. Also, it is

72 Rousseau, *Emile,* 253.

a description of the Enlightenment. That is, it is Pierre Manent's description of the Enlightenment: Just in order to drive out supernature, the moderns drive out nature as well.[73] For if nature remains, we shall still be taught to appreciate, desire, pursue supernatural goods on the basis of knowing them as something better even than natural perfections. So, if we appreciate human pity, and if human mercy is something admirable, we shall be led to adore the surpassing mercy of Christ and want to imitate it.

It would be possible to contest the modern view in the first place, therefore, by criticizing Rousseau's psychology. Rousseau turns what is in fact good for me—the exercise of mercy as a virtue—into something I enjoy if not choose as my good, and indeed, as nothing more than a good of pleasure. That I want your good in mercy is in fact good for me; but that is not why I want it, and if I did, it would not be good for me: I would not in fact be attaining to the good of the transcending character of love. As it were, Rousseau's account invites us to turn all *amor amicitiae* into *amor concupiscentiae* on the ground that *amor amicitiae* is good for us. What presents itself as the love of friendship must be a form of concupiscence, because nothing by nature sublime can exist in the scientifically explicable universe he inhabits. He thinks sublimation real, but it is hard to see it as anything but self-deception.[74]

If he really has deformed the data, therefore, then it might be sufficient to ask whether it is plausible to say that the father of the prodigal is pleased at comparing his happiness to his son's wretchedness. It would perhaps be sufficient to examine the quality of mercy displayed in the life of St. Vincent de Paul or St. Philip Neri or St. Benedict the Moor.

On the other hand, perhaps it is wasted energy to try to refocus human pity and reinvigorate our purchase on human nature. It is, moreover, no accident that the really splendid examples of mercy are Christian ones. What ancient hero is celebrated for the quality of his mercy? It may be best to confront the modern view more directly and efficaciously on the field of Christology. Issues of closeness and distance, resolved for both divine and human pity, are clearest in Christ. Rather than asking after the father of the prodigal son, we will ask whether it be plausible that the Christ of the gospels takes pleasure at seeing the people as sheep without a shepherd (Mt 9:36).

To answer Rousseau expressly, we look to St. Thomas's evocation of Christ on the cross. The magnitude of his suffering, St. Thomas says, is in part a function of his perfect knowledge of the causes of sadness, the sin of

[73] Pierre Manent, "Christianity and Democracy," in *Modern Liberty and Its Discontents*, 101–3.

[74] See Bloom, Introduction to Rousseau, *Emile,* 15–16, 21, on sublimation.

mankind prominent among them.[75] If we think Christ pities us most of all on the cross, however, then we cannot follow Rousseau. "When one is suffering one pities only oneself," he says.[76] In which case, Christ's words to the Good Thief, and indeed, the Good Thief's observations about the innocent suffering of Christ, give the lie to the modern account. Christ's compassion for us in our sin and his interior sorrow are not, in fact, to be separated. Christ's sorrow *(dolor)* was the greatest among all the sorrows of this life, and as to the interior sorrow he experienced, this was a function of its cause, sin, in fact, all the sins of the human race, "for which he satisfied by suffering, whence he ascribed them as to himself."[77] He "ascribed them as to himself." We arrive at *Salvifici Doloris* (§18), according to which Christ "perceives in a humanly inexpressible way this suffering [of sin] which is the separation, the rejection by the Father, the estrangement from God." Moreover, Christ perceives this, the Holy Father says, precisely because of "the divine depth of his filial union with the Father." This is very exact. It is not the suffering of the sinner that Christ shares, but a greater suffering. For the sinner, darkened in mind by sin, cannot have perfect awareness of his misery. Christ, illumined in mind by the depth of his filial union with the Father, knows this evil through and through, and suffers accordingly. This suffering, moreover, just is the suffering that mercy is. It is pity for the other, and in that very pity the remedy for the plight of the other. I return to this remarkable concentration of the features and facets of mercy shortly.

The convincing answer to Rousseau's construction of pity takes us to the cross, the cross as understood by St. Thomas and the Holy Father. In this way, Christ's pity is the guardian and guarantor of human pity in the modern world. In the same way, revelation guards reason and theology philosophy according to the Holy Father in *Fides et Ratio*.[78] In this light, it is astonishing to realize how little we have traveled from *Gaudium et Spes*, §22.

Nietzsche

The difficulty of speaking exactly about the divine mercy is illustrated well by an article of some years back by Michael Dodds.[79] I set aside the

---

75 *ST* III, q. 46, a. 6; and on the causes of Christ's suffering, a. 5.

76 Rousseau, *Emile*, 229.

77 *ST* III, q. 46, a. 6: "[P]ro quibus satisfaciebat patiendo: unde ea (peccata) quasi sibi adscribit."

78 *Fides et Ratio*, §§48, 81–83.

79 Michael Dodds, "Thomas Aquinas, Human Suffering, and the Unchanging God of Love," *Theological Studies* 52 (1991): 330–44.

host of those who immediately and straightforwardly make the divine mercy a principle of divine suffering, and who admit frankly that they think the transcendence and infinity of God does not imply impassibility.[80] Dodds is important precisely because his gesture toward the modern sensibility seems so slight.

Dodds makes prominent use of St. Thomas's reply to the second objection of article 1 of Question 30, the opening article of the question on the virtue of mercy we visited above. Here, speaking of human mercy and pity, St. Thomas explains that mercy is properly directed to the evil of others, while sorrow *(dolor)* regards our own suffering. Therefore, if someone is closely related to us, belongs to us, we do not pity them so much as suffer "sicut in vulneribus propriis." We suffer "as in our own wounds." Now, "between human beings and God there is the most perfect sort of love, the most intimate kind of unity," Dodds writes, which is true enough.[81] It follows that God compassionates us, although this is a matter, not of affection, but of will, God's effective will to alleviate suffering, and this too is true enough.[82] Further, Dodds thinks, because one closely related to one who suffers suffers as in his own wounds, we can say that our suffering is God's suffering.[83] And this is not well said. The application of this text to God, where one suffers for another as in one's own wounds, is problematic. It seems to depend on the idea that God could have "his own wounds." But if he cannot have his own wounds, then we ought not to say, and even granted the qualifications Dodds makes, that our suffering is God's suffering. It is true indeed that we who suffer belong to God, and that he loves us more intimately than one human being another. Even so, that we who suffer are God's is one thing; that our suffering is God's suffering is another.

The issue here is not only one of metaphysical coherence, but of not falling into the arms of Nietzsche, our second exponent of the modern sensibility about pity. If we say that our sufferings are God's, then we begin to make of Christianity the religion of pity in the way that Nietzsche says it is, and its god after having grown "old and soft and mellow and compassionate, more like a grandfather than a father, most like a tottery old grandmother," will one day die, "suffocated through his excessive pity."[84]

---

80 For a good brief introduction to this issue, see Thomas Weinandy, "Does God Suffer?," *First Things* 117 (November 2001): 35–41.

81 Dodds, 337.

82 Ibid., 338.

83 Ibid., 336, 340.

84 Friedrich Nietzsche, *Thus Spoke Zarathustra,* trans. R. J. Hollingdale (Baltimore: Penguin Books, 1961), IV, "Retired from Service," 273.

In this way lies the collapse of the distinction between the creature and the Creator, and in this way lies the collapse of our hope from a God who is powerful to save and whose mercy endures forever just because his love is changeless and everlasting, and just because his joy knows no shadow of alteration or decay. His capacity to wipe away all tears is strictly one with his inhabitation of a place, a place we long to go to, where there are no tears to be wiped away.

Where Rousseau recommends pity, Nietzsche attacks it, and they therefore stand very differently toward it. But they stand toward the same thing. They both make a self-regarding comparison something essential to pity.[85] Nietzsche hates pity because it makes the strong soft and the bold hesitant.[86] Rousseau likes it for the same reason and thinks it necessary for modern post-Christian polity. So it is, and for that reason it is to be despised according to Nietzsche. Moreover, too much pity would be a bad thing for Rousseau, too. Too much of this societal glue, and the springs of action cannot move; too much attention to dirt and disease, and the capacity of the healthy to be happy is enervated. This is Nietzsche's fear. While the noble man might enjoy his strength in alleviating the suffering of some wretch,[87] too much pity exhausts energy, saps strength, kills. Pity puts us on the path to nihilism, for the weak make the strong feel bad, guilty, for their strength.[88] God dies from too much pity.

What Rousseau prepares for as replacement of Christendom, the modern democratic state, Nietzsche hates as its logical consequence, the last unfolding of Christianity—something softer and more effeminate than even Christianity.

Let us sum up for Nietzsche. Far from twice blessed, mercy is twice cursed. To attempt to elicit pity is the stratagem of the poor and the weak, the servile and the base; succumbing to it, the noble and strong debase themselves and exhaust their substance.

If we escape Rousseau by looking to the genuineness of the suffering of Christ over our sin and suffering, we have not for all that done with Nietzsche. Is Christ then brought down? If we leave things there, at the cross, then it would be difficult to avoid characterizing mercy as twice cursed, in a cosmic way cursed. We shall only have eroticized suffering,

---

[85] They both speak of its object as "mankind" rather than the neighbor, too; see Nietzsche, *Beyond Good and Evil,* trans. Walter Kaufmann (New York: Vintage, 1966), nos. 82, 81. It is as if, absent Christ, we can no longer have a neighbor.

[86] Friedrich Nietzsche, *Beyond Good and Evil,* nos. 62, 75; nos. 202, 116; nos. 206, 126.

[87] Ibid., nos. 260, 205.

[88] Friedrich Nietzsche, *On the Genealogy of Morals,* trans. Walter Kaufmann (New York: Vintage, 1969), Preface, nos. 5, 19.

dabbled in a sort of mysticism of pain and trouble, and envisioned a tragic universe, one more tragic than Aristotle's.

The solution is not just a simple invocation of the resurrection, though it certainly depends on the shout of Easter Alleluias. We must in the first place recover the sense of the cross as a deed, and not just a display. True, it is a display of the compassion of God. God's mercy, the mercy shared by the three Persons, is manifested in the obedience of the Son unto death, displayed in his human sorrow for our sin. We see human mercy as the vehicle of divine mercy. Because it is a human mercy, it is an effective communication of divine mercy than which none greater can be imagined. Also, the cross is a deed, a work; it changes things; it changes, not God, but our relation to God because it is satisfaction for sin.[89] Let us hear St. Thomas again: "The cause of his interior suffering was, in the first place, all the sins of the human race, for which he was satisfying by suffering."[90] The very sorrowing of Christ is his satisfying for sin. Christ's compassion is therefore the heart of the atonement psychologically grasped. His sorrow for sin, which is his pity on us, pleases the Father more than our sins displease him. Here, sorrow is the effective remedy of our plight, as stated above, for it is something created, economic, that outweighs the created, economic evil of sin. Here there is established the "superabundance" of the justice of the cross the Holy Father refers to in *Dives in Misericordia*.[91] At the same time, this human compassion of Christ, because it is the compassion of a divine person and the vehicle of divine mercy, is a mercy in both its object, including sin, and its efficacy, powerful for a new creation, beyond any purely human mercy. It is a human mercy than which no greater can be conceived; it is a divine mercy than which no greater can be received.

In the second place, the solution depends also on what we take the person to be. It is therefore a matter of seeing what the person of Christ is. To paraphrase the Holy Father, the love that is displayed in the cross is a love that not only fixes trouble, but connects persons together in such a way that they become more personal. Especially, with the person of Christ, what is manifested is the expansiveness of the divinized humanity of Christ, an instrument whereby all are included, all invited to the wedding feast of the Lamb. What we behold in the fullness of the Paschal

[89] For the cross as deed and not just display, see David S. Yeago, "Crucified Also for Us under Pontius Pilate," in *Nicene Christianity: The Future for a New Ecumenism*, ed. Christopher R. Seitz (Grand Rapids, MI: Brazos Press, 2001), 87–105.

[90] *ST* III, q. 46, a. 6: "Doloris autem interioris causa fuit, primo quidem, omnia peccata humani generis, pro quibus satisfaciebat patiendo."

[91] *Dives in Misericordia,* §7.

Mystery is the completion of the incarnate person of Christ by his inclusion of other persons in his own mission, and the perfection of our persons in being so included.[92] It is at this personal level that the Holy Father directs us to the twice blest character of mercy.

Of course St. Thomas understands that mercy is twice blest, redounding to the good also of the one who is merciful since, after all, he counts it as a virtue, and the virtues are perfections of the one who exercises them. But does he have a sense of the precise Christological point that is being made by the Holy Father? He seems, perhaps, to have gone beyond St. Thomas as St. Thomas has gone beyond Aristotle. Of course, we may look to Thomas's commentaries on Colossians 1:24, where our satisfaction fills out Christ's because enabled by Christ, and Ephesians 1:23, where we find the reality of Christ as Head dependent on the Body. Even so, we do not find so stark a statement as this, when, speaking of the love elicited by Christ's mercy in us, the Holy Father says of it that it is "a kind of 'mercy' shown by each one of us to the Son of the eternal Father." He adds: ". . . could man's dignity be more highly respected and ennobled, for, in obtaining mercy, he is in a sense the one who at the same time 'shows mercy'?"[93] He does not want to say only that dignity is restored when the heart of stone is plucked out and the heart of flesh inserted, nor even also to advert to our share in the sufferings of Christ. The strength of the Holy Father was his aliveness to the truly personal level, where we interact with Christ the Lord face to face.

The history of Jesus, the unfolding of his humanity in his human perceptions, insights, evaluations, choices, actions are the revelation of a divine person. And this is so in a context where he cannot perceive, see, choose, act by himself alone, in isolation. He cannot be alone because it is a human context, and human beings are political animals, finding their proper perfection because enabled fully to act only in the company of other men. So, other persons necessarily enter into display of his person and the accomplishment of his mission: which is a matter of the human dignity of a divine person. This is why the contemplation of the Lord includes and is furthered by the contemplation of Peter, and John, of the

[92] Hans Urs von Balthasar, *Theo-Drama,* vol. 4: *The Action*, trans. Graham Harrison (San Francisco: Ignatius, 1994), 456: "In concrete terms, Christ only exists together with the community of saints united in the Immaculata, together with the communion of the ministerial office visibly united in Peter and his successors. . . ." This is the obverse of the truth that we derive our theological "persons" from Christ, for which see, e.g., *Theo-Drama,* vol. 3: *Dramatis Personae: Persons in Christ,* trans. Graham Harrison (San Francisco: Ignatius, 1992), 246–49, 270–71.

[93] *Dives in Misericordia,* §8.

Syrophoenician woman, of the man born blind, of the man let down on a pallet, of the lepers, and all those who come in his way. We cannot fully contemplate him and know him apart from also knowing them. All these are sinners. Never more do we know him, therefore, than when we behold them as targets of his love, which in a sinful world is to say targets of his mercy. So, they enable to the Lord to be the Lord; they let the Son show himself and in that way be who he is in the economy of salvation.

Not everything has been inscribed in St. Thomas. We can allow the Holy Father to say something St. Thomas did not. Even so, I seem to hear the Common Doctor speak to this topic, too:

> Christ by his humanity wanted to manifest his divinity. And therefore by living with men, which is proper to man, he showed his divinity to all by preaching and by doing miracles, and by living innocently and justly among men.[94]

Apart from conversation and commerce with men, his mission could not be accomplished.

Let us end as the Holy Father was wont to end so many of his writings. If we never know Christ except in knowing his mercy and so in contemplating his relation to sinner, we must add that this contemplation is itself aided by contemplating him in his relation with Mary. Because of her sinlessness, Mary becomes all the more important for our knowledge of her son. We need to see him interact with human beings who are sinners, but also, just so we can judge that the more nicely, also we need to see him interact with a human person who is not a sinner. We need to see that human person who is not a sinner interact with us on the strength of his prior love. Our appreciation of Mary as the Mother of Mercy is a part of our appreciation of Mercy Incarnate who drew his flesh from her—perhaps, never more than in contemplating him in his relation to Mary, the mother of mercy. This, too, the Holy Father knew.[95]

---

94 *ST* III, q. 40, a. 1, ad 1: "Christus per humanitatem suam voluit manifestare divinitatem. Et ideo, conversando cum hominibus, quod est proprium hominis, manifestavit omnibus suam divinitatem, praedicando et miracula faciendo, et innocenter et iuste inter homines conversando."

95 *Dives in Misericordia,* §9.

The Christian Humanism of Karol Wojtyla and Thomas Aquinas

ROBERT BARRON
Mundelein Seminary
Mundelein, Illinois

KAROL WOJTYLA AND THOMAS AQUINAS are separated by seven hundred years. One was a twentieth-century diocesan priest and bishop, the other a thirteenth-century Dominican friar. One came of age in the maelstrom of one of the darkest periods of recorded history, caught between the pincers of two maliciously anti-Christian totalitarianisms, the other in a conflicted but still relatively stable Christian culture. One entered into the philosophical conversation as the modern world was giving way to the postmodern, while the other dialogued and debated in an unambiguously premodern context. Despite these significant differences, the two thinkers can illumine one another precisely because of the overwhelmingly important thing that they had in common, that is, their faith in the God/man Jesus Christ. Both believed that the mystery of creation and the mystery of God are most richly disclosed in the Incarnation and hence both took that event as the lens through which all of reality is properly surveyed.

In this article, I will concentrate on the Christian humanism that emerges in the writings of Wojtyla and Aquinas, a perspective that is a thoroughgoing paradox. For both thinkers, the human being is fully alive precisely in the measure that he conforms himself to the radical obedience of Jesus Christ, which is to say, Jesus' utter surrender in love to the Father. For both, authentic human freedom is had in an act of self-forgetting and self-abandonment. What makes this a paradox and not a contradiction is the oddness of the person to whom the surrender is offered: a God whose entire being is a being for the other, a God who is nothing but the giver of gifts. I will develop this insight in two basic stages. First, I shall examine some key texts of Thomas Aquinas dealing with Incarnation, Creation, and the nature of God, in the hopes of explicating Thomas's understanding of God as non-competitively and non-contrastively transcendent to the world. Next, against this background, I shall examine some themes in the theological ethics of Karol Wojtyla, endeavoring to show that, for him, robust human flourishing is possible only through a Christ-like abandonment to God, or to state it more abstractly, that freedom is most itself when it is placed in correlation to the truth.

The Distinction in Thomas Aquinas

In his dismissive assessment of Thomas Aquinas, Bertrand Russell said that Thomas was a competent commentator on Aristotle, but no more, and that this modest achievement was out of all proportion to his enormous reputation. Such a construal is possible only for someone who read Aquinas inattentively, for what makes Thomas so interesting is precisely the way he twists and turns Aristotle's language, struggling to make it speak a truth that Aristotle himself never envisioned. Thomas Prufer said that Aquinas spoke "a fractured Aristotlese," implying that, when Aquinas employed it, the rhetoric of the Philosopher broke under the weight of something it couldn't quite bear, viz. the Incarnation of God. It is my contention that the entire theology of Thomas—especially as he articulates it in the second *Summa*—is conditioned by this great fact and hence becomes unintelligible apart from it. Therefore, if we want to understand his view of God, cosmos, and the human, we must turn first to the texts on the enfleshment of the Son of God.

The opening question of the third part of the *Summa theologiae* is this: whether it is *conveniens* (fitting) that God become a creature. After entertaining objections on both metaphysical and aesthetic grounds, Thomas answers that the Incarnation was supremely fitting because God is the ultimate good and the good, as the pseudo-Dionysius argued, is *diffisivum sui* (diffusive of itself), and there could be no greater self-gift than that God would become a creature out of love. In a word, the Incarnation was fitting because it was peculiarly characteristic of the one whose very nature is self-offering. Now, to press the matter a bit, this act on the part of God could be seen as good only in the measure that it benefited the one who received it. In so many of the ancient mythologies, gods and goddesses "become" human, but this takes place in an invasive and manipulative way. What stands behind Thomas's discussion, of course, is the great anti-pagan formulation of the Council of Chalcedon, that the Incarnation takes place through the hypostatic joining of two natures, divine and human, that remain, even in the union, distinct and integral. This means that God "becomes" a creature without ceasing to be God or violating the integrity of the creature he becomes. The closeness of God does not undermine humanity, but rather enhances it.

Robert Sokolowski has pointed out with with great insistence that such a state of affairs could hold only if there is an absolutely basic distinction between God and the world. Were God in any sense a creaturely or finite nature, a being *in* the world, he could not become a creature without some sort of compromising either of his own being or that of the thing that he becomes.[1] This is true because there is a mutual exclusivity at the ontological level between any two finite natures: An antelope "becomes" a lion only by being devoured, and a house becomes ash only by being destroyed. But since in Christ God enters into creation in the most intimate sense without undermining creaturely integrity, without ontological violence, God must be utterly unlike that which he enters. Were he of the same type as a worldly nature, he couldn't establish the closeness to a worldly nature that is described in the doctrine of the Incarnation. Here we begin to sense the high paradox of the central Christian claim. This divine otherness that we have been describing cannot be construed simply and one-sidedly as "transcendence," as though God were, in Karl Barth's phrase, a distant planet or a Greek philosophical idol.[2] Were God simply "spatially" or even "quantitatively" other—a highest or supreme being among many—he would still be a worldly nature and still therefore incapable of affecting the Incarnation. The God of Jesus Christ must be qualitatively other, not so much somewhere else, but some*how* else, this peculiar otherness allowing him to establish an unheard of intimacy with that which he is not.

Kathryn Tanner has expanded upon Sokolowski's formula by speaking of God's non-competitive and non-contrastive transcendence to the world. She implies that God is other but precisely not the way that one worldly nature is contrastively over and against another.[3] God's to-be does not facedown the to-be of a creature, competing with it for time, space, or ontological primacy. God differs from the world to be sure, but he differs differently than creatures differ from one another. When in the *Proslogion*, St. Anselm "defines" God as "that than which no greater can be thought," he is giving voice to this same paradox.[4] If God were a being in

1 Robert Sokolowski, *The God of Faith and Reason* (Washington, DC: Catholic University of America Press, 1982), 34–39.

2 Karl Barth, *The Humanity of God* (Westminster: John Knox Press, 1960).

3 Kathryn Tanner, *Jesus, Humanity, and the Trinity: A Brief Systematic Theology* (Minneapolis: Fortress Press, 2001), 1–8.

4 Anselm of Canterbury, *Proslogion,* in *St. Anselm: Basic Writings*, trans. S. N. Deane (LaSalle, IL: Open Court, 1974), 7.

or alongside of the world (like a classical god or goddess), he would not be that than which no greater can be thought, since he plus the rest of the world would be greater than he alone.[5] God must exist in such a way that the universe's existence neither adds to nor subtracts from his own being; while retaining his complete otherness, he must be, in Nicholaus of Cusa's phrase, the *non Aliud*. And this is why, furthermore, Thomas Aquinas rarely used the phrase *ens summum* (highest being) when speaking of God, preferring instead the more mysterious *ipsum esse subsistens* (the sheer act of to-be itself). The unreceived energy of existence is, obviously, radically unlike any existing thing, even as it enters "by essence, presence, and power" into all existing things, from archangels to atoms.

What Sokolowski calls "the Christian distinction" is especially on display in Aquinas's doctrine of creation. In the mythologies and cosmologies of the ancient world, the universe comes into being through some act of primordial violence, one god defeating another, or a divine principle wrestling some recalcitrant force into submission. The rational cosmologies of Plato and Aristotle retain a good deal of this mythic quality. Plato holds that matter is shaped by the Demiurge in accord with the patterns of the forms, and Aristotle argues that prime matter is drawn into form through the attractive power of the prime mover. In both cases, the divine influence is aggressive and external: Something that stands over and against God is brought into order through divine action. There is none of this in Aquinas. Following the Church Fathers, Thomas speaks of *creatio ex nihilo*, the bringing of the universe in its entirety into being from nothing. Creation in the proper sense is not the shaping of matter (since prime matter is itself a creature); it is not a spatial event (since space is a creature); and it does not take place in time (since time itself is the result of creation). There is, quite literally, nothing "outside" of God that would be ontologically capable of receiving the act of creation. In the third question of the *De potentia*—where Thomas develops this counter-intuitive notion most thoroughly—we find a remark that is paradoxical to an almost Zen-like degree: "[T]hat which receives the creative act is created by that which it receives."[6] In a word, absolutely everything that exists in the world derives its being completely, and in every aspect, from the creative power of God. This means, on the one hand, that the creature is utterly dependent on God, but it entails, on the other hand, that there is absolutely nothing in the creative act that is violent, aggressive, or invasive. The world in its totality is from God, and God, in the

---

[5] Sokolowski, *The God of Faith and Reason,* 8.

[6] Thomas Aquinas, *Quaestio disputata de potentia Dei,* q. 3, a. 3 in *Quaestiones disputatae*, Vol. II (Turin: Marietti, 1965), 43.

most radical sense, lets the world be. What comes forth from God is utterly of God, yet, as finite and created, it is infinitely other than God, so that the integrity of creation is a function of its absolute dependency upon the Creator. Admittedly, none of this makes sense in the context of our ordinary speech about worldly things. If a person came too close to me, I would accuse him of being domineering and manipulative; if a woman were utterly dependent upon a man (or vice versa), we would properly describe their relationship as dysfunctional. But once more, it is just this sort of over-and-againstness and mutual exclusivity that is being denied in the doctrine of *creation ex nihilo*. It is not despite the divine closeness, but rather precisely because of it, that the creature can be itself.

Correlative to the doctrine of creation from nothing is the doctrine of the *analogia entis*. For Thomas, God cannot be construed, as we have seen, as one being among many; rather he must be conceived as the act of being which is otherly other than the realm of beings. God and creatures are not—as in Duns Scotus—beings categorized as varying types in the genus "existence." Rather, created things are participants in the primordial act of existence and hence are beings in only a mitigated and analogical sense. None of this implies pantheism of course, but it does mean that all of finite existence, while retaining its creaturely integrity, shares here and now in the to-be of God. Furthermore, the analogical conception of being entails the connectedness of all finite things to one another through God. Since all created realities come into being through a continual act of creation, they are all, despite their enormous differences at the surface level, linked together at the deepest ground of their existence. When St. Francis spoke of "brother sun and sister moon," he was using language that was, at the same time, poetically evocative and metaphysically exact. To be sure, creaturely connections can never be utterly non-competitive or non-contrastive, but when they are affected at the level of *creatio ex nihilo*, they participate in something of God's way of relating. This is why Augustine could remark that one person loves another more and better when he loves him "in God." As I have argued elsewhere, the gothic rose windows—composed of the many medallions arranged in interconnected harmony around the central image of Christ—are symbolic expressions of this participation metaphysics.[7]

Now what does this Incarnational ontology have to do with Thomas's understanding of human flourishing? In a word, everything. Like all creatures, human beings are most integrally themselves in the measure that they are totally dependent upon the non-competitive God. The difference

---

[7] Robert Barron, *Heaven in Stone and Glass* (New York: Crossroad, 2000), 33–34.

is that human beings can consciously and freely either affirm or deny this ontological paradox; they can cooperate with the non-contrastive transcendence of God, or they can resist it. At the heart of the moral life, for Thomas Aquinas, is the realization of our freedom (our choice for the good) in surrender to the God who not only transcends all earthly values, but whose very goodness consists in a letting-be of the other. Our freedom is properly correlated to the truth of things (organic interconnection) and to the Truth who is God (non-competitive transcendence).

The Compromise of the Distinction

What we have been describing is the extremely subtle equilibrium that characterizes the Christian worldview. Because the relationships between God and the universe and among created things are so "delicate" in their metaphysical structure, it is quite easy to misconstrue them. It required the graced genius of an Aquinas to articulate them with even relative adequacy. In both Protestantism and its secular counterpart, philosophical modernity, we witness a fudging of *the* distinction and a concomitant misunderstanding of the rapport between the divine and the non-divine, a mistake that has had far-reaching theoretical and practical consequences. Before turning to the writings of Karol Wojtyla, it is necessary at least to sketch the contours of this dissolution, since his humanism is in many ways a response to it.

It is commonly remarked that Martin Luther placed great stress on the transcendence of God, but it is less often appreciated how his particular interpretation of that transcendence flowed from his reading of the two-natures doctrine of Chalcedon. As we saw, the classical tradition—very much including Aquinas—stressed the non-competitiveness of the natures joined in the one person of Christ, but Luther construed the natures in a much more contrastive manner, so that the divinity of Jesus threatened to swallow up his humanity. This led to the dichotomization between Creator and creature that can be seen throughout Luther's theology: For God to get all of the glory, humanity and the cosmos as a whole must be stripped of glory. God is placed by Luther in a transcendent realm almost as a gesture of protection, as though any closer contact with the world would compromise him. This distantiation was made possible, furthermore, through the univocal conception of being introduced by Scotus and given fuller expression by Ockham and his nominalist successors who in turn helped to shape Luther's philosophical vision.[8]

---

[8] Colin Gunton, *The One, the Three, and the Many: God, Creation, and the Culture of Modernity* (Cambridge: Cambridge University Press, 1993), 56–58.

This Protestant misinterpretation of the God/world relationship was bequeathed to the secular philosophers of modernity, who in various ways, sought to resolve the tension between humanity and a fundamentally competitive God. Descartes, Berkeley, and the Deists rendered God a somewhat distant and diffident justification for the essentially secular projects of politics and science. Spinoza solved the problem by simply dissolving the distinction between God and the world altogether: *Deus sive natura.* And most dramatically, Hobbes, Nietzsche, Feuerbach, Marx, and Sartre saw that a competitive God had to be eliminated if humanity is to reach full political, social, and personal flourishing. Nowhere is this principle more clearly stated than in Sartre's pithy syllogism: "[I]f God exists, I cannot be free; but I am free. Therefore God does not exist."[9] If Luther separated God and humans in order to protect God, the atheists did so in order to protect us. Michael Buckley has shown that as modernity unfolded, the competitive God took on more and more the features of the devil, the ancient "enemy of the human race."[10]

It has been central to the project of Louis Dupré to demonstrate that modernity involved the unweaving of the intertwined tapestry of God, world, and self that classical Christianity had maintained.[11] As we saw, when God is understood as the sheer act of being itself, then cosmos and soul find their integral meaning in relation to the divine. But when God is demonized, world and psyche lose their ontological moorings and hence their connection to God and to one another. The loss of objective meaning is correlative to the characteristically modern positing of the subject as source of meaning. Dupré has shown that it was not subjectivism itself that marks the modern—for a kind of turn to the subject can be found in Plato, Plotinus, Augustine, and Bonaventure—but rather the view that the subject creates value rather than recognizing it. Sartre's existentialism is therefore but the explicitation of what was implicit in modernity from Descartes on.

Karol Wojtyla and the Problem of Freedom

As a twentieth-century son of Poland, Karol Wojtyla was perhaps uniquely positioned to survey and understand the tension between the

---

9 Jean-Paul Sartre, *Existentialisme est un humanisme* (Paris: Les Editions de Nagel, 1970), 21.

10 Michael Buckley, "Modernity and the Satanic Face of God" in *Christian Spirituality and the Culture of Modernity: The Thought of Louis Dupré* (Grand Rapids, MI: Eerdmans, 1998), 101.

11 Louis Dupré, *Passage to Modernity: An Essay in the Hermeneutics of Nature and Culture* (New Haven: Yale University Press, 1993), 93–105.

systems we have been describing. As a young man, in the twenties and thirties of the last century, Wojtyla took in through every pore a vibrantly Catholic culture. In the liturgy, public devotions, poetry and drama, personal prayer, and the political/social life itself, the young man witnessed a world permeated by the Catholic attitude and spirit. Then commencing in the late 1930s and continuing through the 1940s, 50s, and 60s, Wojtyla found himself caught between two ideological systems—Nazism and Communism—that were made possible by the breakdown of the Catholic synthesis.[12] As he wrestled with these especially fierce outgrowths of modernity, both of which claimed to be an authentic humanism, he felt compelled to articulate why the true friend of humanity was precisely the incarnational Christianity that both Nazism and Communism repudiated.

The Catholicism that Wojtyla asorbed viscerally through prayer and aesthetically through drama came to him in a more intellectual form during his studies in Rome. There under the inspiration of Garrigou-Lagrange and others at the Angelicum, Wojtyla studied the philosophy and theology of Aquinas, as well as the mysticism of John of the Cross. Upon his return to Poland as a priest, he did pastoral work for a brief period and then, at the prompting of the Cardinal Archbishop of Cracow, Adam Sapieha, he began studies for a second, civily recognized doctorate.[13] The topic he chose for his research was the phenomenological ethics of Max Scheler, one of the most gifted and spiritually alert disciples of Husserl. In the prologue to his major work *The Acting Person*, Wojtyla admitted that, despite his disagreements with him, Scheler has remained perhaps the profoundest influence on his own work.[14] Therefore, to understand precisely how he sought to engage modernity philosophically, it is important for us to explore Wojtyla's relationship to the Schelerian project.

What Wojtyla immediately appreciated in phenomenology was what attracted figures such as Dietrich von Hildebrand and Edith Stein to the discipline, viz. its robust objectivism. Over and against the tired Kantianism of his time, Husserl had famously cried *"zu den Sachen selbst"* ("to the things themselves"). The Kantian distinction between noumenon and

---

[12] See George Weigel, *Witness to Hope: The Biography of Pope John Paul II* (New York: Harper Collins, 1999), especially 44–87.

[13] Jaroslaw Kupczak, OP, *Destined for Liberty: The Human Person in the Philosophy of Karol Wojtyla/John Paul II* (Washington, DC: Catholic University of America Press, 2000), 6–7.

[14] Rocco Buttiglione, *Karol Wojtyla: The Thought of the Man Who Became John Paul II* (Grand Rapids, MI: Eerdmans, 1997), 118.

phenomenon Husserl took to be wrong-headed and counter-productive, and he accordingly encouraged his disciples to describe the objectively real as it appeared to a properly intentional consciousness. Max Scheler applied this method to the problems of ethics, arguing that morality flows ultimately from certain basic intuitions of objective value *(Wert)*. The suspicion of Kant that Scheler inherited from Husserl took an even more pointed form in the context of this ethical analysis. Kant had driven a wedge between the interior and purely formal realm of the categorical imperative and the exterior dimension of feeling and inclination, insisting that the former was alone the ground for proper moral deliberation. Scheler reacted strongly against this excessive rationalism and formalism and held that moral intuition is largely affective, embodied in nature, a feeling with the values that show themselves.[15] This Schelerian stress on bodiliness and passion would exert a powerful influence on Wojtyla's moral thinking. Another feature of the Kantian moral system that Scheler found unpalatable was the element of autonomous self-regard. The claim that "the only thing that can be described as unambiguously good is a good will" led, Scheler felt, to a sort of Pharisaism, a fussily introspective obsession with the integrity of the will itself. Better for the moral subject to lose himself in the intuition of objective value.[16]

Wojtyla's analysis of Scheler touched on both of these reactions to Kant. Though he reverenced the importance of the body in moral assessment, Wojtyla held that feelings as such could never ground the ethical life. He was convinced that values had to be apprehended primarily by intellect, lest one devolve into an unstable and relativizing subjectivism. He thought that the Kantian autonomy, rightly understood, was not Pharisaism but rather a gathering or creation of self that was indispensable to the moral project. As he reflected further, he came to see that Kant and Scheler situated themselves on opposing sides of a whole series of unhealthy dualisms: between duty and inclination, autonomy and passivity, freedom and truth. His own project then took shape as a bridging of these divides, especially the last. As a phenomenologist, Scheler stood, however inadequately, for the great classical value of objective truth, while Kant stood for the central modern value of freedom and self-determination. What they lacked was the integrating Catholic worldview that would allow for the co-existence of both values.

Wojtyla's mature thought came to expression in two texts, *Love and Responsibility*, essentially lectures from his Lublin course on the morality

---

15 Kupczak, *Destined for Liberty,* 34–36.

16 Ibid., 11–12.

of marriage and sexuality, and *The Acting Person*, an extremely dense philosophical meditation on freedom and action, which he penned while attending the sessions of the Second Vatican Council. The very difficulty of the prose in *The Acting Person*—even seasoned philosophers often found it impenetrable—led some to speculate that Wojtyla was trying to keep his deepest intentions hidden from Communist censors. Then again, perhaps it was simply the result of blending the two quite disparate philosophical systems of Thomism and phenomenology.

The best way to get at Wojtyla's argument in *The Acting Person* is to revisit the classical Thomistic distinction between an *actus humanus* and an *actus hominis*.[17] The latter, of course, is something that a man happens to do, like sneezing or reacting instinctively upon being startled, whereas the former is an act that proceeds from the deliberation of intellect and the choice of will. An *actus hominis* is accidental to the person, whereas an *actus humanus* is the product of the gathered and responsible self. Against this Thomistic background and in accord with his Schelerian training, Wojtyla endeavored to analyze more precisely the nature of such an act. On the one hand, a properly human act is a response to an objective value that appears in the world, to some good that is consciously appreciated as desirable. Here Wojtyla thinks that Scheler's phenomenology is more correct than Kant's deontology. On the other hand, a truly human act is also supremely subjective in the measure that it contributes to the process of self-creation. Here Kant's characteristically modern stress on autonomy is more correct than Scheler's insistence on passivity before the world of value.

We have to proceed with some care at this point, for it is quite easy to misconstrue Wojtyla's language in an almost Pelagian direction. What he means is that there are two objects—one direct and the other indirect—to every deliberate moral act. First, the good to be sought—food, shelter, fame, friendship—is desired, but secondly, the good of the self, the excellence of the moral subject as such, is simultaneously sought. In moral choice, one is always desiring a particular end and choosing the kind of person one wants to be, so that the subject itself is treated quasi-objectively. Wojtyla went so far as to say that the person, as efficient cause of his own deliberate action, is at the same time, the efficient cause of his own self.[18] The debt to Aristotle's theory of habit and character formation should be clear here, but Wojtyla radicalized Aristotle in light of modernity's stress on freedom and autonomy. The will's active shaping of character "adds to the world a perfection no one else can add," a new *kind*

[17] Karol Wojtyla, *The Acting Person,* trans. and ed. Andrzej Potocki and Anna-Teresa Tymieniecka (Dordrecht: Reidel, 1979), xiii–xiv.

[18] Buttliglione, Karol Wojytla, 129–40.

of value. Borrowing from the Kantian tradition, he speaks of this capacity to stand over and freely shape the moral self as "transcendental." In this emphasis on self-determination, Wojtyla sounds like Kant, Jefferson, and Rousseau and does in fact push beyond the insufficiently dynamic anthropology of Aquinas.[19] What makes all the difference—and here we come to the heart of it—is that this act of self-creation does not proceed from the dynamism of the will itself nor from an arbitrary choice, but from the always concomitantly chosen objective good. The objective transcendentals—the good, the true, and the beautiful—ground and make possible the subjective "transcendentalism" that Wojtyla described. This is the same dovetailing of freedom and truth that stood at the very heart of Aquinas's Christian humanist project.

Jesus Christ as Subjective and Objective Norm

To this point, we have seen how Karol Wojtyla reconciled, through his own version of transcendental anthropology, the modern concern for autonomy and the classical concern for truth, but we haven't yet considered the rapport between freedom and the truth of God, especially as that truth has been made manifest in Jesus Christ. This relationship, which, for reasons both methodological and prudential, was relatively muted in Wojtyla's philosophical writings, came to rich and explicit expression in the encyclical letters that he would write as Pope John Paul II. As many commentators have noted, the passage from *Gaudium et Spes*, no. 22—"it is only in the mystery of the Word Incarnate that light is shed on the mystery of man"—has served as a *leitmotif* and hermeneutical key for John Paul II.[20] The adoption of this theme has extremely important methodological implications, for it reverses the momentum of so much liberal theological speculation that has tended to read (and hence misread) Christ in light of man instead of vice versa. But for John Paul, it has a more substantive meaning as well, viz. that Jesus Christ is the truth about humanity in both the objective and subjective sense, that is to say, he is the goal that the will seeks and he is the proper structure of the autonomous person. In the last section of this essay, I will sketch the outlines of this Christocentric anthropology.

The opening chapter of John Paul's 1993 encyclical *Veritatis Splendor* is an analysis of Matthew's account of the conversation between Jesus and the rich young man. Found in all three of the synoptic Gospels, this scene has been identified by N. T. Wright as a turning-point and hinge in the

---

[19] Kupczak, *Destined for Liberty,* 57.
[20] Weigel, *Witness to Hope,* 169.

Gospel narrative, and for John Paul as well it is a key text. For the pope, to grasp the meaning of this story is to understand the central dynamic of the New Testament, the free response to Jesus' offer of eternal life. Stanley Hauerwas has exulted that this major statement of Catholic moral theology commences, not with philosophical abstractions, but with Jesus. Though it certainly represents a departure from more standard accounts, the Christocentrism of *Veritatis Splendor* should not be surprising to the attentive student of Karol Wojtyla's thought, for what is on explicit display here, I maintain, is the Christianity that had, from the beginning, characterized all of Wojtyla's moral philosophy, even in its most abstruse expressions. The truth to which subjective freedom is oriented has always been ultimately the truth who is the person of Christ.

In Matthew's telling, a young man comes to Jesus and asks, "Teacher, what good must I do to have eternal life?" For the pope, this honest and searching question symbolized the universal longing of the human being for moral integrity.[21] As such, it is not primarily a question regarding rules, commandments, and prohibitions, but a quest for "the full meaning of life." Jesus' initial response is the somewhat enigmatic: "Why do you ask me about what is good? There is only one who is good" (Mt 19:17). In fact, this cuts to the heart of the matter. The greatest mistake that the moral searcher can make is to presume that the goal of his quest can be found in any good or truth other than God. One of the most insistently repeated themes of the Bible is that, since we are made according to God's image, we will not find fulfillment in anything other than God, or in any simulacrum of divinity. This insight is repeated by practically every major figure in our tradition, most famously and poetically by Augustine ("our hearts are restless until they rest in thee"), more rationally but just as clearly by Thomas Aquinas in the opening questions of the *Prima secundae*.

How is this prime objective value to be sought? Jesus asks the rich young man whether he has followed the commandments—"you shall not murder; you shall not commit adultery; you shall not bear false witness; honor your mother and father . . . love your neighbor as yourself"—and the young man responds affirmatively. Here we are at the first stage of moral development, but the distinctive mark of biblical ethics is already visible. Since the one we seek is himself an act of self-forgetting love, we attain him only to the degree that we become internally conformed to his way of being. Hence all of those egregious violations of love—murder, adultery, hatred of one's neighbor, etc.—must be eliminated in the seeker

[21] John Paul II, *Veritatis Splendor* in *The Encyclicals of John Paul II*, ed. J. Michael Miller, CSB. (Huntington, IN: Our Sunday Visitor, 1996), 679.

after God. The pope cites the clearest New Testament affirmation of this principle: "If anyone says, 'I love God,' and hates his brother, he is a liar; for he who does not love his brother whom he has seen, cannot love the God whom he has not seen" (1 Jn 4:20). The reaching of the goal presupposes, in a word, a preliminary gathering of the self around the precepts of love.

But the real drama of this story begins precisely at the point where one might be tempted to say that ethical reflection ends. Somewhat plaintively, the young man says, "I have kept all these; what do I still lack" (Mt 19:20)? Though we may suspect that it is only someone very young who could claim that he has kept all of the commandments, we still notice something of great importance in his intuition and question. Because the human being is made in God's image, his soul has a kind of infinite *capax*, an expansiveness that corresponds, however imperfectly, to the fullness of the divine reality. Therefore the simple keeping of the fundamental commandments—most of which are negative in character—can never be enough to satisfy the spirit. In Mark's version of the story, Jesus then looks at the man with love and says, "Go, sell what you own, and give the money to the poor, and you will have treasure in heaven; then come and follow me" (Mk 10:21). The look of love, of course, is a marvelous detail, for it signals, not only Jesus' encouragement of the young man and an approval of his question, but also the divine grace that is required for the next step in the moral itinerary. Once the soul has been shaped in the direction of love through the discipline of the commandments, it is now ready for a more complete and dramatic self-emptying. It is ready for the *sequela Christi*, the following of Christ on the path of discipleship. This is a matter, not only of external imitation, but of the deepest inner conformity to Christ, a walking with him in the manner of an apprentice shaping his life in accord with his master's. It goes beyond the commandments, because it involves a total gift of self, even to the point of death, for Christ leads the disciple in one direction, the cross. This "law of the gift," as George Weigel describes it, comes to more explicit expression at the end of *Veritatis Splendor* when the pope analyzes the limit case of Christian martyrdom.[22] Though he doesn't court death, the disciple of Jesus accepts death when circumstances are such that there is no other way to bear witness to the holiness of God and the dignity of human life.

A first theme to which we should attend in the story of the rich young man is that of freedom. Of his own free will, the man comes up to Jesus and poses his question. Jesus answers him and then stands open to further

---

22 Weigel, *Witness to Hope,* 136–37.

dialogue; finally, he invites him to the deepest form of life. At no point in this conversation is there a hint of violence or coercion. Even at the end, when the young man walks away sad, unable to respond to Jesus' demand, the Lord lets him go. The true God, as we have seen, does not compete with freedom; rather he awakens it and directs it. Second, we notice a dovetailing of the inner and outer, of the objective and the subjective, that we remarked in Wojtyla's philosophical treatment of the human act. The choice of the proper object for freedom—viz. God—corresponds at every stage to the choice to be conformed unto Christ. The *sequela Christi* is hence freedom's objective and subjective norm. In choosing Christ, the person opts for his proper end (because Jesus is the God he seeks), and he creates his proper self (for Jesus is the paradigm of a renewed humanity). When Paul says, "it is no longer I who live but Christ who lives in me," he implies that the fully gathered self is the self that is conformed to the point of identity with the thoughts and desires of Jesus. Thomas Aquinas confirms this intuition in saying that Christ is, simultaneously, the Truth and the Way, the former because he is God and the latter because he is human.

Conclusion

It begins and ends with the law of the gift. Thomas Aquinas thought that the Incarnation was *conveniens* because it corresponds so fully with the kind of reality God is, namely one that is *diffusivum sui*. As God gives himself away, humanity is lifted up. By the same token, Thomas thought that full human flourishing was accomplished in the act of surrender to the ultimate good who is God. Karol Wojtyla, speaking in a more modern idiom, said that human freedom is realized in a surrender to the truth of God; and then he announced that that truth is none other than a God who hands over his life to us. For both thinkers, the most authentic humanism, therefore, consists in a meeting of two ecstacies, divine and human, a dovetailing of two freedoms, a coming-together of an infinite and finite mode of being-for-the-other.

In a word, for both Thomas Aquinas and Karol Wojtyla, authentic humanism *is* Jesus Christ.

John Paul II's Theology of Truth and Freedom: A Dissident Phenomenology in a Thomistic Anthropology

MICHAEL SHERWIN, OP
University of Fribourg
Fribourg, Switzerland

IN THE SUMMER OF 1940 during the brutal Nazi occupation of Poland, the twenty-year-old Karol Wojtyla penned a play titled *Jeremiah: A National Drama in Three Acts*. In the very first act, the young playwright proclaims that "One must throw truth across the path of lies. One must throw truth into the eye of a lie." This is so, because "in truth are freedom and excellence," while the betrayal of truth leads only to slavery.[1] Already at this early date, Karol Wojtyla was expressing a conviction that would become a principal refrain of his pontificate: Freedom depends on fidelity to the truth.[2] In this, he showed himself a faithful disciple of his theatrical

1 Karol Wojtyla, *The Collected Plays and Writings on Theater,* translated with introductions by Boleslaw Taborski (Berkeley: University of California Press, 1987), 109 and 103, respectively. Cited by Kenneth Schmitz, *At the Center of the Human Drama: the Philosophical Anthropology of Karol Wojtyla/Pope John Paul II* (Washington, DC: Catholic University of America Press, 1993), 7.

2 The centrality of freedom's dependence on fidelity to the truth in the theology of John Paul has been recognized by a number of authors. See Rocco Buttiglione, *Karol Wojtyla: the Thought of the Man Who Became Pope John Paul II* (Grand Rapids, MI: Eerdmans, 1997 [first published in Italian in 1982]), 151–56; David Hollenbach, "Christian Social Ethics after the Cold War," *Theological Studies* 53 (1992): 94; Stanley Hauerwas, "In Praise of *Centesimus Annus*," *Theology* 95 (1992): 419–28; Avery Dulles, "John Paul II and the Truth about Freedom," *First Things* 55 (1995): 36–41; George Weigel, *Soul of the World: Notes on the Future of Public Catholicism* (Grand Rapids, MI: Eerdmans, 1996), 125–49; Michael Novak, "Truth and Liberty: the Present Crisis in Our Culture," *Review of Politics* 59 (1997).

mentor, Mieczyslaw Kotlarczyk. For Kotlarczyk and the Rhapsodic Theater he founded, the spoken word was a force for change. Deeply imbued with the Johannine spirituality of the Word made flesh, a Living Word that comes to bear witness to the truth, Kotlarczyk believed that truth publicly proclaimed was the most effective cultural resistance against the forces of violent oppression.[3] This conviction and the experience of living it among his fellow artists made an indelible impression on the young Wojtyla. As George Weigel suggests, Wojtyla would remember the power of bearing witness to the Living Word when called to act on another larger stage, in the face of other forms of oppression.[4]

But the poetic wellsprings of John Paul's theology of truth and freedom also point to the principal challenge confronting anyone attempting to understand this theology. Even after becoming pope, Karol Wojtyla retained the heart of a dramatist and poet. Faithful to the tradition of the Rhapsodic Theater, he preserved a love for the richness of words and a Johannine sense of their levels of meaning. Consequently, John Paul did not speak of truth and freedom in only one way, but followed the Gospel of John in applying the terms analogically.[5] The primary burden of this essay will be to sketch these various analogous uses.

The goal of this sketch, however, is not merely to explain the meaning of these terms, but to suggest that John Paul's theology of truth and freedom contains an implicit anthropology, an anthropology intimated in his phenomenological analysis of freedom's dependence on truth. Moreover, I shall highlight the relevance of this anthropology by placing it in the context of the dissidents of Central and Eastern Europe, especially the thought of Vaclav Havel. This will enable us to see John Paul's theology as grounding the phenomenology of the dissidents upon the Gospel message and a broadly Thomistic anthropology.

Phenomenology means different things to different people. Here, however, I employ it in the broad sense and take it to mean a method

---

3 George Weigel, *Witness to Hope: the Biography of John Paul II* (New York: Harper Collins, 1999), 37–38, 65–66.

4 Ibid., 66.

5 For example, in John's Gospel, when Jesus says, "I have come into the world to bear witness to the truth" (Jn 18:37b), does truth here mean the same thing as when he says "I am the way, the truth and the life" (Jn 14:6)? It would seem not, since Jesus himself says, "If I bear witness to myself, my testimony is not true" (Jn 5:31). Jesus is the truth, but he also bears witness to a truth that is somehow distinct from but related to him. Thus, in the Gospel of John, truth has several analogically related meanings. The same can be said of John Paul's theology: The pope did not have a univocal conception of truth and freedom, but employed these terms in several analogically related ways.

whereby one engages in an attentive openness to and an analysis of human experience, an experience that is always simultaneously an experience of concrete things and of the conscious self.[6] In developing his theology of truth and freedom, John Paul employed terms drawn from John's Gospel and from contemporary philosophy. My contention, however, is that this papal theology only becomes intelligible when placed within a broadly Thomistic framework. Specifically, the several analogously related meanings of truth and freedom developed by John Paul become intelligible only from within a Thomistic understanding of nature, grace, and the human person's vocation in Christ. This further implies that if theologians want to help the faithful understand this aspect of papal teaching, they would do well to develop a renewed Thomistic anthropology.

John Paul's Fourfold Conception of Truth

An attentive reading of John Paul's encyclicals reveals that he applied truth in four distinct but related ways. Truth refers (1) to God as the beginning and end of all things, (2) to Christ as the Living Word (Logos) who is the pattern of all things, (3) to existential humanity as graced human nature, fallen but redeemed, and lastly, (4) to the Gospel as the proclamation of redemption. Following John Paul's own practice we shall begin with truth as the Living Word. We should note first, however, that by employing truth in this fourfold way, John Paul underlines an aspect of truth that is only secondary for Aquinas. For St. Thomas, who defines truth as the "conformity" between intellect and thing,[7] truth is primarily in the mind and only secondarily in things.[8] For John Paul, however, truth is primarily in things. It is the pattern or structure that gives reality its inner coherence. In other words, while Thomas's preferred word to express reality is "being," John Paul's preferred term is "truth." While for Thomas, God is most properly being or existence itself (the I-Am-Who-Am), for John Paul, God is most properly Truth. Although these two perspectives are not necessarily opposed, the emphasis is clearly different and this difference has consequences for how each author presents the mysteries of revelation.

[6] For a concise presentation of John Paul's mature understanding of the phenomenological method, see Jaroslaw Kupczak, *Destined for Liberty, the Human Person in the Philosophy of Karol Wojtyla/John Paul II* (Washington, DC: Catholic University of America Press, 2000), 66–76. Colin McGinn describes phenomenological analysis as "analysis of consciousness as it presents itself to the subject of consciousness." Colin McGinn, *The Making of a Philosopher: My Journey through Twentieth-Century Philosophy* (New York: Harper Collins, 2002), 43.

[7] *ST* I, q. 16, a. 2; *SCG* I, ch. 59.

[8] *ST* I, q. 16, a. 1.

Truth as Christ

At the very outset of his pontificate, John Paul established the Johannine tone of his theology by including in the opening paragraph of his first encyclical, *Redemptor Hominis,* the opening words of John's prologue: "The word was made flesh and dwelt among us."[9] Later in the same encyclical the pope appeals to John to describe Christ as the truth:[10] "I am the way, the truth and the life" (Jn 14:6). As the eternal Word (Logos), the Son of God is the pattern of all creation, or what the pope elsewhere describes as the "intimate truth of being."[11] Yet, as the Word made flesh, he is the "prototype" of perfect humanity, or what the pope describes as the "intimate truth of human being."[12] When the Word becomes flesh, he not only fully reveals the Father—"he who has seen me, has seen the father" (Jn 14.9)—he reveals the full truth about the human person.[13]

In revealing the full truth about humanity, Christ not only reveals the perfect pattern of the human, he reveals the truth about historical humanity (its sinfulness, its need for forgiveness and the forgiving love held out to it by the Father). Thus, Jesus before Pilate proclaims: "[F]or this I have come into the world, to bear witness to the truth" (Jn 18:37).[14] One feature of this revelatory action that John Paul underlines is precisely freedom's dependence on truth. He explains:

> Jesus Christ meets the man of every age, including our own, with the same words: "You will know the truth, and the truth will make you free" (Jn 8:32). These words contain both a fundamental requirement and a warning: the requirement of an honest relationship with regard to truth as a condition for authentic freedom, and the warning to avoid every kind of illusory freedom, . . . every freedom that fails to enter into the whole truth about man and the world.[15]

Knowledge of the truth will set us free if we live in honest relationship with the truth. Yet, John Paul offers a further precision. The freedom to which we are called is only possible through the action of Truth itself. Jesus through his life, death, and resurrection sends the "Spirit of truth" who both guides us into full knowledge of the truth and empowers us to live in harmony with this truth. The Spirit sets us free in and for the truth.[16]

[9] *Redemptor Hominis,* §1.

[10] Ibid., §7

[11] *Dominum et Vivificantum,* §36.

[12] Ibid., §59.

[13] *Redemptor Hominis,* §7

[14] Ibid., 12.

[15] *Redemptor Hominis,* §12. See also *Veritatis Splendor,* §§34 and 87.

[16] *Dominum et Vivificantem,* §59.

Truth as Existential Human Nature

The pope's encyclical on moral theology famously begins with the words *Veritatis Splendor*: the splendor of truth. The context of this utterance, however, is much less well known. "The splendor of truth shines forth in all the works of the Creator and, in a special way, in man, created in the image and likeness of God." On one level this truth is the Logos, the eternal Word shining forth in all creation, especially in the human intellect. On another level, for John Paul this truth is a created participation in the Logos. As existing in things, truth is the inner order or essence of the thing. It is what John Paul calls "the truth of creation."[17] It is what enabled the pope elsewhere to describe human life as being "indelibly marked by a truth of its own."[18]

John Paul underlines the human person's unique way of participating in the Truth, which he describes as "the truth within humanity."[19] This truth has several facets. On one level there is the truth of creation that John Paul portrays as the "law of reason."[20] This is "the truth about the moral good," which, John Paul tells us, "is a witness to the universal truth of the good" present in the mind of even the most hardened sinner.[21] In other words, John Paul used the term "truth" as a synonym for what St. Thomas calls the first principles of practical reason and of the natural law.[22]

But in relation to humanity, John Paul more frequently employed a broader sense of truth. Truth then refers to what we could call existential human nature. For John Paul the "truth about man" is that although he suffers many limitations, being subject to suffering and death, he has a deep and restless desire for something greater (both a desire for truth and for freedom). Moreover, he experiences an inner summons to a higher life.[23] For John Paul this truth (this human reality) is experienced by all people, even by non-Christians. Although they might not formulate it in these terms, all people experience their limitations, their aspirations to something greater, as well as a mysterious inner call to a higher life. As John Paul explains, "there already exists in individuals and peoples an expectation, even if an unconscious one, of knowing the truth about God, about man, and about how we are to be set free from sin and death."[24]

---

17 *Veritatis Splendor,* §41.
18 *Evangelium Vitae,* §48.
19 *Redemptor Hominis,* §14.
20 *Veritatis Splendor,* §§41, 61,
21 Ibid., §61.
22 *ST* I, q.79, a. 12; I–II, q. 94, a.2.
23 *Redemptor Hominis,* §14.
24 *Redemptoris Missio,* §45.

Clearly, this "truth within humanity" signifies the existential state of fallen but graced human nature.

Lastly, John Paul refers to the "full truth" of the human person. This is the truth about the human person made known through revelation.[25] John Paul explains: "[W]e are not dealing with the 'abstract' man, but the real, 'concrete,' 'historical' man. We are dealing with 'each' man, for each one is included in the mystery of the Redemption."[26] Truth on this level leads us to see that our earthly limitations are somehow related to sin; that our aspirations for truth and freedom are fulfilled in union with the Trinity through the humanity of Christ; and that it is by means of the incarnation, death, and resurrection of Christ through the gift of the "Spirit of truth" that we are able to know these things and to live them. The full truth leads us to see that it is through the missions of the Word and Spirit that we are able to attain the truth and freedom that comes from union with the Trinity; in short, the full truth enables us to recognize that it is through union with the Trinity that we are able to live in the truth.

Truth as the Gospel Message

John Paul recognized, however, that the full truth about the human person is something that must be revealed. He thus also refers to truth in a way that makes it synonymous with the Gospel message. Yet, in John Paul's lexicon, even the word "Gospel" has analogous meanings. The Gospel we proclaim is Christ himself; but the Gospel is also the narrative of what Christ does for us and of how we are called to live in Christ.

John Paul emphasizes that acceptance of the Gospel requires the action of the Spirit leading us to conversion. The pope reminds us that in John's Gospel (16:13) Jesus states that "when the Spirit of truth comes, he will guide you into all the truth."[27] Initially this truth has a twofold aspect. It reveals our sinfulness and need for conversion, while at the same time revealing God's unfailing mercy on our behalf. Through the action of the Spirit we discover that as beings who search for the truth, our freedom comes from living in harmony with the deepest truth about ourselves.

The beginning of this freedom is to live the commandments according to the truth about the good inscribed in our hearts. Most fully, however, to live in harmony with the truth is to live according the Truth who is Christ. Christ as Truth is the prototype of human freedom and fulfillment. To be free, therefore, we must live the life of Christ in a complete gift of self, which is only made possible by the action of the

---

[25] *Redemptoris Hominis,* §11.

[26] Ibid., §13.

[27] *Dominum et Vivificantem,* §6.

Holy Spirit. This gift of self ultimately leads us to perfect union with the Truth who is God. John Paul refers to this union in Trinitarian terms as resulting from the Trinitarian processions. He describes it as the "mysterious radiation of truth and love" (namely the processions of the Son and Spirit) that leads the human person "to become a sharer in the truth and love which is in God and proceeds from God."[28]

Truth as God

When John Paul described God as truth, he sometimes did so in the context of human fulfillment and happiness. As creatures whose very essence is to seek the truth, this restless search only finds its completion in the vision of God in heaven. Thus, in *Redemptor hominis*, John Paul quotes Augustine's famous phrase, "you have made us for yourself, O Lord, and our hearts are restless until they rest in you."[29] Commenting on this passage, John Paul portrays it as expressing the human person's restless search for truth and desire for the good, both of which are fulfilled only in God. God is the truth who alone satisfies our restless hearts.[30]

Freedom's Dependence on Truth

The Meanings of Freedom

When we turn our attention to freedom, we discover that John Paul also employed this term analogously. At times he spoke of it as something given to and radically present in all people.[31] Indeed, the presence of this freedom is one of the truths about humanity that we are called to respect.[32] At other times he referred to freedom as something we can lack,[33] and as something for which we search and long to attain.[34] Of course, most fundamentally for our current study, there are numerous references in John Paul's encyclicals to freedom's dependence on fidelity to the truth. There are clearly tensions here. For example, if freedom depends on fidelity to the truth that we are free, there seems to be a certain circularity in the argument.

Here again, however, a careful reading of John Paul's descriptions of freedom reveals that they presuppose a broadly Thomistic anthropology. We can

---

[28] *Dives in Misericordia*, §§6, 7.
[29] *Confessions*, I.1.
[30] *Redemptor Hominis*, §18.
[31] Ibid., §21; *Veritatis Splendor*, §86.
[32] *Redemptor Hominis*, §16.
[33] *Centesimus Annus*, §39.
[34] *Redemptor Hominis*, §18.

discern three related meanings of freedom. Freedom signifies (1) the principle of free action; (2) the absence of constraint, whether internal or external; and (3) freedom as the capacity for excellence. In *Veritatis Splendor*, John Paul distinguishes between freedom's origin and freedom's situation.[35] In its origin, freedom is a gift from God given to all humans. On this level it is like a seed. It exists in germ as something we must develop before it can become perfect. Here John Paul is merely describing the spiritual character of the intellect and will. These two powers are the spiritual principles that enable us to transcend the constraints of the material creation. They are what enable us to act from our own free decision *(liberum arbitrium)*.

Yet, freedom's situation, which is another word for the experience of freedom, reveals that freedom is often limited. Human freedom can be constrained both by the interior disorder of our passions and inclinations or by exterior constraints on our actions imposed by society or the State.[36] As noted earlier, John Paul affirms that freedom begins by obeying the commandments, but only reaches perfection in the life of graced virtue that enables us to live according to the truth.[37] Here again there is a tension. Freedom depends on obedience to truth, while only when freedom is perfected in us can we fully live according to the truth. The tension is resolved when we recognize that the first assertion refers to freedom as freedom from constraint: External freedom depends on society respecting the truth about the human person, while internal freedom depends on our having ordered our passions to the true good. On this level we only become free from constraint when we have ordered our passions to the truth about ourselves and when society has ordered its institutions to this same human truth.

Freedom at this level, however, is only the beginning. Freedom from internal constraint is the necessary but not sufficient condition for perfect freedom.[38] Perfect freedom refers to the capacity for excellence.[39] It is the graced ability to live completely and creatively in the truth. It is the graced ability to bear witness to the Truth who is Christ and to the Gospel truth about our concrete vocation in Christ. Ultimately, for John Paul, the

---

35 *Veritatis Splendor,* §86.

36 *Centesimus Annus,* §§38, 39.

37 *Veritatis Splendor,* §11.

38 *Evangelium Vitae,* §75.

39 On freedom as the capacity to live a certain creative excellence, see Servais Pinckaers, OP, *Sources of Christian Ethics,* trans. Mary Thomas Noble, OP (Washington, DC: Catholic University of America Press, 1995), 354–78; for the implications of this notion of freedom in relation to fidelity to truth, see George Weigel, "A Better Concept of Freedom," *First Things* 121 (2002): 14–20.

perfect freedom integral to living in the truth is a life configured to Christ's loving self-offering to the Father for the good of humanity.[40]

Truth and Freedom in Secular Society

There is, however, another tension in John Paul's reflections on truth and freedom, a tension that some commentators find particularly troubling. On the one hand John Paul presented the Church as championing freedom of conscience and the freedom of the individual, especially religious freedom.[41] He portrayed the practice of the Early Church as having recognized and respected the necessary link between freedom of conscience and the effective proclamation of the Gospel.[42] He regarded this freedom as an essential feature of human dignity that must always be respected. On the other hand, as we have seen he vigorously affirmed freedom's dependence on fidelity to truth: "[F]reedom negates and destroys itself, and becomes a factor leading to the destruction of others, when it no longer recognizes and respects its *essential link with the truth*."[43] Understanding this tension and John Paul's response to it will help situate the pope's theology of truth and freedom within the social and political context from which it emerged. It will allow us to see his theology as an attempt to place the insights of the dissidents from Central and Eastern Europe on a firmer theological foundation.[44]

Free Society and the Fear of Totalitarianism

Many find the assertion that freedom depends on fidelity to truth deeply troubling in light of the totalitarian tendency to impose one's truth on others. This fear is well expressed by the economist and Nobel laureate Milton Friedman. In his brief commentary on *Centesimus Annus*, Professor Friedman states:

> As a non-Catholic classical liberal, I find much to praise and to agree with in this letter, . . . But I must confess that one high-minded sentiment, passed off as if it were a self-evident proposition, sent shivers down my back: "*Obedience to the truth* about God and man is the first

[40] *Veritatis Splendor,* §87.

[41] *Redemptor Hominis,* §12.

[42] Ibid.

[43] *Evangelium Vitae,* §19.

[44] The fact that John Paul's teaching has deep affinities with the teachings of other dissidents from Central and Eastern Europe was early noted by Rocco Buttiglione. See Buttiglione, *Karol Wojtyla: the Thought of the Man Who Became Pope John Paul II,* 152, n. 41. See also Allen White, "Magna est Veritas et praevalebit," *New Blackfriars* 71 (1990): 196.

> condition of freedom." Whose "truth"? Decided by whom? Echoes of the Spanish Inquisition?[45]

Friedman pinpoints a major concern, a concern eloquently formulated years before by Isaiah Berlin in his classic studies on the nature of liberty.[46] Berlin famously distinguishes between negative and positive liberty. Negative liberty is freedom *from* coercion (it is the unhindered ability to do as one pleases as long as this freedom does not infringe on the freedom of others), while positive liberty is freedom *for* excellence (it is a self-mastery that empowers a person to live according to a concrete conception of human fulfillment). Berlin argues that the positive conception of liberty is inherently dangerous, because those who believe that freedom depends on living according to a specific way of life sooner or later succumb to the temptation to "free" their fellows by imposing this way of life on them by force. At issue here, therefore, is the extent to which institutions such as the Catholic Church that regard freedom as dependent upon the acceptance of a certain conception of the human person are a danger to liberal institutions and the civil rights these institutions seek to preserve. In Berlin's view, such institutions advance a view of freedom that leads to totalitarianism. Berlin regards this judgment as confirmed by the long and bloody history of Europe.

Berlin's solution was to embrace a vigorous "pluralism of values," where each citizen can without interference "choose ends without claiming eternal validity for them."[47] A popularized version of this view has recently been paraphrased as follows: "Only openness guarantees freedom, and only one who believes in the relativity of truth can be genuinely open. The true believer is a threat to liberty."[48] Berlin, however, also recognized the opposite peril of portraying individual freedom as the sole value in public life. Even liberal societies place limits on individual freedom, which, Berlin argues, we justify through a form of utilitarian calculus: "We justify them on the ground that ignorance, or a barbarian upbringing, or cruel pleasures and excitements are worse for us than the amount of restraint

---

45 Milton Friedman, "Goods in Conflict?" in *A New Worldly Order: John Paul II and Human Freedom*, ed. George Weigel (Washington, DC: Ethics and Public Policy Center, 1991), 77.

46 Isaiah Berlin, *Four Essays on Liberty* (Oxford: Oxford University Press, 1969); see also the recent collection of his essays, *The Proper Study of Mankind: An Anthology of Essays* (New York: Farrar, Straus and Giroux, 1998).

47 Isaiah Berlin, "Two Concepts of Liberty," in *Proper Study of Mankind*, 242.

48 Jonathan Sacks, *The Politics of Hope* (London: Vintage, 2000), 34. As we shall see, Sacks offers this paraphrase in order to critique it.

needed to repress them."[49] Berlin acknowledges that this type of calculus presupposes judgments concerning good and evil, which in turn presuppose some conception of human flourishing. How, then, do the requirements of negative liberty differ from those of positive liberty? Berlin's response is twofold: The conception of human flourishing proper to negative freedom is recognized as provisional and is rooted in a society's emotional revulsion before violations of this conception. Berlin argues for this view from within the liberal tradition of rights.

> [For] the liberal tradition . . . no society is free unless it is governed by at any rate two interrelated principles: first, that no power, but only rights, can be regarded as absolute, so that all men, whatever power governs them, have an absolute right to refuse to behave inhumanly; and, second, that there are frontiers, not artificially drawn, within which men should be inviolable, these frontiers being defined in terms of rules so long and widely accepted that their observance has entered into the very conception of what it is to be a normal human being, and, therefore, also of what it is to act inhumanly or insanely; rules of which it would be absurd to say, for example, that they could be abrogated by some formal procedure on the part of some court or sovereign body.[50]

Rights are absolute and express the domain of non-interference in which each individual should be left alone. Rules delineate the frontiers of these rights and are based in a traditional conception of what it means to be "a normal human being," and what it means to act "inhumanly or insanely."

Berlin affirms unflinchingly that normality is determined according to a society's emotional response to specific actions. A normal person is one who "could not break these rules easily, without a qualm of revulsion."[51] Berlin lists as examples the rules governing due process in courts of law, as well as an army's conduct in war. Among the acts that violate these rules are torture, murder, and the massacre of innocent minorities. "Such acts, even if they are made legal by the sovereign, cause horror even in these days."[52] In essence, Berlin seeks to ground the rights that underpin negative liberty upon Humean emotivism. We protect negative liberty by outlawing actions that an educated gentleman would find emotionally repulsive. In Berlin's view, therefore, the best defense against tyranny is to promote a collective recognition of the provisional and limited character of our understanding of the human good and to trust in the emotional

---

[49] Isaiah Berlin, "Two Concepts of Liberty," in *Proper Study of Mankind*, 240.

[50] Ibid., 236.

[51] Ibid.

[52] Ibid.

good sense of an educated majority. In this, Berlin well expresses the dominant moral perspective in Europe and America. It is a view ably proclaimed by contemporary intellectuals such as Richard Rorty and popularly expressed by the major outlets of western art and culture.[53]

Yet, is this view sufficient? Does trusting in the majority's emotional "horror" and "revulsion" before evil provide a sufficient foundation to protect even the negative freedom that our societies so cherish? A careful reading of recent history suggests otherwise. The fact that the Nazis succeeded in persuading lifelong public servants *voluntarily* to execute innocent women and children and very quickly to do so without any emotional horror or revulsion should cause defenders of liberty some pause.[54] Moreover, as Rabbi Jonathan Sacks has observed, the popularized version of Isaiah Berlin's perspective seems to have fostered a surprising result: a culture that is unable even to articulate rational objections to mass murder.[55] Rabbi Sacks offers the example of the Harvard professor who discovered to his dismay that among his students "there was no general agreement that those guilty of the Holocaust itself were guilty of a moral horror. 'It all depends on your perspective,' one said. 'I'd first have to see those events through the eyes of people affected by them,' another remarked."[56] If civil servants can murder the innocent without feeling "horror" and if sixty years later students at Harvard can feel no "moral horror" over those functionaries' actions, then something is deeply amiss in the defense of negative liberty proposed by Isaiah Berlin. As Rabbi Sacks notes, contemporary moral relativism appears to be the product of a "sincere determination of a post-war, post-Holocaust generation to avoid the possibility of any future 'final solution.'"[57] In fact, however, this moral perspective is possibly preparing the groundwork for just such solutions in the future.

Berlin based his utilitarian emotivism on something he believed to be empirically demonstrable: Humans pursue a plurality of ends that are essentially irreconcilable. These ends are irreconcilable because there is no one conception of the human person that all people are able rationally to

[53] See especially Berlin's conclusion at the end of "Two Conceptions of Liberty" (242) which expresses a view virtually identical to the one advanced by Richard Rorty in *Contingency, Irony and Solidarity* (Cambridge: Cambridge University Press, 1989), 44–95, 189–98.

[54] See Christopher Browing, *Ordinary Men: Reserve Police Battalion 101 and the Final Solution in Poland* (New York: HarperCollins, 1992).

[55] Jonathan Sacks, *Politics of Hope,* 34–35.

[56] James Q. Wilson, *The Moral Sense* (New York: Free Press, 1993), 8; cited by Jonathan Sacks, *Politics of Hope,* 35.

[57] Jonathan Sacks, *Politics of Hope,* 34.

discover and embrace. One might agree with Berlin in rejecting a version of Enlightenment rationalism that sought to impose its type of "rationality" on whole societies.[58] Yet, might it be possible to make lesser claims for reason without falling into moral relativism or moral authoritarianism? In other words, might it be possible to defend the area of non-interference proper to negative freedom by advancing a non-Enlightenment view of practical reasoning? It is here that the experiences of the dissidents from Central and Eastern Europe acquire unique importance, especially for our efforts to understand John Paul's theology of truth and freedom.

Truth and the Dissidents from Central Europe

If the dominant attitude in the west toward freedom's relationship to truth can be paraphrased as "only belief in the relativity of truth guarantees freedom," a very different view has developed in Central and Eastern Europe. For thinkers such as Aleksandr Solzhenitsyn and Vaclav Havel, freedom depends on "living within the truth."[59] Indeed, as the Czech philosopher Erazim Kohák noted at the time, "The entire tenor of Czech dissent . . . has been on *life in the truth*. . . . In word and deed, Czech dissidents have demonstrated their conviction that there is truth, that there is good and evil—and that the difference is not reducible to cultural preference."[60] This was also true in Poland and even earlier for the dissidents in Russia. Thinkers throughout Central and Eastern Europe have each in their own way recognized that freedom—as an individual as well as a social/political reality—depends on fidelity to certain basic truths about what it means to be human.[61]

In his now-classic study of political resistance to repression, penned while he was still under house arrest, Vaclav Havel offers his reflections on

---

58 See, for example, *Centesimus Annus* 46, where John Paul recognizes "the danger of fanaticism or fundamentalism among those who, in the name of an ideology which purports to be scientific or religious, claim the right to impose on others their own concept of what is true and good."

59 Vaclav Havel, "The Power of the Powerless," trans. Paul Wilson, in *The Power of the Powerless: Citizens Against the State in Central-Eastern Europe*, ed. John Keane (Armonk, NY: M. E. Sharpe, 1985), 23–96; Aleksandr Solzhenitsyn, *The Oak and the Calf* (San Francisco: Harper and Row, 1979).

60 Erazim Kohák, "Can There Be a Central Europe?" *Dissent* 37 (1990): 195–96; cited by David Hollenbach, "Christian Social Ethics after the Cold War," *Theological Studies* 53 (1992): 94.

61 For the role of this insight in the transformations that occurred in Central and Eastern Europe, see George Weigel, *The Final Revolution: the Resistance Church and the Collapse of Communism* (Oxford: Oxford University Press, 1992), especially pages 37–57, 125–58, 174–90, and 199–209.

the role of truth in emancipating a society from oppression.[62] Havel explains that the totalitarian regimes of Central Europe developed a system of control that forced their members to participate in a vast network of deception, so thoroughly permeated with hypocrisy and lies that virtually everything became described by its opposite:

> [T]he complete degradation of the individual is presented as his or her ultimate liberation; depriving people of information is called making it available; . . . the repression of culture is called its development; the expansion of imperial influence is presented as support for the oppressed; the lack of free expression becomes the highest form of freedom.[63]

The rules of this game of make-believe required that every member of society, from the greengrocer to the president, perpetuate the illusion. They were all pushed to participate daily in the many tiny public rituals that validated the ideology of the regime. Havel notes that it was not necessary to believe the lies. Few in fact did. It was only necessary to act as if the lies were true, or at least to remain silent about them. Havel describes this as "living within the lie" and emphasizes human receptivity to living a lie as a necessary component of a totalitarian regime's success: "[H]uman beings are compelled to live within a lie, but they can be compelled to do so only because they are in fact capable of living in this way."[64] Modern totalitarianism is able to function as it does because of the human capacity—whether from fear of pain or the desire for comfort—to adapt itself to living a lie. This accommodation comes at a price. Living within a lie alienates the person from himself, and leads to a "profound crisis of human identity."[65]

Havel affirms, however, that the experience of human alienation has a curious result. It points beyond itself. "Individuals can be alienated from

[62] Vaclav Havel, "The Power of the Powerless," 23–96. Havel draws here on the work of his philosophical mentor, the Czech philosopher and signer of Charter 77, Jan Patocka, whose death under police interrogation was one of the catalysts that led to Prague's Velvet Revolution. Patocka had labored since the 1930s to find a synthesis between Husserl's (and later Heidegger's) theoretical insights into the crisis of European society and the ethical activism of Thomas Masaryk, Czechoslovakia's first philosopher president. For Patocka, the solution was to rediscover philosophy's essential character as a "life in truth." See Edward F. Findlay, *Caring for the Soul in a Postmodern Age: Politics and Phenomenology in the Thought of Jan Patocka* (Albany, NY: SUNY Press). For Rorty's perspective on Jan Patocka and the Czech dissidents, see Richard Rorty, "The Seer of Prague," *The New Republic* (July 1, 1991): 35–40.

[63] Vaclav Havel, "The Power of the Powerless," 30.

[64] Ibid., 38.

[65] Ibid., 45.

themselves only because there is *something* in them to alienate." The violence of human alienation reveals "living within a lie" to be the distorted image of another way of living.

> Living the truth is thus woven directly into the texture of living a lie. It is the repressed alternative, the authentic aim to which living a lie is an inauthentic response. Only against this background does living a lie make any sense: it exists *because* of that background. In its excusatory, chimerical rootedness in the human order, it is a response to nothing other than the human predisposition to truth. Under the orderly surface of the life of lies, therefore, there slumbers the hidden sphere of life in its real aims, of its hidden openness to truth.[66]

The pain of alienation points to the "hidden sphere" of human life. Havel describes this hidden sphere in various ways. It is the reality underlying the deepest desires of the human heart, desires that are naturally ordered toward certain specific ends. "The essential aims of life are present naturally in every person. In everyone there is some longing for humanity's rightful dignity, for moral integrity, for free expression of being and a sense of transcendence over the world of existences."[67] In essence, Havel is asserting that there exists in all people an inclination toward something more than the mere satisfaction of their material needs. First, there is an inner urge to pursue life's needs in a free, responsible, and creative way. Second, rooted in the human recognition of something within us that transcends the material world, there is the urge to pursue the truth about this hidden reality and the human person's place in it. Third, there is the urge to pursue these creative aims and this openness to truth *with others* from within a network of responsibility and social solidarity. Those who are true to the promptings of this hidden sphere of life and attempt to live in harmony with its aims are attempting to "live within the truth."

Havel sees the inner human urge to live according to the truth, to live according to the "real aims of life," as the authentic source of resistance to oppression. Reacting against the widely held view that resistance movements are largely the work of elite groups of artists and intellectuals, Havel portrays these movements as springing from all parts of society.[68] The greengrocer who stops placing propaganda posters among his vegetables or the master brewer who tries to improve his product are both responding to the same human urge: the urge to act freely and responsibly before values they recognize to be higher than the State and

66 Ibid., 41.

67 Ibid., 38.

68 Ibid., 47.

not subject to its ideology. These citizens do not necessarily seek to become dissidents, but are thrown into it by circumstances that bring out their sense of personal responsibility before the truth of things. "It begins as an attempt to do your work well, and ends with being branded an enemy of society."[69]

Havel views living within the truth as multidimensional. It has an existential dimension ("returning humanity to its inherent nature"), a cognitive dimension ("revealing reality as it is"), a moral dimension ("setting an example for others"), and an "unambiguous *political* dimension."[70] Since living within the lie is essential to an oppressive regime's ability to maintain itself in power, living within the truth becomes a deadly threat to it. Havel explains that once individuals start to live within the truth in concrete ways there arises within oppressed societies "the independent spiritual, social and political life of society."[71] Gradually, individuals living within the truth begin to work together to develop "parallel structures" or even a "parallel polis," where the members of society can together pursue the real ends of human life. Havel has in mind here underground universities, theatres, trade unions, and any other free association that provides space for the collective pursuit of the authentic aims of human life. Writing in 1978, Havel judged that this was as far as the resistance movements had gotten. "These parallel structures, it may be said, represent the most articulated expressions so far of 'living within the truth.' "[72] He predicted, however, that one possible outcome would be for these efforts to lead to the peaceful collapse of the regime and a collective commitment to protect the "independent life of society" and every individual's ability to pursue with others a life within the truth. In essence, Havel sketched the features of the Velvet Revolution that would irrupt ten years later.

Living within the Truth and the Protection of Negative Liberty

Vaclav Havel presents the defense of human rights as a core aspect of any movement to resist oppression. "As we have seen, the 'dissident movement' grows out of the principle of equality, founded on the notion that human rights and freedoms are indivisible."[73] The parallel structures created by communal efforts to live within the truth act as "a defence of the individual and his or her right to a free and truthful life (that is, a

[69] Ibid., 63.
[70] Ibid., 41.
[71] Ibid., 65.
[72] Ibid., 79.
[73] Ibid., 60.

defence of human rights and a struggle to see the laws respected)."[74] In short, Havel affirms that the goal of all resistance to oppression is to preserve a realm within which individuals are able "to live freely in dignity and partnership."[75] In this respect, Havel's goal does not differ greatly from Isaiah Berlin's. Like Berlin, Havel sees his position as expressing "humanity's revolt against an enforced position."[76] Like Berlin, Havel views his efforts as "an attempt to regain control over one's own sense of responsibility."[77] Indeed, in the final analysis, Berlin and Havel are both defending the classical liberal position that the role of government is to create and protect a private realm where individuals are free to pursue their own goals without interference.

There is, however, an important difference between them. They seek to protect negative liberty in vastly different ways. As we have seen, Isaiah Berlin wants to protect liberty by promoting a vigorous pluralism of values, whose only unifying principle is society's present collective sentiment concerning which acts are "normal" and which "abnormal" or "repulsive." Vaclav Havel, on the other hand, although he recognizes the importance of allowing individuals to pursue a variety of disparate aims, nevertheless sees these ends as rooted in a common humanity, having common characteristics. While Berlin affirmed that there is no one bedrock conception of the human person into which the plurality of human ends can be reconciled, Havel affirms the absolute necessity of recognizing such a bedrock conception for the defense of liberty. Indeed, for Havel, experience shows that we share a common humanity.

> Historical experience teaches us that any genuinely meaningful point of departure in an individual's life usually has an element of universality about it. In other words, it is not something partial, accessible only to a restricted community, and not transferable to any other. On the contrary, it must be potentially accessible to everyone; it must foreshadow a general solution and, thus, it is not just the expression of an introverted, self-contained responsibility that individuals have to and for themselves alone, but responsibility to and for the *world*.[78]

Thus, while for Berlin moral pluralism flowing from a relative agnosticism concerning what it means to be human offers the only real defense of civil rights and negative liberty, Havel holds that lasting liberty can

---

[74] Ibid., 78.
[75] Ibid., 46.
[76] Ibid., 45.
[77] Ibid.
[78] Ibid., 80.

only exist from within a collective recognition of the foundational aims of human life, aims that are not subject to the sentiment of a manipulated majority nor the ideology of a regime. By contrast, Berlin embraces a resigned relativism.

> It may be that the ideal of freedom to choose ends without claiming eternal validity for them, and the pluralism of values connected with this, is only the late fruit of our declining capitalist civilization: an ideal which remote ages and primitive societies have not recognised, and one which posterity will regard with curiosity, even sympathy, but little comprehension.[79]

With serenity Berlin even affirms that "principles are not less sacred because their duration cannot be guaranteed. Indeed, the very desire for guarantees that our values are eternal and secure in some objective heaven is perhaps only a craving for the certainties of childhood or the absolute values of our primitive past."[80] Havel displays no such insouciance concerning the permanence of human values. He recognizes that the discovery of truths that transcend any given culture or regime is the foundation of any attempt to live freely and with dignity. Far from being a childish or primitive craving for certainties, the affirmation that "there is truth, that there is good and evil—and that the difference is not reducible to cultural preference" (as Kohák so well expresses it) is the only sure defense of civil rights and human liberty. Stated in Berlin's terms, the dissidents from Central and Eastern Europe discovered that some measure of positive liberty (the freedom to live according to the real aims of human life) is needed to promote and protect negative liberty (the political freedom not to be interfered with in one's pursuit of one's freely chosen aims). It is here that John Paul's theology of freedom's dependence on truth comes into historical focus.

Living within the Truth and John Paul's Theology of Truth

As we have seen, the aspect of John Paul's teaching with which Milton Friedman objects is the pope's assertion that "*obedience to the truth* about God and man is the first condition of freedom."[81] Friedman asks, "Whose 'truth'? Decided by whom?" This is a legitimate question. If the pope means here that political freedom depends on society embracing and imposing on its members the fullness of Catholic doctrine, then this

---

[79] Isaiah Berlin, "Two Concepts of Liberty," in *Proper Study of Mankind*, 242.
[80] Ibid.
[81] *Centesimus Annus,* §41.

would indeed be problematic for supporters of negative liberty and a free society. The pope would then be supporting a theocratic view of the State with totalitarian features not unlike those exhibited by the now defunct repressive regimes of Central and Eastern Europe. Yet, the fact that the dissidents who helped topple those regimes regard a similar fidelity to truth as an integral component of their success suggests that there is another way to read the pope's assertion. Once again, to understand John Paul's teaching, we must remember that he regards freedom's dependence on truth as a reality existing on several concentric levels.

John Paul does indeed affirm that the fullness of human freedom is properly a Christian reality: It belongs to those who participate in someway in the life of Christ and his Church. The pope, however, also affirms that this fullness cannot be forced upon another. An essential component of the "truth about man," obedience to which is a prerequisite of freedom, is that each person's freedom of conscience must be respected: "[T]otal recognition must be given to *the rights of the human conscience*."[82] Although the human conscience is bound to obey the truth,[83] this obedience is lived by means of one's inner freedom. It cannot be imposed upon us by others. Thus, among the human rights defended by the Church are "the right to religious freedom together with the right to freedom of conscience."[84] Indeed, John Paul adds that, "the curtailment of the religious freedom of individuals and communities is not only a painful experience but it is above all an attack on man's very dignity, independently of the religion professed or of the concept of the world which these individuals and communities have."[85] As if responding to Friedman's concern, John Paul describes "obedience to truth" as entailing, among other things, "the duty to respect the rights of others."[86] Knowing the truth will set us free, but only if that truth is accepted freely. The pope argues, therefore, that the primary function of the State is to protect and promote its citizens' ability, individually and collectively through free associations, to seek the truth and to live creatively according to the truth. Echoing Havel's teachings concerning the "independent life of society," John Paul affirms that the State must respect and promote the "subjectivity of society."[87] For John Paul, as for Havel, this level of social life exists between the individual and the State and is the level at

---

82 Ibid., §29.

83 Ibid.

84 *Redemptor Hominis,* §17.

85 Ibid.

86 *Centesimus Annus,* §17.

87 Ibid., §46.

which we learn to live within the truth. John Paul portrays the Church as functioning on this level. In relation to the State, the Church is a free association of individuals that seeks to help its members and all people of good will to know the full truth about themselves and attain full freedom in Christ. In essence, the pope is arguing that one of the functions of the State is to promote social conditions that enable intermediate institutions like the Catholic Church to exist and pursue their ends.

It is in the context of the Church's role in society that John Paul responds directly to the type of objection advanced by Milton Friedman, characterizing it as follows:

> Nowadays there is a tendency to claim that agnosticism and skeptical relativism are the philosophy and the basic attitude which correspond to democratic forms of political life. Those who are convinced that they know the truth and firmly adhere to it are considered unreliable from a democratic point of view, since they do not accept that truth is determined by the majority, or that it is subject to variation according to different political trends.[88]

John Paul responds to this objection in two ways. First, he argues that unless some truths about the human person transcend society and the State, then we have no way of defending ourselves from the arbitrary use of power: "[I]f there is no ultimate truth to guide and direct political activity, then ideas and convictions can easily be manipulated for reasons of power."[89] Indeed, freedom itself (the negative liberty proper to political life) depends on respect for basic truths about human nature that are not subject to society: "In a world without truth, freedom loses its foundation and man is exposed to the violence of passion and to manipulation, both open and hidden."[90] The pope affirms tirelessly, therefore, that the experiment of democratic government and free society will collapse and become an "open or thinly disguised totalitarianism"[91] unless the members of a free society protect several basic truths about the human person.

> Among the most important of these rights, mention must be made of the right to life, an integral part of which is the right of the child to develop in the mother's womb from the moment of conception; the right to live in a united family and in a moral environment conducive to the growth of the child's personality; the right to develop one's intelligence and freedom in seeking and knowing the truth; the right to

[88] Ibid.

[89] Ibid.

[90] Ibid.

[91] Ibid.

> share in the work which makes wise use of the earth's material resources, and to derive from that work the means to support oneself and one's dependents; and the right freely to establish a family, to have and to rear children through the responsible exercise of one's sexuality. In a certain sense, the source and synthesis of these rights is religious freedom, understood as the right to live in the truth of one's faith and in conformity with one's transcendent dignity as a person.[92]

John Paul offered this list of rights from within his view that the basic unit of culture—the basic unit of a society's subjectivity—is the family.[93] Like Havel, John Paul described the individual and communal search for truth and the capacity to live in harmony with this truth as fundamental rights that society and the State must respect. The pope, however, went far beyond Havel by offering a concrete list of human rights that must be protected if society is to remain free. The challenge that John Paul placed before classical liberals such as Milton Friedman and Isaiah Berlin was simply this: Can the political freedoms you cherish be preserved without ensuring the fundamental right to life—especially among the most vulnerable members of society: the unborn, the elderly and the disabled—and the social conditions for the integral development of human life? Throughout his encyclicals, the pope affirmed that the experience of the twentieth century revealed that freedom cannot be preserved unless these rights are protected.

Note, however, that John Paul did not seek to impose even this crucial truth upon society. It is a truth that can only be lived by being freely accepted. Thus, in relation to secular society and the secular State, John Paul claimed for the Church only the freedom to bear witness to the truth. In essence, John Paul recognized and respected man's freedom to destroy himself and his society; the human person's freedom to embrace slavery instead of liberty. Nonetheless, he reserved the right for the Church and for all Christians to bear witness to the truth.[94] With confidence in the inherent attractiveness of the truth about the human person, a truth that is animated by *the* Truth with a capital T (the mysterious radiation of truth and love), John Paul was confident that Christians and all people of good will who bear witness to the truth by how they live their lives can move whole populations to live differently, to change their form of government, to change their scale of values.[95]

---

92 Ibid., §47.
93 Ibid., §39.
94 Ibid., §5.
95 Ibid., §23.

John Paul further responded to the view that "true believers" are a danger to democracy by affirming that in fact the opposite is the case. Looking back over the remarkable events of 1989, the pope described the changes as in great part due to "the non-violent commitment of people who, while always refusing to yield to the force of power, succeeded time after time in finding effective ways of bearing witness to the truth."[96] In this context, "the Christian upholds freedom and serves it,"[97] while working in dialogue with others to build a society that respects basic human rights.

In John Paul's view, only those who recognize freedom as integral to human dignity will work to ensure negative liberty in society. Moreover, for labors on behalf of negative liberty to succeed, one must have an accurate understanding of what freedom means. Only those who recognize that human freedom means more than merely the ability to choose between material goods, that it signifies the capacity to live according to the truth about the human person (according to the real aims of life), will be able to promote a society that protects its members' ability to pursue their goals without interference. This insight is also present in thinkers from Central Europe. John Paul went beyond thinkers like Havel, however, in showing how the Christian is doubly able to promote negative liberty and civil rights: A Christian inspired by the true aims of the Gospel will promote civil rights because he or she recognizes freedom of conscience as a necessary component of any individual response to the grace of Christ and the Gospel message. Moreover, the Christian will be animated by such a zeal to bear witness to these values that at times it will even move him to shed his blood for them.

In this context, one way of interpreting John Paul's teaching on truth and freedom is to regard it as an extended effort to give a theological foundation (a largely Johannine foundation) to the insights of the dissidents of Central and Eastern Europe. They learned from bitter experience the importance of fidelity to truth. They learned as well the interior joy and liberating power of this fidelity.[98] John Paul's theology can partly be viewed as an effort to show how this truth ultimately finds its foundation in the mystery of the Living Word of God, the Truth become human in the humanity of Christ and acting among us in the love of the Spirit. In the final analysis, therefore, John Paul remained faithful to the Johannine insights of the Rhapsodic Theater. He remained faithful to the power of the Living Word as a force for cultural liberation.

---

[96] Ibid.

[97] Ibid., §46.

[98] *Dives in Misericordia,* §6.

Toward a Thomistic Anthropology of Truth and Freedom

In these pages I have outlined the various meanings of truth and freedom in John Paul's theology and have tried to place them in their social and political context. I have argued at key points that the pope's theology of truth and freedom becomes most fully intelligible within a broadly Thomistic anthropology. This fact, however, presents us with a problem. Many would argue that Thomistic anthropology is outmoded because the philosophy of nature underpinning it has been proved false by modern science. Thus, any theology that rests upon Thomistic principles is doomed to failure. Some, therefore, try to ground freedom's dependence on truth upon a phenomenological analysis not easily reconcilable with Aquinas's thought.[99] Others, enthralled by the apparent power of Hume's critique of the "Is/Ought fallacy" or G. E. Moore's critique of the "naturalistic fallacy," try to ground morality on a neo-Kantian version of Aquinas.[100] Yet, is St. Thomas's anthropology in fact outmoded? Has modern science truly disproved the philosophy of nature that underlies Aquinas's Christian anthropology? My own contention is no: On the level of its principles, Thomas's anthropology is not outmoded, because modern science has not, in fact, disproved the basic insights of Aquinas's philosophy of nature. Indeed, as several recent studies suggest, a growing number of scientists are beginning to pose questions about the philosophical underpinnings of their own methods and are offering answers to these questions that have affinities with Aquinas's philosophy of nature.[101] To my knowledge, however, no one has yet drawn together in one monograph the insights of these studies nor placed them in conversation with the views of contemporary analytic philosophers who draw similar conclusions. Nonetheless, I would like to suggest that John Paul's theology of truth and freedom will become more accessible to the faithful by being grounded in a renewed Thomistic anthropology and philosophy of nature. Although these concluding remarks are not the place to develop

---

[99] See for example Erazim Kohák, *The Embers and the Stars: A Philosophical Inquiry into the Moral Sense of Nature* (Chicago: University of Chicago Press, 1987).

[100] See, for example, John Finnis, *Natural Law and Natural Rights* (Oxford: Clarendon Press, 1980).

[101] John Haught, *Science and Religion: From Conflict to Conversation* (New York: Paulist Press, 1995); Mariano Artigas, *The Mind of the Universe: Understanding Science and Religion* (Radnor, PA: Templeton Foundation Press, 2000); William E. Carroll, *La Creación y las Ciencias Naturales: Actualidad de Santo Tomás de Aquino,* trans. Oscar Velásquez (Santiago: Ediciones Universidad Católica de Chile).

such a perspective, I would like to end by sketching what I believe to be the key elements of such a renewal.[102]

When St. Augustine expresses his longing for God in the *Confessions*, he famously does so in the plural: "You have made us for yourself, O Lord, and our hearts are restless until they rest in you."[103] Although we may be tempted to view spiritual longing or the experience of human alienation as solitary events, they both have profoundly social dimensions. To live within the truth or within a lie both require socialization. Even though, from the Thomistic perspective, each of us is born with the spiritual powers of intellect and will, both of which contain principles orienting us toward the true and the good, we only learn to know the truth and to love the good through a community. In other words, although the primary precepts of the natural law and the inclinations of the will are present in everyone, we learn to act according to these principles in and through a moral apprenticeship whereby we are initiated into the life of a community. Freedom's dependence on truth is a community-based dependence. We grow in freedom in and through communities that have a greater or lesser grasp of the truth. A renewed Thomistic anthropology, therefore, will be one that has a deeper understanding of the communal aspects of moral development.

The social character of moral development, however, is only one component of renewal. Humans are not just social, they are animal. As we have seen, Vaclav Havel suggests that the experience of human alienation reveals "living within the lie" to be the distorted image of something richer: It points to the authentic human joy of "living within the truth." Similarly, we can view the effects of Enlightenment attempts to remove animality from the definition of Man as equally revelatory. Once humans were no longer "rational animals" and became "thinking beings," the last thread linking morality with nature was severed. This history is complex. It is linked to a changed understanding of "nature" and of the place of the "spiritual" within nature. The change in definition was part of an effort to save human freedom from the perceived determinism of nature and the physical. Yet, it contradicts what is most evident about us: We are primates, members of the animal kingdom, sharing characteristics present

---

102 In what follows I am deeply influenced by the work of Alasdair MacIntyre, especially *After Virtue: A Study in Moral Theory*, 2nd ed. (Notre Dame, IN: University of Notre Dame Press, 1984); *Three Rival Versions of Moral Enquiry* (Notre Dame, IN: University of Notre Dame Press, 1990); and *Dependent Rational Animals: Why Human Beings Need the Virtues* (Chicago: Open Court, 2001).

103 *Confesiones* 1.1: *"fecisti nos, domine, ad te, et inquietum est cor nostrum donec requiescat in te."*

in other primates and in other animals. This does not mean, however, that we are merely primates. St. Thomas recognized that we are strange amphibians: made to breathe the air of the spiritual while living in the waters of the material. A renewed Thomistic anthropology will thus also take seriously what we share developmentally with other animals, while identifying our unique way of living these common aspects. Such an approach will require that we address squarely the concerns of those who are persuaded that no moral "ought" can be discerned from an "is." In other words, any effort to return animality to the definition of the human would require a clear explanation of how knowing what a thing is also implies knowing something about how it ought to act. As noted earlier, this also implies a renewed understanding of practical rationality, one that shows how knowledge of what constitutes human flourishing shapes our practical judgments concerning what we should do here and now.

An approach that takes more seriously human animality and the social dimensions of moral development will also provide a renewed context for understanding the mystery of sin. While Havel speaks of the human capacity freely for reasons of fear or comfort to live within the lie, John Paul squarely places these actions in the context of sin: the human person's capacity to act contrary to what he or she knows to be right, and to do so even while retaining an awareness that such actions are contrary to the wisdom and will of God. A moral theology that grasps the role of the emotions and of one's social context in shaping our moral judgments will better explain the dynamics of sin and the means of freeing ourselves from it. In other words, the deeper we understand the social and animal components of human nature, the better we will be able to explain (a) why "living within the lie" can be so appealing, (b) why living within the lie brings such sorrow and confusion, and (c) how "living within the Truth" both liberates us from the sorrowful confusion of sin and empowers us to live the joy of virtue.

But perhaps the biggest obstacle to centering more clearly John Paul's theology of truth and freedom in a Thomistic anthropology is the obstacle posed by the philosophy of nature. Thomistic anthropology will continue to have limited appeal as long as it fails to show that the philosophy of nature upon which it depends is compatible with the discoveries and methods of contemporary science. The standard narrative of the emergence of modern science portrays the scientific method as born from the defeat of Aristotelian science. Indeed, many of the early discoveries of modern science were discoveries that overturned time-honored assumptions of the Aristotelians. Disciples of Aquinas, therefore, will have to show how the principles of the philosophy of nature differ from the outmoded science of Aristotle. Specifically, they need to show convincingly how the natural world has qualitative as well as quantitative aspects, and that these qualitative aspects can be known and studied.[104] The time seems ripe for such an undertaking because scientists themselves are turning to questions that transcend the merely quantitative aspects of nature. Indeed, some are even searching for a holistic approach that will help them understand the human community's place in creation, and the role of the scientist as a member of that community.[105]

The challenge, therefore, for those who wish to give John Paul's theology of truth and freedom a deeper grounding in Thomistic anthropology is threefold. It calls for an anthropology that underlines the social dimensions of moral development, returns animality to the definition of the human, and springs from a renewed philosophy of nature. Responding to this threefold challenge will facilitate our understanding of the Johannine proclamation that "You will know the truth, and the truth will make you free" (Jn 8,32). It will help us convince our contemporaries that what the young Karol Wojtyla asserted in *Jeremiah: A National Drama* is equally true today during our own national dramas: "One must throw truth across the path of lies" because "in truth are freedom and excellence," while the betrayal of truth leads only to slavery.

---

[104] William E. Carroll, "The Scientific Revolution and Contemporary Discourse in the Relationship between Faith and Reason," in *Faith and Reason*, ed. Timothy L. Smith (South Bend, IN: St. Augustine Press, 2001): 195–216.

[105] See Dominique Lambert, *Sciences et théologie: Les figures d'un dialogue* (Bruxelles: Lessius, 1999); Benedict Ashley, *Theologies of the Body* (Boston: National Bioethics Center, 1995).

The Common Good in St. Thomas and John Paul II

MICHAEL WALDSTEIN
International Theological Institute
Gaming, Austria

WHEN ONE COMPARES St. Thomas and John Paul II on communion and community, one sees that "common good" plays a central architectonic role for St. Thomas, but apparently not for John Paul II. "Gift of self" plays a central architectonic role for John Paul II, but apparently not for St. Thomas. In addition, St. Thomas hardly ever draws on Trinitarian theology to illumine communion among creatures, because his account of the Trinity focuses on processions within one knowing and loving subject. John Paul II, by contrast, speaks about the Trinity primarily in interpersonal terms and draws on this understanding frequently and systematically in his account of communion among human beings. I have been struggling with these differences for quite a while because I am writing a book on *Common Good and Gift of Self: The Communion of Persons in St. Thomas and John Paul II.* It was a sharp delight to run into John Paul II's *Letter to Families*, §§10 and 11 because they weave the common good and gift of self into a very suggestive unity. There are many connections to think through.

Let me start with some introductory remarks on "common good." A common good is a good in which many persons can share at the same time without in any way lessening or splitting it. When I drink wine, it becomes exclusively my own personal or private good. If I drink it, you cannot. We might have a cask of wine, and in some real sense the wine can then be common. Yet it is only imperfectly common, common only in the sense of being sufficient to provide for the personal or private good of more than one person. Conversely, it is not the whole cask that is my personal good, but only a part of it.

By contrast, the Pythagorean theorem is a common good in the strict and full sense. If I understand it well, I do not in any way deprive you of understanding. Conversely, I do not take only part of the theorem to myself to be my private possession. The more I personally understand it, the more it becomes mine in its totality.

The peace of a state or a family is also a common good in the strict sense, provided that it is a genuine peace of the whole, from which no one is excluded. When I share in this peace, I do not lessen your share in it. In fact, without my share, your share in it would decrease, since peace can exist in the full sense only if each and every person shares in it.

The Common Good of Marriage and Family

John Paul II's point of departure in §10 of his *Letter to Families* is the marriage vow. "The words of consent define the common good of the couple and of the family. First, the common good of the spouses: love, fidelity, honor, the permanence of their union until death." John Paul II adds a general point about the common good. "The common good, by its very nature, both unites individual persons and ensures the true good of each." One of the most common errors about the common good is that it is an alien good, not really the good of the persons to whom it is supposed to be common, and therefore not really a common good. When the state collects income tax from me to put it into the common pot, it is true that my money is gone and someone else has it. My money has become an alien good. The state, of course, should use the money for purposes that eventually flow back to me and others in the state, but money is by its very nature a private good. It can only be imperfectly common. The common good of the spouses, by contrast, is truly common. It unites them and is the good of each. This is, in fact, what it means for a good to be truly and fully common.

As part of their vow, the spouses promise to accept children. The children become part of "the genealogy of the person"[1] that begins with the generation of the Son from the Father, continues in the creation of persons, and reaches its highpoint in the vision of God. In this genealogy, the Trinity is the first exemplar of communion. Communion of creatures is made in the image of that exemplar.

When children are born, the common good of husband and wife extends itself. "Through the genealogy of persons, conjugal communion becomes a communion of generations. *Per ipsam personarum originem coniugalis communio fit generationum communio*" (§10).

---

[1] The "genealogy of the person" and its Trinitarian origin is the subject of *Letter to Families*, §9.

Some Connections between Common Good and Gift of Self

John Paul II concludes §10 as follows.

> Families today have too little "human" life. There is a shortage of people with whom to create and share the common good; and yet that good, by its nature, demands to be created and shared with others: *"Bonum est diffusivum sui"* ["good pours itself out"]. The more common the good, the more properly one's own it will also be: mine, yours, ours. This is the logic behind living according to the good, living in truth and charity. If man is able to accept and follow this logic, his life truly becomes a "sincere gift."

This text functions as the bracket between §10, which deals with the common good, and §11, which deals with the gift of self. The connecting thread that John Paul II uses is the axiom so dear to St. Thomas, *bonum est diffusivum sui*. In this axiom one finds both of these concepts: the good, which means preeminently the common good, and self-communication or, in the realm of persons, self-gift.

In *De potentia*, question 2, article 1, St. Thomas asks whether generative power belongs to God. He responds:

> It is the nature of any act that it communicates itself as much as possible. For this reason every agent acts inasmuch as it is in act. Now, acting is nothing else than communicating as much as possible that by which the agent is in act. But the divine nature is most of all and most purely act. Therefore it itself communicates itself as much as possible. It communicates itself by mere likeness to creatures, which is clear to all, because any creature is a being according to its likeness to that [divine nature] itself. The Catholic faith posits also another mode of communication, namely, as [the divine nature] itself is communicated by a natural communication, as it were, so that just as the one to whom human nature is communicated is human, so the one to whom divinity is communicated is not only similar to God, but is truly God.[2]

St. Thomas usually formulates the principle of self-communication or self-diffusion in these very general terms: Actuality as such communicates itself, the good as such diffuses itself, pours itself out. If one applies the principle to persons in particular, one can express it in personal terms as *someone giving* something belonging to himself or giving *himself*. An example of this way of speaking is found in St. Thomas's *Pange Lingua*: At the last supper Jesus "gives himself with his own hands, *se dat suis*

[2] St. Thomas Aquinas, *De potentia,* 2.1 c.

manibus."[3] Such self-communication, he argues, belongs to the very nature of the love of friendship.

> Love is twofold, namely, love of friendship and love of concupiscence, but they differ. In the love of concupiscence we draw to ourselves what is outside of us when by that very love we love things other than ourselves inasmuch as they are useful or delightful to us. In the love of friendship, on the other hand, it is the other way around, because we draw ourselves to what is outside. For, to those whom we love in that love we are related as to ourselves, communicating ourselves to them in some way.[4]

All love of friendship, according to this text, involves a self-communication. Following the Gospel of John, St. Thomas uses this way of speaking also in his Trinitarian theology.

> To be given can belong both to the divine essence, as we say that the Father gives his essence to the Son, and it can belong to the Father, so that the Father is said to give himself, and similarly to the Son and to the Holy Spirit. . . . And thus we concede simply that the person gives himself and is given by himself.[5]

One can see this specifically personal way of speaking very clearly in John Paul II's Trinitarian theology, for example, in §10 of *Dominum et Vivificantem*:

> In his intimate life, God "is love," the essential love shared by the three divine Persons: personal love is the Holy Spirit as the Spirit of the Father and the Son. Therefore he "searches even the depths of God," as *uncreated Love-Gift*. It can be said that in the Holy Spirit the intimate life of the Triune God becomes totally gift, an exchange of mutual love between the divine Persons and that through the Holy Spirit God exists in the mode of gift. It is the Holy Spirit who is *the personal expression* of this self-giving, of this being—love. He is Person-Love. He is Person-Gift. Here we have an inexhaustible treasure of the reality and an inexpressible deepening of the concept of person in God, which only divine Revelation makes known to us. At the same time, the Holy Spirit, being consubstantial with the Father and the Son in divinity, is love and uncreated gift from which derives as from its *[living] source all giving of gifts* vis-à-vis creatures (created gift): the gift of existence to all things through

---

[3] "In supremae nocte coenae recumbens cum fratribus, observata lege plene cibis in legalibus, cibum turbae duodenae se dat suis manibus." St. Thomas Aquinas, *Officium for the Feast of Corpus Christi*.

[4] St. Thomas Aquinas, *Super Ioannem,* cap. 15, lect. 4, Marietti, §2036.

[5] St. Thomas Aquinas, *Sent.* I.15.3.1 c.

> creation; the gift of grace to human beings through the whole economy of salvation. As the Apostle Paul writes: "God's love has been poured into our hearts through the Holy Spirit which has been given to us."[6]

According to St. Thomas, the divine nature, inasmuch as it is perfect, communicates itself. More exactly, the Father, who is identical with the divine nature, begets the Son, giving to him the entire divine nature, and the Spirit proceeds from both in virtue of the same divine communicative power, which always involves both person and nature.[7] According to John Paul II a life of giving takes place in the Trinity and is concentrated in the person of the Holy Spirit. St. Thomas only speaks of the Holy Spirit's name "gift" in relation to human beings who receive this gift. John Paul II speaks about it also as a properly Trinitarian name belonging to the Holy Spirit in his procession from the Father and the Son. I do not think they contradict each other, but the perspectives are complementary.

St. Thomas invokes the principle of the self-communication of a perfect nature also at the very beginning of the *Tertia pars* when he addresses the question whether the Incarnation was fitting.

> I answer that what is fitting to every thing is that which belongs to it according to the account of its own nature. Thus it is fitting for man to reason because this belongs to him inasmuch as he is rational in his nature. Now, the nature of God is goodness, as Denys says in Divine Names 1. Therefore, whatever belongs to the account of the good is fitting to God. It belongs to the account of the good that it communicates itself to others as Denys says in Divine Names 4. Therefore it belongs to the nature of the highest good that it communicates itself in the highest way to creatures. This comes about most of all by this, that he joins a created nature to himself in such a way that there is one person from these three, the Word, the soul and the flesh, as Augustine says in *De Trinitate* 13. Therefore it is clear that it was fitting to God to become incarnate.[8]

According to St. Thomas, one and the same principle can be seen in the generation of persons in the Trinity, in creation and in the incarnation. It belongs to the very account of actuality and goodness to communicate itself.

The same principle lies also at the root of the commonness of the common good. According to De Koninck, "The common good differs

---

[6] John Paul II, *Dominum et Vivificantem,* §10.

[7] "Generative power signifies simultaneously the essence and (personal) notion, *potentia generandi simul essentiam et notionem significat.*" *De potentia,* 2.2 c.

[8] St. Thomas Aquinas, *Summa theologiae* III, q. 1, a. 1.

from the singular good by this very universality. It has the character of superabundance and it is eminently diffusive of itself insofar as it is more communicable: it reaches the singular more than the singular good: it is the greater good of the singular."[9] The *Letter to Families* says the same thing in §10, "The more common the good, the more properly one's own it will also be: mine, yours, ours." I can have and treasure the Pythagorean theorem or the peace of my family in a more intimate sense than wine. Wine *does* become mine when I drink it, but it remains in a certain way external to me even when it enters into my stomach. When the wine is assimilated into my body, it is no longer wine. By contrast, the Pythagorean Theorem does not remain external to me. It is deeply drawn into my mind, but remains itself in this diffusion of itself. The case of peace is similar. It remains itself and is shared by many as a whole. The greater communicability of more perfect being is the reason for its commonness as a common good.

Again, when the perfection of being is understood specifically as personal being, the self-diffusion of the good is the self-gift of the person. There is thus a deep connection between these two doctrines: the common good and the gift of self.

Gift of Self

In §11, John Paul II uses the concept "gift of self" in tandem with "common good" and brings out some of the light they throw on each other.

He begins by quoting *Gaudium et Spes,* §24, which is perhaps the most important leitmotif running through his pontificate.[10]

> Indeed, the Lord Jesus, when he prayed to the Father, "that all may be one . . . as we are one" [John 17:21–22] opened up vistas closed to human reason, for he implied a certain likeness between the union of the divine Persons, and the unity of God's sons in truth and charity. This likeness reveals that man, who is the only creature on earth which God willed for itself, cannot fully find himself except through a sincere gift of himself.[11] (cf. Lk 17:33)

According to this text, the Trinity is the first exemplar of unity among persons. The text closely connects two statements: First, the unity of the divine persons is reflected in the unity of god's sons in truth and charity. Second, this relation between exemplar and its image shows that man can

[9] Charles De Koninck, "On the Primacy of the Common Good against the Personalists," *Aquinas Review* 4 (1997): 1–71, here 16.

[10] See Pascal Ide, "Une théologie du don: Les occurrences de Gaudium et spes, n. 24, §3 chez Jean-Paul II," *Anthropotes* 17 (2001): 149–78, 313–44.

[11] Vatican II, *Gaudium et Spes,* §24.

only find himself in a sincere gift of himself. One can conclude from these two statements that the original paradigm, not only of unity, but also of giving must lie in the Trinity. An analysis of the word "give" in the Gospel of John and the Revelation to John would be able to show the deep biblical roots of this truth.

John Paul II comments:

> After affirming that man is the only creature on earth which God willed for itself, the council immediately goes on to say that he cannot "fully find himself except through a sincere gift of self." This might appear to be contradiction, but in fact it is not. Instead it is the magnificent paradox of human existence: an existence called to serve the truth in love. Love causes man to find fulfillment through the sincere gift of self. To love means to give and to receive something which can be neither bought nor sold, but only given freely and mutually. (§11)

In §11 John Paul II returns to the marriage vow and explains it through the logic of the gift of self. In their gift of themselves to each other, the spouses participate in the gift that Christ makes of himself by shedding his blood. Marriage is rooted in the Eucharist.

As in §10, John Paul II passes from the vow and its common good to the transmission of life (§11). The transmission of life is part of "the logic [or as the Latin text has it, the consistent proposal] of the sincere gift." The child is a gift of the creator to the spouses. John Paul II draws the conclusion that the child is the common good of its parents and of the family. St. Thomas says likewise, "offspring is the common good of husband and wife."[12]

An important distinction St. Thomas makes is that between intrinsic and extrinsic common good. The example he usually uses to illustrate this distinction, following Aristotle, *Metaphysics Lambda,* is an army. The intrinsic common good of an army, which is its internal order and unity, is ordered to victory, which is the army's extrinsic common good. A universal principle can be seen here. "Whenever we see a multitude ordered to each other, it must be ordered to some external principle."[13] This principle applies also to marriage. The intrinsic common good of marriage, which is the unity of love between husband and wife on the basis of the marriage vow, is ordered to the child, which is the extrinsic common good of marriage.

In §11 John Paul II defends the truth of the statement that the child is the common good of the family. He concludes with a rather dense and difficult passage.

---

[12] St. Thomas Aquinas, *Sent.* IV.33.2.1 c.

[13] St. Thomas Aquinas, *De veritate,* 5.3 c.

> The common good of the whole of society dwells in man; he is, as we recalled, "the way of the Church." Man is first of all the "glory of God": *"Gloria Dei vivens homo,"* in the celebrated words of St. Irenaeus, which might also be translated: "The glory of God is for man to be alive." It could be said that here we encounter the loftiest definition of man: The glory of God is the common good of all that exists; the common good of the human race.

In the first sentence of this text, John Paul II moves from the family to society as a whole. The common good of the whole of society "dwells in man, *in homine immoratur.*" The common good he has in mind at this point is the glory of God, which is something distinct from man, although it is closely united with him because it "dwells in man, *in homine immoratur.*"

According to St. Thomas, "the whole universe with its single parts is ordered to God as to the end, inasmuch as in them through a certain imitation the divine goodness is represented to the glory of God."[14] In rational creatures, St. Thomas goes on to say in the same place, this ordination to God is present in the most eminent way, because they are not only similar to God, but can attain God by knowing and loving him. His glory is more fully revealed in this gift of himself to created persons.

Since the common good of God's glory is so intimately tied to rational creatures and the operations of their life, Irenaeus is right to include man and the operations of human life in a quasi definition of glory. "The glory of God is for man to be alive." John Paul II turns this definition around as a quasi-definition of man: [F]or man to be alive is to have the glory of God dwelling in him. Irenaeus himself makes a similar reversal when he writes, "This is the glory of man, to persevere and remain in the service of God."[15]

What is the glory that comes to dwell in man? It is the glory of the Trinity. It is a glory inseparable from the power of self-communication that lies in the infinite goodness of the divine nature, that is, it is a glory inseparable from the gift in which "just as the Father has life in himself, so has he given to the Son to have life in himself" (John 5:26). It is the glory of the Holy Spirit as the person in whom "God exists in the mode of gift."

John Paul II offers in §11 a statement for which I do not know any immediate parallel in St. Thomas. "Yes! Man is a common good: a common good of the family and of humanity, of individual groups and of different communities." What sense does it make to call man, every man, a common good? One way of access lies in observing how John Paul II

---

[14] *ST* I, q. 65, a. 2.

[15] St. Irenaeus, *Adversus Haereses,* 4.14.1.

responds to a widespread attitude of the culture of death, namely, "the temptation not to want another birth. . . . A child comes to take up room when it seems that there is less and less room in the world" (§11). In this anti-life mentality each additional human life appears as an attack on the population or the environment or the planet. Against this mentality John Paul II insists that, just as every child is a common good for its family, so every human being is a common good for the various forms of community. He is not contradicting the important principle that the ultimate and deepest reason for loving others is their ordination to a common good that transcends individual persons.[16] He clearly states that the common good par excellence is the glory of God, that is, God himself in the self-communication of his goodness. Human dignity lies in being ordered to this end and even more so in reaching it. Yet, on a more elementary level, it is a good for the whole state—and this means it is a common good—when a child is born. The state regards the child in some measure impersonally as part of a mass of children that ensure the state's survival. In the family, the child is treasured and affirmed as a common good in more personal fashion (§11). The child becomes even more a good for entire communities when it matures and gains in goodness. John Paul II's formulation "man is a common good" is certainly startling for a disciple of St. Thomas, but it is intelligible, particularly in the culture of death which can see each new human being only as occupying space needed for others.

In §11 John Paul II also links the paschal mystery with St. Irenaeus's definition *"gloria dei vivens homo"* (see John 10:10). The paschal mystery communicates a more primal glory that lies in the eternal giving that takes place in the Trinity. It is made accessible in the gift of the Holy Spirit. John Paul II concludes with a dense formulation.

> It is the Gospel truth concerning the gift of self, without which the person cannot "fully find himself," which makes possible an appreciation of how profoundly this "sincere gift" is rooted in the gift of God, creator and redeemer, and in the "grace of the Holy Spirit" which the celebrant during the Rite of Marriage prays will be "poured out" on the spouses. Without such an outpouring, it would be very difficult to understand all this and to carry it out as man's vocation. (§11)

This paragraph should be taken together with the paragraphs on the "logic" of life, or, as the Latin text of §11 has it, "the consistent proposal, *consentaneum propositum*."

---

16 See De Koninck, *Primacy of the Common Good,* 16–17.

> This is the logic behind living according to the good, living in truth and charity. If man is able to accept and follow this logic, his life truly becomes a "sincere gift." (§10)
>
> When a man and woman in marriage mutually give and receive each other in the unity of one flesh, the logic of the sincere gift of self becomes a part of their life. Without this, marriage would be empty; whereas a communion of persons, built on this logic, becomes a communion of parents. (§11)

The remarkable thing about *Letter to Families* §10 and 11 is that John Paul II succeeds in showing how a number of mysteries are connected in a coherent "logic" of life, in a "consistent proposal": the mystery of the Trinity as a mystery of giving; the paschal mystery as a mystery of giving; and human life, again as a mystery of giving. He shows how the common good is a harmoniously suited part of this overall logic. One important connecting point between St. Thomas and John Paul II is the axiom *"bonum diffusivum sui,"* which John Paul II, following St. John of the Cross, unfolds in his teaching on the gift of self, first in the Trinity, then among creatures, particularly in the relation between man and woman.

Intellect and Will in the Encyclical *Fides et Ratio* and in Thomas Aquinas

REINHARD HÜTTER
Duke Divinity School
Durham, North Carolina

The Will in *Fides et Ratio*: A Stowaway[1]

The Question

ATTENDING AT LENGTH to the question of faith and reason and allowing the question of the will to remain unthematized is like embarking upon a perilous sea passage with the helmsman attempting to hide as a stowaway. Indeed, only by identifying the stowaway as the helmsman, that is, by explicitly thematizing the will's relationship to faith and reason, can we circumvent the frequently committed fallacy of treating faith and reason as fundamentally extrinsic to each other or, worse, as fundamentally opposed—perpetually engaged in negotiation between sometimes peaceful and sometimes warring encampments. As we can learn from Thomas Aquinas and as we will discuss below in some detail, attending to the question of the will avoids this problematic move because the will, as one distinct power of the soul, moves all its other powers, first among them, reason, to their respective operations. Furthermore, according to Thomas Aquinas, the will plays a central, albeit complex, role in the act of faith in which reason is to some degree commanded by the will to

[1] The encyclical is cited according to the new translation as offered in *Restoring Faith in Reason: A New Translation of the Encyclical Letter Faith and Reason of Pope John Paul II together with a commentary and discussion*, ed. Laurence Paul Hemming and Susan Frank Parsons (London: SCM Press, 2002). For a more critical engagement of the encyclical, and especially its original English and German translations, cf. chapter 11 in my book *Bound to Be Free: Evangelical Catholic Engagements in Ecclesiology, Ethics, and Ecumenism* (Grand Rapids, MI: Eerdmans, 2004).

assent to the truth of faith.[2] Hence, it is to be expected that, similar to complex force fields, faith and reason interact and overlap in complex ways as a function of the will's central, if not constitutive, role in their respective operations. But this is not all. It is also the case that faith, as assenting reason, reasons in order to explore the reasons of faith: *fidei ratio*. And reason in its own comprehensive reaching toward truth constantly anticipates—in a kind of faith, that is, in a primordial intellective trust in the intelligibility of being—an antecedent meaningful coherence of reality that is already presupposed in any process of inquiry: *rationis fides*. Moreover, as an inherently teleological activity, rational inquiry needs to anticipate the existence of the goal for which it aims (this goal being not a particular object but an insight in which the inquiry's investigative motion comes to rest).[3] This primordial intellective trust in the intelligibility of reality is the basis on which *Fides et Ratio* is able as well as entitled to encourage a "restoring [of] faith in reason."[4]

The *rationis fides*, of course, differs fundamentally from the *fides* that ultimately is the gift of the Spirit. Hence, *fides,* in its strict theological sense, must be categorically distinguished from *rationis fides*. For *fides* is the active reception of an inexhaustible yet concrete personal truth, a reception in

---

[2] *ST* I, q. 111, a. 1, ad 1: "[N]on quasi convictus ratione, sed quasi imperatus a voluntate." (Unless otherwise noted, all citations from the *Summa theologiae* in English are taken from the translation of the Fathers of the English Dominican Province, *St. Thomas Aquinas Summa Theologica* [New York: Benziger Brothers, 1948]. The Latin original offered in the footnotes is taken from Sancti Thomae de Aquino, *Summa Theologiae,* 3rd ed. [Turin: Edizioni San Paolo, 1999], which offers an improved version of the Leonine edition.) Yet this is only the tip of the iceberg. Aquinas nuances this teaching by developing the notions of an affective cognition *(cognitio per connaturalitatem)* that is moved by an inner instinct *(instinctus interior)*. Cf. *ST* II–II, q. 2, a. 9, ad 3 and II–II, q. 45, a.2. Cf., in detail, Max Seckler, *Instinkt und Glaubenswille* (Mainz: Matthias Grünewald Verlag, 1961).

[3] Cf. on this dynamic the pathbreaking work by Michael Polanyi, *Personal Knowledge: Towards a Post-Critical Philosophy* (Chicago: University of Chicago Press, 1958). Polanyi offers a condensed and accessible account in his "Faith and Reason," *Communio* 28 (2001): 860–74.

[4] To quote the felicitous title of the new translation of the encyclical (with commentary and discussion) edited by Laurence Paul Hemming and Susan Frank Parsons, cited above. For a profound metaphysical meditation (in the form of an intense interpretation of Thomas Aquinas's metaphysics of *esse*) that demonstrates why this trust is a genuine ontological enactment of the intellect itself and therefore the deepest enactment of the *anima intellectiva*, cf. Ferdinand Ulrich, *Homo Abyssus: Das Wagnis der Seinsfrage,* with an introduction by Martin Bieler, 2nd ed. (Einsiedeln: Johannes Verlag, 1998), esp. 289–320.

and through which eternal life inchoately begins in the believer.[5] *Fidei ratio* signifies faith's intellectual exploration *(fides quaerens intellectum)* of this received truth, an exploration that draws upon concepts forged by a reason that enacts its own faith *(rationis fides)* in the prolepsis of the unity of truth.[6]

The Will as the Unthematized Other of Reason

It is safe to say that as long as the will remains unthematized, reason, our faith in reason, and reason's own faith *(rationis fides)* remain largely untroubled. But as soon as we attend to the will, questions—about the will's "incurvature"[7] from human sin and its effect upon reason—emerge with irresistible force. The reason is this: The very fact that *rationis fides* must anticipate the unity of truth that is the telos of any ordered inquiry entails the tacit assumption of the will itself being properly ordered and therefore able to guide appropriately the process of reasoning. Yet what allows us to assume that *sub conditione peccati*, under the condition of sin, the will is properly ordered? Hence, the *rationis fides* might very well operate on an assumption that transcends its capacity of anticipation and for which it might be unable to offer an account: the quality of the willing that moves the process of reasoning. Thus attending to the dynamic of the *rationis fides* unavoidably raises the specter of the will and the role of the will in reason's epistemic and discursive operations.

How does this problem affect *Fides et Ratio* as it presses for and encourages a "philosophia naturae *vere metaphysicae*"[8] (§83) that does justice to

---

5 *ST* II–II, q. 4, a. 1: "[W]e can say that 'faith is a habitus of soul (habitus mentis) through which eternal life begins in us by causing our intellect to adhere to invisible realities." Cited from Jean Pierre Torrell, OP, *Saint Thomas Aquinas, Vol. 2: Spiritual Master,* trans. Robert Royal (Washington, DC: Catholic University of America Press, 2003), 324ff.

6 My reading of the "coniunctio" in §48.

7 On Aquinas's complex doctrine of sin, cf. Otto Hermann Pesch, *Theologie der Rechtfertigung bei Martin Luther und Thomas von Aquin. Versuch eines systematisch-theologischen Dialogs* (Mainz: Grünewald, 1967), 468–516. Two aspects of sin are of interest here: "aversio a Deo" in the case of mortal sin (*ST* I–II, q. 72, a. 5; q. 73, a. 1, ad 2; q. 77, a. 8) and "inordinatus actus" (*ST* I–II, q. 71, a. 1, ad 3; q. 71, a. 6, ad 3 and ad 4). In *ST* I–II, q. 109, a. 7, Thomas states: "Natural good is corrupted, inasmuch as man's nature is disordered by man's will not being subject to God's; and this order being overthrown, the consequence is that the whole nature of sinful man remains disordered."

8 In this instance the new translation does not convince me. It renders the above "a *truly metaphysical* philosophy of nature." But the whole section discusses metaphysics and not "physics," that is, a philosophy of nature proper. Hence, the passage should be rendered, as in the original translation, "a philosophy of *genuinely metaphysical* range."

the ultimate unity of truth? On the one hand, reason's implicit faith *(rationis fides)*, by anticipating a teleologically structured order of reality as a function of reason's own analytic, synthetic, and intentional processes of inquiry, itself invites the rigorous pursuit of metaphysics. Yet on the other hand, precisely the same implicit faith of reason is constrained—bound to respond to the way things are "out there," and bound by the human condition itself and therefore the ways in which reason is shaped not only by humanity's practical needs but even more so by humanity's concrete existence under the condition of sin. We arrive, then, at the pressing question: How do reason and will interrelate in *Fides et Ratio*?

The Hidden Will

We find the dynamic of *rationis fides* and the specter of will most clearly entailed in the encyclical's central mandate: "Fidei parrhesia respondere debet rationis audacia," which can be rendered "The boldness of reason ought to match the freedom of faith" (§48). How so? If the boldness of reason ought to match the freedom of faith, we must suppose that the "boldness of reason" emerges from rectitude of mind and not from reason possibly misdirected by a will that, *sub conditione peccati,* is turned in upon itself. Otherwise, the boldness of reason could as well lead—and de facto did lead—to the hubris of a totalitarian grasp of reality exercised by a reason bent into a purely instrumental rationality or inflated into a quasi-absolute faculty, falsely assuming speculative self-transparency. In short, while the boldness of reason clearly seems to presuppose rectitude of mind, the question remains what precisely the will's role is in relationship to rectitude of mind and, even more so, how the will's incurvature *sub conditione peccati* might affect the boldness of reason precisely insofar as it depends on its discursive operation. Moreover, the encyclical's central mandate implies a dynamic relationship between *fidei ratio* and *rationis fides*, since the freedom of the former presupposes the rectitude of the latter, while the latter's rectitude and subsequent proper boldness presuppose the implicit horizon of the former. Yet again, what is the role of the will in this mutual dynamic implication?

According to *Fides et Ratio*, created reason has the autonomy and freedom to investigate the mystery of human life. Yet as soon as this reason encounters the ultimate truth, it is obliged to open itself to transcendence and in that be truly liberated. Yet we might ask, liberated from what? *Fides et Ratio* would answer, from reductively immanentist limitations of the mind and constrictions of a technocratic logic.[9] But are those purely

[9] Cf. §§85–91.

accidental deteriorations of reason's activity? Or could they possibly be the result of reason and will interacting in problematic ways? In other words, the question again arises of how the will affects reason and, more specifically, rational inquiry. This Augustinian question is by no means an attack on reason or its capacities but rather a questioning of what looks like the tacit, albeit central, assumption that, *sub conditione peccati,* reason being moved by a curved will should as such still be capable of sustaining a tradition of inquiry that would lead into a truthful metaphysical investigation of the human mystery. Furthermore, if, as the encyclical emphasizes, reason's *autonomia* and *libertas* are in need of a liberation that is nothing less than fundamental, what is the point of asking for a "philosophia naturae *vere metaphysicae*" (§83)? Would this metaphysics itself not need to presuppose the will's rectification? Would it not need to be enfolded in the antecedent reality of prevenient grace?

The Will's Incurvature and the Wisdom of the Cross

It might seem that we carry too much of an Augustinian concern into the heart of the encyclical. Yet, on the contrary, the encyclical itself addresses this concern with theological boldness by drawing upon the Apostle Paul's theology of the cross—albeit without making the will an explicit theme. In the way St. Augustine read and received Paul's theology, the cross stands for the ultimate and most radical questioning of any wisdom humans can muster. Simultaneously, the cross stands for the ultimate and most radical establishment of wisdom received in faith. And the reception of this wisdom entails the rectification of the will now being salutarily absorbed by its ultimate good, that is, conformed to God's will. The rectification of the will constitutes the rectitude of mind on the basis of which reason can confidently develop again its genuine and original metaphysical range of inquiry. But how does this look in detail in *Fides et Ratio*—and is this the way it works in *Fides et Ratio*?

According to *Fides et Ratio*, in Romans 1 Paul makes "plain a philosophical argument in popular language" (§22). For *Fides et Ratio*, the upshot of Rom 1:20 is that "[i]n philosophical terms, it can justifiably be said that in this important Pauline text the metaphysical capacity of humanity is affirmed" (§22). However, is this alleged metaphysical capacity not fundamentally undercut, or at least severely incapacitated, by the will's incurvature? According to *Fides et Ratio*, in an act of disobedience "in . . . full and absolute freedom," human beings opposed themselves to God. At this very instant, the will should have become explicitly thematic, since "preferring in full and absolute freedom to oppose" is, if it is anything at all, an operation of the will. Asserting itself "in its full and absolute freedom," the will's act of disobedience undercuts reason's original capacity *ad conditorem Deum revertendi*, "of returning to God the Creator" (§22). The blindness of pride led the first human beings *ut se supremos esse crederent*, to believe themselves to be "supreme and in control." The (willful?) grasp for supremacy inflicts such wounds on reason *(atque rationi humanae vulnera intulerunt)* that "reason became more and more a prisoner to itself" (§22). Despite the obvious importance of the will for disobedience and pride, *Fides et Ratio,* in this crucial reflection on the *conditio peccati*, does not discuss the will and the loss of its integrity in relationship to reason's original capacity to know the truth.

Yet *Fides et Ratio* clearly emphasizes that only the coming of Christ redeems reason from its weakness and liberates it from its self-imprisonment. Christ achieves this liberation of reason's self-imprisonment by being wisdom incarnate. Thus faith in him reopens participation in divine wisdom. And by implication, I would argue, it is only in the context of this participation in Christ, the Wisdom, that the original metaphysical range of reason in *statu integritatis* is restored.

The Wisdom of Philosophari in Maria

As I see it, the key to the unresolved problem of the will in *Fides et Ratio* is wisdom. Wisdom holds a place of such prominence in the encyclical that clearly the encouragement to reason authentically can pertain only to redeemed, or liberated, reason—not to reason *sub conditione peccati*. Let us remember that, according to *Fides et Ratio*, the *telos* of all human life is deification, the participation in the life of the triune God (§7). The ultimate freedom that human freedom can receive is to be liberated in faith in order to participate in divine freedom by receiving the new telos of God's life.

It is thus by no means accidental that *Fides et Ratio* ends with a short meditation on *philosophari in Maria*, the "seat of wisdom" (§108). To repeat here an earlier point: For *Fides et Ratio*, wisdom, personified in the Logos, is identical with the ultimate good, the life of the triune God. Insofar as wisdom becomes a human attribute, it is completely directed to and inchoately embraced by this ultimate good. The will that is drawn to this good can lose itself in that embrace. Thus transformed, the will finds itself again as freedom received. Hence, true freedom stands for liberation from *incurvature*, in which the will asserts its own *libido dominandi* (the self-assertion of the subject and the subjugation of the world, be it by way of modern metaphysics or technology).

To sum up: In pressing the genuine autonomy of philosophical inquiry, *Fides et Ratio* simultaneously represses the question of the will's effect on the epistemic and discursive operation of reason. Restoring "faith in reason" seems to come at the price of avoiding questions such as: How, *post lapsum,* does the will's *libido dominandi* affect reason such that reason's grasp of reality unavoidably ends in a knowledge that is nothing else than an extension of power? *Fides et Ratio* is clearly aware of the deeply reductionist tendencies that certain strands of post-Nietzschean thinking involve, strands that can arguably be identified as voluntarist. I think it is right in light of these tendencies that *Fides et Ratio* reemphasizes reason's fundamental epistemic capacities and, by implication, its epistemic primacy over against the will. Furthermore, I regard it as crucial that the encyclical encourages a renewal of a philosophy of being.[10] However, it strikes me as detrimental to the encyclical's fundamental mandate—"fidei parrhesia respondere debet rationis audacia" ("the boldness of reason ought to match the freedom of faith")—to omit an explicit reflection of the will's relationship to reason. Only when the relationship between reason and will is clarified can two questions successfully be addressed: first, why and how, *sub conditione peccati,* "reason became more and more a prisoner to itself" (§22) and, second, in what way (namely, by "naturalizing" the *conditio peccati*) the distinctively voluntarist philosophies of modernity constitute such a profound problem. In short, restoring "faith in reason" can succeed only when we squarely attend to reason's other, the will. While omitting to do so itself, *Fides et Ratio* at least points in the direction from which decisive help for this task is to come. For *Fides et Ratio* identifies Thomas Aquinas as the paradigmatic point of orientation for how faith and reason, theology and philosophy, should rightly interrelate. It is indeed Thomas Aquinas who offers an account of the will's relationship to reason that not only fills the encyclical's lacuna but also opens fruitful horizons for fulfilling the encyclical's central mandate, precisely by rigorously engaging the question of the will.

Intellect and Will in Aquinas: Back to the Way Forward[11]

Up to this point, following the practice of *Fides et Ratio*, I have used "reason" rather generically. Now it is time to introduce the crucial distinction

---

[10] For rightly emphasizing this point, cf. John F. X. Knasas, "*Fides et Ratio* and the Twentieth Century Thomistic Revival," *New Blackfriars* 81 (2000): 400–408.

[11] In the following part of the chapter I am drawing heavily on my essay "The Directedness of Reasoning and the Metaphysics of Creation," in *Reason and the Reasons of Faith,* ed. Paul Griffiths and Reinhard Hütter (New York/London: T&T Clark International, 2005), 160–93.

between "intellect" and "reason(ing)." In this I follow Thomas Aquinas, for whom "intellect" and "reason" are fundamentally the same faculty. Yet each stands for a particular and fundamentally different aspect of this faculty, insofar as "reason(ing)" denotes the discursive movement of the intellect. That is, "reason" carries the active connotation of the verbal form "to reason." The one implication of this internal differentiation that matters most in the following is that the faculty of the will has a larger and, *sub conditione peccati,* much more problematic effect on the discursive movement of reason(ing) than on the most basic intellective act of apprehending intelligible truth. I also follow Aquinas in regarding speculative and practical reason(ing) as particular aspects of the same faculty.[12]

The Human Being—Made in God's Image

Before plunging into the deep waters of Aquinas's account of the complex interaction between intellect and will, we need to acknowledge the warning that a noted Aquinas scholar recently expressed: "No one can do justice to Aquinas' theory of the will in a few pages. It is rich, complicated, and controversial, and a thorough treatment of it would require a book-length study."[13] Moreover, it is important to realize that in his *Summa theologiae*, Aquinas places his inquiry into the nature of the human being squarely into an explicitly *theological* horizon. He does so by drawing upon Augustine's imago-doctrine, which he received by way of Peter Lombard's *Sentences*. Yet this dependence upon Augustine is not simply a matter of the history of ideas. It is, rather, a matter of substance. Aquinas's anthropology represents nothing less than a philosophically argued yet theologically motivated and driven line of reasoning about the human being as created in the image of God. If it indeed obtains that the human being is created in God's image, this quality must constitute the first formal principle of any subsequent claims about human nature. Aquinas locates this first formal principle in the form of the human, that is, the soul. He does so by distinguishing between, on the one hand, the end *(terminus)* of God's act of creation and, on the other, perfection of this image through grace and the light of glory, that is, the gratuitous gift of

---

12 Cf. especially his *ST* I, q. 79, aa. 8–11.

13 Eleonore Stump, "Intellect, Will, and the Principle of Alternate Possibilities," in *Christian Theism and the Problems of Philosophy*, ed. Michael D. Beaty (Notre Dame, IN: University of Notre Dame Press, 1990), 266. I am indebted to Stump's concise summary of Aquinas's complex teaching. Since her warning was uttered, at least one such book has been written: Robert Pasnau, *Thomas Aquinas on Human Nature* (Cambridge: Cambridge University Press, 2002).

communion with the triune God.[14] In short, Aquinas's anthropology is governed by a multilayered, complex structure: the human created in the image of God yet deeply wounded by the reality of sin and gratuitously directed toward restoration and perfection of the image, which reaches its completion only as human beings find themselves in personal communion with God, a communion gratuitously granted by the triune God through the Spirit in Christ and enacted as a communion of knowing and loving.[15]

Intellect and Will

In order accurately to appreciate Aquinas's analysis of the intricate interrelationship between intellect and will, we need to distinguish between his earlier, intellectualist leaning, up to the completion of *Summa theologiae* I, and a later, more voluntarist leaning that comes to the fore with the inception of *Summa theologiae* I–II and especially in *De malo* 6.[16] We need to gain first a solid appreciation of the earlier, intellectualist emphasis[17] in order to appreciate the nature of the specific shift to the later, nuanced voluntarism.

---

[14] Cf. D. Juvenal Merriell, *To the Image of the Trinity: A Study in the Development of Aquinas' Teaching* (Toronto: Pontifical Institute of Medieval Studies, 1990), 153–235, esp. 168f.

[15] *ST* I, q. 93, especially aa. 5 and 8; but cf. *ST* I, q. 45, a. 7 and q. 43, a. 3. The subsequent 114 questions of the *Prima secundae* and 189 questions of the *Secunda secundae* need to be read as an interpretation of this dynamic *imago Dei* or, better, as an investigation of all those aspects through which the human being already is the image of God and still—gratuitously—is to be restored and perfected in that image. Cf. Otto Hermann Pesch, *Die Theologie der Rechtfertigung bei Martin Luther und Thomas von Aquin* (Mainz: Matthias-Grünewald Verlag, 1967), 401ff. and Yves Congar, "Le sens de l'économie' salutaire dans la 'théologie' de S. Thomas d'Aquin (Somme theologique)," in *Festgabe Joseph Lortz*, vol. 2, ed. Erwin Iserloh and Peter Manns (Baden-Baden: Bruno Grimm, 1958), 73–122, at 105.

[16] Rather than a radical change of mind, I want to interpret this shift as a change of emphasis and as a final clarification of the will as a power of the soul that is fully independent from the intellect. My account of Aquinas's later, more voluntarist emphasis depends on Otto H. Pesch's detailed study "Philosophie und Theologie der Freiheit bei Thomas von Aquin in quaest. Disp. 6 De malo," *Münchener Theologische Zeitschrift* 13 (1962): 1–25. I find convincing Pesch's chronological arguments that suggest that *De malo* was written shortly after *ST* I–II, qq. 1–21 (i.e., between 1270 and 1272, during Aquinas's second stay in Paris) and thus represents the latest state of Aquinas's reflections on the relationship between intellect and will. On the particular historical cause for Aquinas's change of emphasis, cf. Pesch, 4ff.

[17] For the sake of economy, I will draw exclusively upon *Summa theologiae* I in order to establish Aquinas's earlier account in its most accomplished and concise form.

Aquinas understands intellect and will as two distinct yet mutually interrelated powers of the soul, the intellect naturally and of necessity adhering to the first principles[18] and the will adhering to the universal good as its proper object.[19] Thus perceived in abstraction from the concrete enactment of these two potencies, that is, simply according to their proper nature, Aquinas regards the will as the striving that emerges from the intellect's power of cognition. The movement of the will is the inclination toward something. Yet being a property inherent to the intellect's potency, the will is an essentially intellectual capacity and therefore an inclination to a good that is recognized as such. Thus the will inheres in the intellect as that unique ground that moves it toward the good that the intellect has perceived as such.

Despite the clear distinction between intellect and will insofar as they are considered in principle, there obtains an intricate interrelationship between the two, which Aquinas discusses first under the question "Whether the Will is a Higher Power Than the Intellect?"[20] The upshot of Aquinas's complex analysis in this article is that both powers include one another in accordance with their proper natures. For this reason the will itself can be the proper object of the intellect's inquiry.[21] Moreover, for the same reason, the will moves the intellect—but only in one particular way. On the one hand, Aquinas draws upon the distinction between the intellect's inherent relationship to the first principles and the will's orientation toward the universal good, and on the other hand, upon their particular interrelationship in the interplay of all the powers of the soul. This distinction allows for the following relationship: "But if we consider the will as regards the common nature of its object, which is good, and

---

18 *Prima intelligibilium principia*. These principles are the first concepts formed by the intellect when a human being comes into contact with the sensible.

19 *ST* I, q. 82, a. 1.

20 *ST* I, q. 82, a. 3.

21 *ST* I, q. 82, a. 4, ad 1: "If, however, we take the intellect as regards the common nature of its object and the will as a determinative power, then again the intellect is higher and nobler than the will, because under the notion of being and truth is contained both the will itself, and its act, and its object. Wherefore the intellect understands the will, and its act, and its object, just as it understands other species of things, as stone or wood, which are contained in the common notion of being and truth." If, supposedly, the will were superior or prior to the intellect, an investigation of the will would be a futile enterprise, since in this case the will would be both the agent and the object of the investigation, the result of which consequently would be only a play of forces contingent upon the will's particular whims. Interestingly, these "whims," by sleight of hand, assume a certain intellectual capacity of the will itself, yet a capacity clearly in service of desires that have no intellectual ground but rather form a pre-intellectual vortex of forces.

the intellect as a thing and a special power, then the intellect itself, and its act, and its object, which is truth, each of which is some species of good, are contained under the common notion of good. And in this way, the will is higher than the intellect, and can move it."[22] Thus insofar as the intellect's act and its object—that is, truth—are subsumed under the common notion of good, both of them fall under the common nature of the will's object—that is, that toward which the will is unfailingly bent: the good. In other words, because the will moves all faculties of the soul to their proper end, the will moves the operation of the intellect[23] to its proper end. And so Aquinas concludes his reflection upon the interrelationship between intellect and will with the following summary: "From this we can easily understand why these powers include one another in their acts, because the intellect understands that the will wills and the will wills the intellect to understand. In the same way, good is contained in truth, inasmuch as it is an understood truth, and truth in good, inasmuch as it is a desired good."[24] In short, the will moves the intellect as an efficient cause, while the intellect moves the will as a final cause; that is, the will wills the intellect to understand, and therefore the will itself can be a proper object of the intellect's inquiry, while the intellect's understanding offers the will those goods toward which it inclines itself.

As stated above, we can observe a remarkable shift in emphasis between Aquinas's teaching in *Summa theologiae* I, which reflects and systematizes

---

22 *ST* I, q. 82. a. 4, ad 1.

23 Following Aristotle's *De anima*, Aquinas distinguishes between the capacity of abstraction, that is, the agent intellect *(intellectus agens)* that abstracts from sense experience of particular things to form (confused) ideas, and the capacity of understanding, that is, the possible intellect *(intellectus possibilis)* that receives those ideas and develops them via the process of discursive reasoning into concepts. Underlying the agent intellect and the possible intellect is a more fundamental receptive act of the intellect that earlier Aristotelian commentators called *nous pathetikos*. Aquinas gestures to this primal intellective act of undergoing or suffering reality in *De malo* 3, a. 4, where he refers to the intellect as "cuius actus consistit in recipiendo ab exeriori: unde dicitur quod intelligere est pati quoddam." For detailed accounts of Aquinas's complex way of relating active and possible intellect, cf. Robert E. Brennan, OP, *Thomistic Psychology: A Philosophic Analysis of Man* (New York: Macmillan, 1941), especially ch. 6, and most recently, Robert Pasnau, *Thomas Aquinas on Human Nature* (Cambridge: Cambridge University Press, 2002), ch. 10.

24 *ST* I, q. 82, a. 4, ad 1. "Ex his ergo apparet ratio quare hae potentiae suis actibus invicem se includunt: quia intellectus intelligit voluntatem velle, et voluntas vult intellectum intelligere. Et simili ratione bonum continetur sub vero, inquantum est quoddam verum intellectum; et verum continetur sub bono, inquantum est quoddam bonum desideratum" (q. 82, a. 4, ad 1).

his earlier thought, and his later work in *Summa theologiae* I–II and especially in *De malo* 6. Instead of moving the will, as a final cause, the intellect's operation is reduced to that of a formal cause, that is, to the role of presenting the object to the will and thereby offering a specification of the will's act.[25] In other words, the intellect as the will's formal cause does not suffice anymore to activate the will. Rather, lest the origin of the will's movement be thought to rest solely in the will itself—the will thus becoming its own prime mover, which would entail denying the will to be part and parcel of creation—God must be understood as the first mover of the will.[26] This change of emphasis, however, does not at all affect the intellect's distinct and proper mode of operation. Rather, now the will's unique character as completely independent of the intellect's operation comes into much sharper relief. Hence, while most emphatically not being its own first cause, the will is the proximate cause of its own motion: "The will when moved by God contributes something, since the will itself acts even though God moves it. And so the will's movement, although from an external source as the first source, is nevertheless not coerced."[27]

Intellect and Will Affected by Sin

How are intellect and will now affected by sin? Aquinas approaches this question with a fundamental Augustinian commitment, quoting in the *sed contra* of *Summa theologiae* I–II, q. 74, a. 1, St. Augustine's statement that "it is by the will that we sin, and live righteously."[28] On the basis of his previous discussion of the nature of will and intellect as powers of the soul, Aquinas identifies the will, being the principle of voluntary acts, as the principle of sins.[29] This fundamental insight gains crucial importance as

[25] *ST* I–II, q. 9, a. 1.

[26] Cf. *ST* I–II, q. 10, a. 4 and *The De Malo of Thomas Aquinas*, trans. Richard Regan, ed. Brian Davies (Oxford: Oxford University Press, 2001), 463 (*De malo* 6). On the once hotly debated question of the "praemotio physica," cf. the concise discussion in Gallus M. Manser, OP, *Das Wesen des Thomismus,* 3rd enlarged ed. (Freiburg: Paulusverlag, 1949), 603–25.

[27] *De Malo of Thomas Aquinas,* 461 (*De malo* 6).

[28] "Voluntas est qua peccatur, et recte vivitur" (*Retractationes* I.9; PL 32, 596).

[29] "Et ideo sequitur quod peccatum sit in voluntate sicut in subiecto" (*ST* I–II, q. 74, a. 1). Already in *ST* I, q. 17, a. 2 ("Whether Falsity Exists in Things") Aquinas establishes the will as the principle of sin: "In things that depend on God, falseness cannot be found, in so far as they are compared with the divine intellect; since whatever takes place in things proceeds from the ordinance of that intellect, unless perhaps in the case of voluntary agents only, who have it in their power to withdraw themselves from what is ordained; wherein consists the evil of sin. Thus sins themselves are called untruths and lies in the Scriptures."

Aquinas turns to original sin and asks "Whether Original Sin Infects the Will before the Other Powers?"[30] In full consequence of his Augustinian position, he claims that original sin regards first of all the will. Recall Aquinas's earlier claim that the will moves the intellect as its efficient cause and his later claim that the intellect does not move the will, that is, as its final cause, but rather operates merely as its formal cause, presenting the object to the will. Both claims now bear surprising fruit in the specification of original sin. Consider Aquinas's remarks in *Summa theologiae* I–II, q. 83, a. 3, ad 3: "The intellect precedes the will, in one way, by proposing its object to it. In another way, the will precedes the intellect, in the order of motion to act, which motion pertains to sin."[31] Here it is very important to remember Aquinas's earlier distinction between external acts (falling under the category of *poiesis*, making) and internal acts (falling under the category of *praxis*, doing), that is, desire and knowledge.[32] The one internal act we are most interested in here is the act of the speculative intellect *(iudicium speculativum)*, or, in its Aristotelian rendition, *theoria*.[33] However, Aquinas does not ask explicitly how *theoria* might be affected by the will's sinfully misdirecting the intellect. Rather, because of the particular thrust of *Summa theologiae* I–II, where the intellective and volitional movement of humans is perfected by grace and led toward their gratuitous ultimate end, Aquinas focuses on a particular class of internal moral acts, namely, those "acts which do not pass into external matter, but remain in the agent, e.g. to desire and to know: and such are all moral acts, whether virtuous or sinful."[34] Does this mean that *theoria*, the act of knowing that is directed to that which is solely and properly the intellect's object, can never be affected by the will and therefore by sin? In short, are we, according to Aquinas, at least epistemologically free from the effects of original sin? One of the strengths of Aquinas's way of relating intellect and will is his ability to account for how the intellect's proper capacity has not been destroyed by human sin. The intellect is able to come to knowledge and judge properly (yet not inerrantly) in highly complex and nontrivial ways.

When we turn to Aquinas's discussion of the vice of curiosity (indeed, a very Augustinian theme), we will realize that Aquinas allows for *theoria*,

30 *ST* I–II, q. 83, a. 3.

31 "[I]ntellectus quoddam modo praecedit voluntatem, inquantum proponit ei suum obiectum. Alio vero modo voluntas praecedit intellectum, secundum ordinem motionis ad actum: quae quidem motio pertinet ad peccatum."

32 *ST* I–II, q. 74, a. 1.

33 On Aristotle's *bios theoretikos*, cf. Joseph Dunne, *Back to the Rough Ground: 'Phronesis' and 'Techne' in Modern Philosophy and in Aristotle* (Notre Dame, IN: University of Notre Dame Press, 1993), 237–44.

34 *ST* I–II, q. 74, a. 1.

while not being cognitively defective, to be nevertheless deeply affected by a will sinfully bent away from the ultimate good. Aquinas's late and quite restrained voluntarism, still checked by a robust intellectualism, allows for a nuanced account of the will's effect upon reason's discursive operations—without falling into the trap of voluntarist skepticism.

The Virtue of Studiousness and the Vice of Curiosity: Paradigmatic Test-Case for the Relationship between Intellect and Will

We find Aquinas's treatment of the vice of curiosity in the *Secunda secundae* of his *Summa theologiae* an excursus as detailed as it is fascinating on the treatises on the virtues, the vices, and the gifts, beatitudes, and fruits of the Holy Spirit that are discussed in the *Prima secundae*. Curiosity and the respective virtue of studiousness pertain to the cardinal virtue of temperance, that is, the moral excellence that rightly restrains and channels the bodily and intellectual passions that sustain but also endanger human flourishing.[35] In slightly more technical language, Aquinas would regard studiousness as "a subordinate virtue annexed to a principal virtue," that is, temperance, and "to be comprised under modesty," a virtue that in turn is "annexed to temperance as its principal."[36]

Studiousness

Because it provides the crucial backdrop for fully appreciating the deeply problematic nature of curiosity, we will attend first to Aquinas's discussion of the virtue of studiousness. After establishing that the appropriate matter of studiousness is knowledge, Aquinas turns to the question "Whether Studiousness Is a Part of Temperance?"[37] In a striking way, a quote from Augustine in the *sed contra* contrasts the three arguments that deny the question and, more importantly, anticipates Aquinas's telling answer: " 'We are forbidden to be curious: and this is a great gift that temperance bestows.'[38] Now curiosity is prevented by moderate studiousness. Therefore studiousness is a part of temperance." Precisely because the human being is not just a body but a body informed by a soul—and, as we saw above, a soul that is created in the image of God—the human naturally desires what is appropriate to his soul: *cognoscere aliquid*, to know some-

---

35 "[I]t belongs to temperance to moderate the movement of the appetite, lest it tend excessively to that which is desired naturally" (*ST* II–II, q. 166, a. 2).

36 *ST* II–II, q. 166, a. 2; *ST* II–II, q. 160, a. 1.

37 *ST* II–II, q. 166, a. 2.

38 "Curiosi esse prohibemur: quod magnae temperantiae munus est" (*De Moribus Ecclesiae,* cap. 21: PL 32, 1327).

thing.[39] And unsurprisingly, "[t]he moderation of this desire pertains to the virtue of studiousness." The real and exciting complexity of this seemingly straightforward position only emerges in Aquinas's responses to the objections, two responses in which the problematic of reasoning's directedness is immediately and dramatically relevant.

One of the objections raises the problem that knowledge has no connection with the moral virtues of which temperance and therefore also modesty and studiousness are a part. This is because they root in the appetitive part of the soul, that is, in the will. Knowledge, consequently, seems to pertain only to the intellectual virtues (prudence and its subordinate virtues), which arise from the soul's cognitive part, that is, the intellect. In his response, by implicit reference to *Summa theologiae* I–II, q. 9, a. 1, Aquinas first restates the way in which the will directs the intellect: "The act of a cognitive power is commanded by the appetitive power, which moves all the powers." This fundamental insight into the way the will moves all the powers of the soul to their appropriate ends, as discussed above, allows Aquinas to make a critical differentiation. It is the differentiation between the twofold good with respect to knowledge. There is, first, the one that is connected with the act of knowledge itself: "[A]nd this good pertains to the intellectual virtues, and consists in man having a true estimate about each thing." There is, second, the one that belongs to the act of the appetitive power, that is, the will. This good "consists in man's appetite being directed aright in applying the cognitive power in this or that way to this or that thing."[40] Being able to form the appetite aright in order that this power of the will might rightly apply the cognitive power is what makes studiousness a virtue in the first place. To turn Aquinas's point around: Only because the will indeed does have a specific effect on the intellect does a particular moral virtue pertain to the cognitive power.

Let us turn to the other pertinent objection. Studiousness cannot be a subordinate virtue of temperance, because the former does not resemble the latter in the mode of its operation. While temperance is a kind of restraint that opposes the vice of excess, studiousness seems to be first of all the application of the mind to something that opposes the vice of neglect. Aquinas again responds with a distinction, now between contrary inclinations. He prepares this distinction by drawing upon Aristotle's teaching that in order to be virtuous, one must avoid all that to which

[39] It should come as no surprise when Aquinas quotes in this very instance the familiar opening line from Aristotle's *Metaphysics*: "All human beings naturally desire knowledge."

[40] *ST* II–II, q. 166, a. 2, ad 2.

one is most naturally inclined. The virtue of studiousness has two seemingly contrary aspects because of the contrary inclination the human being displays regarding knowledge: "For on the part of the soul, he is inclined to desire knowledge of things; and so it behooves him to exercise a praiseworthy restraint on this desire, lest he seek knowledge immoderately: whereas on the part of the bodily nature, man is inclined to avoid the trouble of seeking knowledge."[41] Consequently, as it pertains to the first inclination, studiousness constitutes a kind of restraint, but insofar as it pertains to the second inclination, "this virtue derives its praise from a certain keenness of interest in seeking knowledge of things; and from this it takes its name." Thus studiousness restrains, channels, directs, and applies the cognitive power in a concentrated, sustained, and keenly interested way to the arduous task of gaining knowledge that is appropriate as well as profound.

Curiosity

With the virtue of studiousness as necessary backdrop, we are now able finally to turn to the vice of curiosity. How does Aquinas treat the vice of curiosity, and how might the intellect's speculative power, *theoria*, be affected by it? In *Summa theologiae* II–II, q. 167, a. 1, Aquinas goes right to the core of the matter by asking "Whether Curiosity Can Be About Intellective Knowledge?" First, he reports three objections, a not untypical assemblage of some of the ways strict intellectualists would want to defend the intellect's supremacy from any incursions from the side of the will. Yet again, Aquinas's choice of the *sed contra*, this time not from Augustine but from Jerome, is quite a foreboding of the kind of response that is about to come: " 'Is it not evident that a man who day and night wrestles with the dialectic art, the student of natural science whose gaze pierces the heavens, walks in vanity of understanding and darkness of mind?' Now vanity of understanding and darkness of mind are sinful. Therefore curiosity about intellective sciences may be sinful."[42]

Fully consistent with what he has previously established, Aquinas maintains that while knowledge as such is always good, the desire for and study in pursuit of knowledge of the truth may be right or wrong. First, acquiring a particular knowledge may be accidentally linked to evil. Second, the appetite and study that is directed at the knowledge of truth may itself be inordinate. This can be the case in four ways: First, in turn-

[41] *ST* II–II, q. 166, a. 2, ad 3.

[42] "Nonne vobis videtur in vanitate sensus et obscuritate mentis ingredi qui diebus ac noctibus in dialectica arte torquetur, qui physicus perscrutator oculos trans caelum levat?" (*In Ephes.,* Lib. II, super IV17; PL 26, 536).

ing from one's primary obligation to a less useful occupation (as the pastor who, instead of persistently studying the Scriptures and continuing to develop the linguistic and conceptual tools necessary for this task, turns to other, more "interesting" intellectual pursuits like computer programs, Web sites with ready-to-go sermons, etc.). Second, in seeking knowledge from persons by whom it is illicit to be taught (as the medical student who wants to study the human response to extreme cold with a Nazi physician who gained his knowledge by systematically freezing concentration camp inmates to death). Since I will dwell longer on the third way, I will immediately move to the fourth: in studying "to know the truth above the capacity of [one's] own intelligence, since by so doing men easily fall into error." Because, as already pointed out above, for Aquinas, reasoning is the discursive activity of the intellect, and because any extended and complex argument about the truth of something that transcends epistemic obviousness (this is a chair, this is a pencil) easily brings the uninstructed person to the limit of his/her own intellectual possibilities, error becomes increasingly likely, and instruction prior to the informed engagement of one's discursive powers in complex inquiries and their discursive disciplines, increasingly necessary. Curiosity in these matters can only amount to dangerous dabbling, while studiousness implies the modesty to acknowledge the necessity of prior instruction.

Finally, we turn to the way most pertinent to our purposes in which the appetite to know can itself be inordinate: in desiring "to know the truth about creatures, without referring [one's] knowledge to its due end, namely, the knowledge of God."[43] Here we finally have Aquinas identifying an inherently restricted—and in this precise sense, misdirected—act of the speculative intellect, or *theoria*. A knowledge of creatures that is not directed to its dutiful end, namely, the knowledge of God, is a distorted, sinful knowledge not because it is faulty in and of itself (that is, there need not be any cognitive defect in this knowledge). Rather, this knowledge becomes distorted, sinful knowledge by its lack of reference to and reverence for the One who grants being in the first place. Knowing "the truth about creatures" unquestionably refers to *theoria*, the speculative act of the intellect directed to everything that is not God or one of God's operations—in short, the full scope of the *ens inquantum ens*. It is Aquinas's response in the *ad primum* that offers additional warrant for this assumption: "Hence there may be sin in the knowledge of certain truths, in so far as the desire of such knowledge is not directed in due manner to the knowledge

43 "Tertio, quando homo appetit cognoscere veritatem circa creaturas non referendo ad debitum finem, scilicet ad cognitionem Dei."

of the sovereign truth, wherein supreme happiness consists."[44] What a sweeping anticipatory indictment of the whole range of modern immanentism, be it in philosophy, natural science, or the so-called humanities!

Thus Aquinas assumes also *theoria* to be affected by sin in that the intellect in its concrete operation is moved in a way that restricts or distracts it from considering its ultimate subject matter, the supreme good, and in this sense misdirects it without necessarily causing a cognitive defect in what is known. Aquinas's nuanced and epistemically restrained voluntarism undercuts the kind of voluntarist skepticism that would arise from the assumption that the will rules unaccountably and irresistibly over reason. The intellect obviously always comes to know things *(res)* in ways appropriate to their nature.

Knowing, Reasoning, and the Will

It is here that Aquinas's subtle distinction between intellect and reason—and hence between knowing and reasoning—to which I alluded earlier does some surprisingly helpful work. It allows us to gain a clearer grasp of the way reasoning, that is, the intellect's discursive activity, can be profoundly misdirected while the intellect's epistemic capacity per se remains largely unaffected.[45] The latter is actually the very presupposition necessary for reasoning to be misdirected in the first place: Even while being discursively misguided, the intellect always continues to perceive some truth, since this is precisely what allows it to remain in error and not in a state of undifferentiated delusion. Therefore, "the intellect cannot be false in its knowledge of simple essences; but is either true, or it understands nothing at all."[46] Hence, it is not in the primal intellective act but

---

[44] "Et ideo potest esse vitium in cognitione aliquorum verorum, secundum quod talis appetitus non debito modo ordinatur ad cognitionem summae veritatis, in qua consistit summa felicitas."

[45] Cf. *ST* I, q. 17, a. 3 ("Whether Falsity Is in the Intellect?"): "Now as the sense is directly informed by the likeness of its proper object, so is the intellect by the likeness of the essence of a thing. Hence the intellect is not deceived about the essence of a thing, as neither the sense about its proper object. But in affirming and denying, the intellect may be deceived, by attributing to the thing of which it understands the essence, something which is not consequent upon it, or is opposed to it. For the intellect is in the same position as regards judging of such things, as sense is as to judging of common, or accidental, sensible objects. There is, however, this difference, as before mentioned regarding truth (Q. 16, A. 2), that falsity can exist in the intellect not only because the knowledge of the intellect is false, but because the intellect is conscious of that knowledge, as it is conscious of truth; whereas in sense falsity does not exist as known, as stated above (A. 2)." [Emphasis added.]

[46] *ST* I, q. 17, a. 3.

in the discursive process of reasoning, of linking intellective judgments in one or another way into complex arguments and theories, that the will, and hence the agent, comes into play.

It is useful to remember at this point Aquinas's insight that similar to the intellect, the will is moved in two ways: first, so far as concerns the exercise of its act and, second, so far as concerns what seems to be—or indeed is—a particular good, that is, "the specification of the act, derived from the object."[47] While the will is not able to influence the intellect's basic operation, it is quite able to will that the intellect not continue thinking about something particular and to direct the intellect instead to consider something else. This accounts for the easy distractibility of reasoning in practical as well as theoretical matters.[48]

Instead of considering complex large-scale examples of misdirected reasoning from the history of science, such as "Aryan physics" (opposing Einstein's theory of relativity), or from dialectical-materialist sociology, economy, and history (acknowledged core disciplines of all the bygone

[47] *ST* I–II, q. 10, a. 2. Eleonore Stump rightly points out that according to Aquinas, "if the will is presented by the intellect with an object which can be considered good under some descriptions and not good under others, then the will is not necessarily moved by that object either. . . . It is open to the will not to will that object by willing that the intellect not think about it" ("Intellect, Will, and the Principle of Alternate Possibilities," 268; cf. *ST* I, q. 82, a. 2).

[48] Aquinas offers a complex discussion of this matter in *ST* I–II, q. 17 ("Of the Acts Commanded by the Will"), in which he applies and extends the intricate feedback system between intellect and will. Command is an act of reason, yet the very fact that reason moves by commanding is due to the power of the will: "Consequently it follows that command is an act of the reason, presupposing an act of the will, in virtue of which the reason, by its command, moves (the power) to the execution of the act" (*ST* I–II, q. 17, a. 1). However, the aspect most pertinent to our concern is found in article 6 ("Whether the Act of the Reason Is Commanded?"), where Aquinas distinguishes between the exercise of the act (which is always commanded "as when one is told to be attentive, and to use one's reason") and the object of the exercise of reason. Here we encounter the crucial distinction between the uncommanded aspect and the aspect that is open to command: "One is the act whereby it apprehends the truth about something. This act is not in our power: because it happens in virtue of a natural or supernatural light. Consequently in this respect, the act of the reason is not in our power, and cannot be commanded. The other act of the reason is that whereby it assents to what it apprehends. If, therefore, that which the reason apprehends is such that it naturally assents thereto, e.g., the first principles, it is not in our power to assent or dissent to the like. . . . But some things which are apprehended do not convince the intellect to such an extent as not to leave it free to assent or dissent, or at least suspend its assent or dissent, on account of some cause or other; and in such things assent or dissent is in our power, and is subject to our command" (*ST* I–II, q. 17, a. 6). Cf. also *De malo* 3, a. 3.

Communist regimes), consider the simple case suggested by Eleonore Stump and applicable by family resemblance:

> Suppose that Anna has just won some money in a contest and that she plans to use the money to buy a frilly pink canopy bed for her daughter, something she has been coveting but unable to afford. As she sits reading a magazine, she comes across an advertisement urging readers to give money to support children in third-world countries and showing a picture of a ragged, emaciated child. Anna no sooner glances at the ad than she turns the page. Why does she do so? The answer to the question will, of course, involve the will's issuing commands which result in Anna's turning the page; *but underlying these commands is something like the will's directive to the intellect not to think about the ad and the needy children it describes.* The will makes this directive in virtue of a hasty calculation on the part of the intellect that looking at the ad is not good. . . . Informing or influencing this calculation will be Anna's coveting of the frilly pink canopy bed for her daughter, a passion in Aquinas' sense. Perhaps without the influence of that coveting Anna's calculation about the ad might have been different.[49]

Aquinas's analysis of the vice of curiosity makes it plain why Stump's example, while pertaining to a matter of practical reasoning, can easily be applied to the act of speculative reasoning as well.[50]

Curiosity's Horizon of Discovery (Metaphysics of Creation) and its Cure (Grace)

If it is the case that curiosity is the vice that affects *theoria* by restricting and distracting the intellect and by misdirecting the discursive process of reasoning, we need now to ask: What constitutes the horizon from which the vice of curiosity can be identified in the first place? And how can a redirected gaze of *theoria* be suggested at all? Aquinas's third argument in *Summa theologiae* II–II, q. 167, a. 1, and especially his response to the first objection, implies that this horizon is nothing less than a theologically

---

49 Eleonore Stump, "Intellect, Will, and the Principle of Alternate Possibilities," 269. [Emphasis added.]

50 Cf. Aquinas's discussion of "Whether Falsity Is in the Intellect?" in *ST* I, q. 17, a. 3 and the concise summary he offers in *De malo* 3, a. 3 of the ways the intellect and the will are moved and are not moved. Here again "regarding the intellect, things necessarily linked to naturally known first principles necessarily move the intellect. . . . But the intellect is not compelled to assent to conclusions if they be not necessarily linked to naturally known first principles, as is the case with contingent and probable things. Likewise, neither does the intellect necessarily assent to necessary things necessarily linked to first principles before it knows there is such a necessary connection" (*De Malo of Thomas Aquinas*, 245, 247).

motivated and informed metaphysics of creation. How so? Let us recall both passages. First, the pursuit of knowledge may be wrong "when a man desires to know the truth about creatures, without referring his knowledge to its due end, namely, the knowledge of God. Hence Augustine says that 'in studying creatures, we must not be moved by empty and perishable curiosity; but we should ever mount towards immortal and abiding things.' "[51] Second, since the sovereign good of humanity consists in the knowledge of the sovereign truth, Aquinas avers, "there may be sin in the knowledge of certain truths, in so far as the desire of such knowledge is not directed in due manner to the knowledge of the sovereign truth, wherein supreme happiness consists."[52]

What happens in both cases is that in order to specify curiosity as an intellectual vice, as sinfully misdirected reasoning, Aquinas consistently presumes what Robert Sokolowski calls "the Christian distinction" between the Creator and everything *(ta panta)*.[53] However, it is precisely this distinction that constitutes the defining mark of the metaphysics of creation over against any other form of metaphysics.

To put it in the form of a thesis: A metaphysics of creation is the necessary horizon (a) to understand why curiosity is a vice and (b) to direct the intellect's gaze to its proper object, the ultimate truth. Yet what do I mean by a *theologically* motivated and informed metaphysics of creation? What differentiates it from other versions of metaphysics, especially an Aristotelian metaphysics, as the science of being as being *(ens inquantum est ens)*? To put it in terms that are possibly too condensed: While a metaphysics of being presupposes the ontological difference between being and beings, a metaphysics of creation admits its dependence "from above" by presuming a second, and ultimately more fundamental, difference. It is the difference between *esse commune/esse ipsum*—an absolute abundant *actus essendi* that is open to both participation (creation) and subsistence (God) and, while abstracting from both, is to be found in both—and *ipsum esse subsistens*, that is, God.[54] Hence, while remaining implicit in the

51 *ST* II–II, q. 167, a. 1.

52 *ST* II–II, q. 167, a. 1, ad 1.

53 Robert Sokolowski, *The God of Faith and Reason: Foundations of Christian Theology* (Notre Dame, IN: University of Notre Dame Press, 1982), 32ff.

54 For a short and accessible account, cf. Josef Stallmach, "Der actus essendi und die Frage nach dem Sinn von 'Sein,' " in *Actus omnium actuum: Festschrift für Heinrich Beck zum 60. Geburtstag*, ed. Erwin Schadel (Frankfurt: Lang, 1989), 47–58. On Aquinas's crucial definition of the *esse* ipsum as "simplex et completum sed non subsistens," cf. the profound commentary in Ferdinand Ulrich, *Homo Abyssus*: "Allein, das ipsum esse ist 'nichts' zwischen Gott und dem Geschaffenen; denn Gott hebt alles Dritte als Mittleres—was nicht heißt: als 'reine Vermittlung'!—

metaphysics of *esse*, the dependence upon *sacra doctrina* and its normative distinction between the Creator and everything else becomes explicit in the metaphysics of creation.

Yet why does the metaphysics of creation antecedently depend upon the metaphysics of *esse*? Precisely because it allows for the only conceptual expression of the "dare *esse*," of the gift of creation, the metaphysics of *esse* is open to being elevated and assumed by the second difference into the metaphysics of creation.[55] Because the metaphysics of creation is an extension of *sacra doctrina* into the metaphysics of being, that is, an expression of *fides quaerens intellectum* that reads the world *(ta panta)* as God's creation all the way down, this move makes the metaphysics of creation vulnerable, dependent upon the conceptual and substantive veracity of the specific metaphysics of being—that is, the metaphysics of *esse*—that it assumes.

A theologically informed metaphysics of creation is constituted by the *second, onto-theological, difference* because the first, or ontological, difference is dramatically insufficient for understanding the world as *creatio ex nihilo* and, moreover, fundamentally incapable of establishing the horizon that enables us to appreciate the true nature of curiosity in the first place. Rather, only the onto-theological difference between *esse ipsum* and *ipsum esse subsistens*, in which *esse* itself is analogically conceived, fulfills the theological requirement to understand the world as creation.[56]

A metaphysics of creation (a) is able analogically to consider and interrelate all of reality, all of what is, thereby reflecting the intelligible unity in the difference of creation; (b) is inherently directed to and participationally dependent upon divine transcendence because of the centrality of the second difference; and (c) is therefore able intellectively to present to the will the ultimate object of desire, its due end. However, *sub conditione peccati,* the intellect cannot reform or redirect the will so that the

---

zwischen sich und den Geschöpfen auf; 'non potest aliquid esse medium inter creatum et increatum' [*De Veritate* 8.17]. Das Andere zum subsistierenden Sein selbst ist 'Nichts'. Dieses 'Nichts' ist die Differenz des Geschaffenen zu Gott" (15).

55 For an extraordinary account of the openness of the metaphysics of *esse* for the metaphysics of creation, cf. Heinrich Beck, *Der Akt-Charakter des Seins* (Munich: Max Hueber Verlag, 1965) and Ferdinand Ulrich, *Homo Abyssus* (Einsiedeln: Johannes Verlag, 1998).

56 Aquinas draws upon both Aristotle and Plato in his metaphysics of creation, yet in the form of a superior synthesis that is made possible by the antecedent assumption of the intellect's due end as also desired by a rectified will, namely, the supreme truth and good. It is precisely the second difference that accounts for why the supreme truth and good do not need to become operative (as knowledge *simpliciter*) in the process of intellectual inquiry.

good of the second difference becomes the will's definitive end of desire. Thus the metaphysics of creation begs the question of the will's primal mover and especially its renewal or healing through grace, so that, as the intellect is being informed by faith, the will may be informed by charity. In short, a genuine metaphysics of creation always begs Christology and can achieve its purpose ultimately only "after Christ."

Hence, following Thomas Aquinas's way of squarely facing the reality of the will in its relationship to the intellect yields at least two crucial insights that give rise to a fruitful further development of *Fides et Ratio*'s central mandate, "Fidei parrhesia respondere debet rationis audacia," that is, "The boldness of reason ought to match the freedom of faith" (§48). First, according to Aquinas, reasoning as the discursive operation of the intellect implies the activity of the will in directing reason's discursive operation in this or in that way. The encyclical's use of "reason," however, begs this implication, which, in turn, profoundly qualifies the relationship between, as *Fides et Ratio* puts it in its opening line, the "two wings by which the human spirit is raised up toward the contemplation of truth." Second, only after the will's rectification can reason's discursive operation genuinely and lastingly open itself for the transcendent truth that can be received only—short of the *visio beatifica*—in faith.

Faith and Reason: John Paul and Aquinas

THOMAS WEINANDY, OFM, Cap.
United States Conference of Catholic Bishops
Washington, DC

POPE JOHN PAUL II wove together, within his encyclical *Fides et Ratio*, a number of multifaceted and interconnected themes bearing upon the relationship between faith and reason. While the pope was aware of many examples of men and women within the history of philosophy and theology who have knitted faith and reason together in a proper and fruitful manner, he nonetheless singled out Thomas Aquinas as the chief exemplar. For the pope, "Thomas had the great merit of giving pride of place to the harmony which exists between faith and reason" (§43, see also §57). In this essay I want, firstly, to examine the various themes interlocking faith and reason and in so doing point out the Thomistic spirit that pervades their relationship. Secondly, I want briefly to provide, from within a biblical and Thomistic setting, a metaphysical and epistemological basis for the pope's teaching.

By way of introduction it must be noted that the pope was actually more concerned with reason than with faith. His concern was twofold. Firstly, within the contemporary climate of philosophical relativism, agnosticism, and even nihilism, he believed that human beings, most especially philosophers, must renew their confidence in reason's ability to come to know the truth, specifically metaphysical truth, for it is only in reason's ability to grasp the truth that men and women obtain their true human dignity (see §§4–5, 45–49, 55).

> Life in fact can never be grounded upon doubt, uncertainty or deceit; such an existence would be threatened constantly by fear and anxiety. One may define the human being, therefore, as *the one who seeks the truth* (§28).

Thus, the Church "sees in philosophy the way to come to know fundamental truths about human life" (§5).

Secondly, this renewed confidence is essential not only for allowing reason to function properly within its own human intellectual sphere, but also for allowing it to function properly in relationship to faith. Reason can facilitate faith, and, most especially, advance a fuller understanding of the mysteries of faith so as to provide for their clearer articulation, and so concurrent defense. Ultimately, for the pope, it was only when reason interacts with faith, that is, with the revelation of God fully manifested in Jesus Christ, that it achieves its highest goal, that of coming to know, in a communion of love, the mystery of the triune God.

John Paul accentuates this twofold concern when he states:

> This is why I make this strong and insistent appeal—not, I trust untimely—that faith and philosophy recover the profound unity which allows them to stand in harmony with their nature without compromising their mutual autonomy. The *parrhesia* [outspokenness] of faith must be matched by the boldness of reason (§48, see also §56).

How then did John Paul perceive this interaction between reason and faith?

Faith—The Friend of Reason

While the pope insisted that the human intellect possesses its own natural or innate ability to come to a knowledge of the truth, faith, in the aftermath of sin, now comes to reason's aid. Faith in the Gospel, containing as it does the Spirit of truth, heals reason of its weaknesses so that it might now freely undertake its natural pursuit of the truth in a more vigorous manner. Moreover, faith opens up to reason new avenues of intellectual enquiry, which, when left to itself, it would never have considered exploring. Thus, for John Paul, revelation is "the true lodestar of men and women as they strive to make their way amid the pressures of an immanentist habit of mind and the constrictions of a technocratic logic" (§15). Faith "sharpens the inner eye, opening the mind to discover in the flux of events the working of Providence" (§16). Even within the context of the Old Testament one finds that

> faith liberates reason in so far as it allows reason to attain correctly what it seeks to know and to place it within the ultimate order of things, in which everything acquires true meaning. In brief, human beings attain truth by way of reason because, enlightened by faith, they discover the deeper meaning of all things and most especially of their own existence (§20).

The basis of the pope's claim is the Thomistic principle that as grace builds upon nature, "so faith builds upon and perfects reason. Illumined by faith, reason is set free from the fragility and limitations deriving from the disobedience of sin and finds the strength required to rise to the knowledge of the Triune God" (§43). John Paul insists that "it is faith which stirs reason to move beyond all isolation and willingly to run risks so that it may attain whatever is beautiful, good and true. Faith thus becomes the convinced and convincing advocate of reason" (§56, see also §75). Faith, therefore, as a theological virtue, "purifies reason" thus allowing it truly to act in a fully rational manner (§76). Moreover, divine revelation has forced philosophy to view "new vistas of further meanings which reason is summoned to penetrate" and thus revelation has been "an undoubted boon for philosophy" (§101). Throughout the encyclical, then, John Paul encourages and exhorts contemporary men and women not to undermine their intellectual dignity by assuming that truth is beyond their reach. Rather, they are called to acknowledge in truth that they are able, as intellectual human beings, actually to know the truth. Faith, far from being its enemy, is ultimately reason's best friend.

While on one level the encyclical ardently endorses reason's natural ability to know the truth and so encourages contemporary men and women to have confidence in reason's ability, yet the pope never, on another level, in accordance with Aquinas's principle, allows reason an autonomy that would divorce it from grace, that is, from the sphere of faith (see §45–58). In the light of sin, reason is now dependent upon faith in order for it to function properly and so reach its full potential. There is then, thoughout the encyclical, a subtle but unmistakable call to conversion, for faith is reason's salvation.

Reason—The Friend of Faith

Reason as the Window to Faith

While faith befriends reason so too, for John Paul, was reason called upon to befriend faith. In accordance with Aquinas, the pope recognized that "faith . . . has no fear of reason, but seeks it out and has trust in it" (§43). This befriending, as seen above, must be predicated upon a robust confidence in reason's ability. Only when reason is allowed to exercise its full philosophical maturity, and so be truly rational, can it assume its noble task of befriending faith. Thus, the foundational expression of friendship is by reason recognizing and utilizing its natural ability to obtain metaphysical truth. For the pope, metaphysical knowledge bore witness to reason's dignity. Human reason is not confined to sensory knowledge, but rather, through the means of the senses, the human intellect is able to discern the being and nature of things, and so obtain metaphysical knowledge (see §22). Philosophy is called upon "to verify the human capacity to *know the truth*, to come to a knowledge which can reach objective truth by means of that *adaequatio rei et intellectus* to which the Scholastic Doctors referred" (§82). Moreover, philosophy must then be *"genuinely metaphysical"* in that it allows men and women to obtain "the metaphysical dimension of reality": "in truth, in beauty, in moral values, in other persons, in being itself, in God" (§83).

While John Paul did not make any explicit reference to a particular epistemology, yet it is evident that he here endorsed a realist position, one that would be in accordance with Aquinas's own epistemology. Only such a realist epistemology, as will shortly become evident, allows reason to befriend faith, for only a realist position espouses reason's ability obtain metaphysical truth about the ontological nature of reality, and so opens the window to faith. The pope, as was Aquinas, was well aware that an idealist, empiricist, relativist, rationalist, or fideist epistemology would not only not serve the interests of faith, but it would also more radically undercut its claim to truth (see §§49–56, 86–91).

Philosophy, then, in authenticating reason's ability to obtain metaphysical truth, does more than merely acknowledge that it can actually know the world around it, but such an epistemological affirmation also perceives that human reason is open to truth that exceeds its natural ability to obtain, that is, the revelation that comes from God. When reason confirms its own ability to know metaphysical truth, it equally endorses its ability to receive revelation, and in so doing befriends faith. As John Paul states:

> At the deepest level, the autonomy which philosophy enjoys is rooted in the fact that reason is by its nature oriented to truth and is equipped moreover with the means necessary to arrive at truth. A philosophy conscious of this as its "constitutive status" cannot but respect the demands and the data of revealed truth (§49).

However, here resides the inadequacy of much contemporary philosophy, an inadequacy that finds its ancestry in the Enlightenment. Human beings lost faith in reason when they lost faith in revelation (see §45). Actually, philosophy lost its faith in reason precisely to avoid the demands of revelation and so avoid the summons to faith. By undermining reason's ability to know the truth, it then became "reasonable" not to believe, and it was this sanctioning of unbelief that philosophy, very often, most desperately wanted to ensure. However, in reason's attempt to shut the window on faith, it has also shut the window on its own dignity of being truly rational (see §§75–76). It is only when men and women become open to revelation and to the faith that it demands will they once more be willing to restore to reason its true nobility. Thus, again, at the heart of the encyclical resides a call to conversion, for only such a conversion can counteract contemporary philosophy's disparagement of reason.

Moreover, as the pope insists, it is only metaphysics that allows the content of revelation to be adequately understood and expressed. "A philosophy which shuns metaphysics would be radically unsuited to the task of mediation in the understanding of Revelation" (§83). Besides providing the opening to revelation, how then does metaphysics befriend faith? Moreover, in what ways does metaphysics aid in the understanding and the expression of faith? The answer to these questions is twofold.

The Guide to Faith

Firstly, metaphysical reasoning ensures and sanctions that the act of faith is not irrational. While the act of faith is distinct in itself, reason can guide the mind to faith. Again, it is here that the pope and Aquinas speak with one voice. Reason, through metaphysics, is able to come to "a natural knowledge of God." It is able to distinguish between divine revelation and other phenomena, and so it is able to discern its credibility. In that metaphysics treats of truths that are ontological in nature, it bears witness to the intellect's ability to know and articulate truth that is beyond the merely observable and phenomenal, and so equally testifies to the intellect's ability to grasp God's action manifested in historical deeds and interpreted in human words (see §10).

> From all these truths, the mind is led to acknowledge the existence of a truly propaedeutic path to faith, one which can lead to the acceptance of Revelation without in any way compromising the principles and autonomy of the mind itself (§67).

John Paul affirms that, for human beings, the act of faith is the most "important act in their lives" for it is here that "freedom reaches the certainty of truth and chooses to live in that truth" (§13, see also §75).

Enhancing the Mysteries

Secondly, reason is a servant of faith in that it enables the mysteries of revelation to be properly conceived and articulated so as to enhance their nobility and clarity, which, in turn, fosters the "communicating of the truth of the Gospel to those who do not know it" (§5). On the one hand revelation "is utterly gratuitous, moving from God to men and women in order to bring them to salvation" (§7), so "there exists a knowledge which is peculiar to faith, surpassing the knowledge proper to human reason" (§8). Thus, "the truth made known to us by Revelation is neither the product nor the consummation of an argument devised by human reason" (§15). Reason, therefore, cannot "pass judgement on the contents of faith, of which it would be incapable since this is not its function" (§42). Nor then can revelation be reduced to or subsumed within some human philosophy contrived by reason alone (such as is found, for example, in Kant, Hegel, or contemporary Process thought), which in turn would radically alter the understanding and interpretation of the mysteries of faith (see §46). Yet, on the other hand, reason's supreme dignity is found precisely in its ability to grasp the truths of faith and so seek to understand them. Faith actually "asks that its object be understood with the help of reason; and at the summit of its searching reason acknowledges that it cannot do without what faith presents" (§42).

It is at this juncture that John Paul's important treatment of the relationship between the *auditus fidei* and the *intellectus fidei*, with regards to the doing of theology, comes into prominence. Firstly, "theology makes its own the content of Revelation as this has been gradually expounded in Sacred Tradition, Sacred Scripture and the Church's Magisterium" (§65). This is in keeping with the nature of revelation itself. God, through historical deeds and the human words that interpret those deeds, establishes the mystery of human salvation (see §10). This is what is to be believed in faith as it has been proclaimed and understood by the apostolic Church through the centuries. Human beings "acknowledge fully and integrally the truth of what is revealed because it is God himself who is the guarantor of that truth. They can make no claim upon this truth which comes to them as gift . . ." (§13). Secondly, following the ancient maxim, *fides quaerens intellectum,* it is precisely these same truths of faith that impel the rational believer, through the indwelling of the Spirit of truth, to seek a deeper understanding. Here the *intellectus fidei*, that is, reason animated by faith, strives to understand more deeply the truths of faith (see §79). The encyclical provides such examples as the use of language when speaking about God, the relations within the Trinity and the relationship between the divinity and the humanity in Christ (see §66). Reason can never fully comprehend the mysteries of faith and so make them fully intelligible, yet reason can further clarify more precisely what the mysteries of faith are and in so doing make them even more illustrious and awe-inspiring.

There is here, then, a circular hermeneutic. First, through the act of faith reason receives the mysteries of faith and so grasps their truth. Second, faith beckons reason to assist it in furthering its understanding of these mysteries. Third, reason performs this task, not apart from faith, but only under faith's guidance, for only faith itself can guide reason to a deeper understanding of faith's content. John Paul holds that, in the pursuit of a fuller understanding of God's word, it is through that very divine word that "reason is offered guidance and is warned against paths which would lead it to stray from revealed Truth" (§73). Were reason to perform its task apart from faith it would naturally tend to distort the mysteries by subsuming them within some rational philosophy that would evacuate them of their divine content. As the pope again states: "The knowledge of faith does not destroy the mystery, it only reveals it the more, showing how necessary it is for people's lives" (§13).

It is evident that the spirit and thought of Aquinas is contained within the pope's understanding of how reason relates to faith's desire to fathom the divine mysteries. It is almost as if one can hear the voice of Aquinas echoing in the pope's very words. For example, in the doing of theology Aquinas takes as his starting point *sacra doctrina*, that is, the teaching of sacred Scripture, which "has no science above itself,"[1] along with the Church's doctrinal tradition and magisterial pronouncements concerning its interpretation.[2] This is what is to be accepted in faith. Neither reason nor philosophy gives rise to *sacra doctrina*. In the very first question of his *Summa theologiae* Aquinas states:

> Whereas man's whole salvation, which is in God, depends upon the knowledge of this truth. Therefore, in order that the salvation of men might be brought about more fitly and more surely, it was necessary that they should be taught divine truths by divine revelation. It was therefore necessary that, besides philosophical science built up by reason there should be a sacred science learned through revelation.[3]

Likewise, the truth of *sacra doctrina* is guaranteed not by reasoned argument, but "its certitude [is] from the light of the divine knowledge, which cannot be misled."[4] In accordance with the encyclical, Aquinas insists then that *sacra doctrina* "does not argue in proof of its principles, which are the articles of faith"[5] for "it accepts its principles not from other

---

[1] *ST* I, q. 1, a. 8.

[2] *ST* I, q. 1, a. 83; I, q. 1, a. 8, ad 2.

[3] *ST* I, q. 1, a. 1.

[4] *ST* I, q. 1, a. 5.

[5] *ST* I, q. 1, a. 8.

[6] *ST* I, q. 1, a. 5; I, q. 1, a. 6, ad 1 and 2.

sciences; but immediately from God, by revelation."[6] Nonetheless, while divine revelation must be accepted in faith, yet, in keeping with the pope's teaching, it seeks philosophy's aid in order to obtain a fuller and deeper understanding. For Aquinas, as for the pope, philosophy is the essential "handmaiden" of *sacra doctrina* "for this science can in a sense depend upon the philosophical sciences, not as though it stood in need of them, but only in order to make its teaching clearer."[7]

> [Similarly,] sacred doctrine makes use even of human reason, not, indeed, to prove faith (for thereby the merit of faith would come to an end), but to make clear other things that are put forward in this doctrine. Since therefore grace does not destroy nature, but perfects it, natural reason should minister to faith as the natural bent of the will ministers to charity.[8]

While Aquinas is not constantly singled out within the encyclical, his teaching on the relationship between faith and reason and the proper use of philosophy within that relationship is not merely hidden beneath the surface but actually embedded within the pope's own principles and teaching. This should not be surprising since, as was acknowledged at the onset, John Paul himself believed that Aquinas gave "pride of place to the harmony which exists between faith and reason" (§43). Thus Aquinas, would in turn, agree with John Paul that "faith and reason are like two wings on which the human spirit rises to the contemplation of truth," which ultimately resides in the knowledge of and in the communion with the triune God (Introduction).

Faith and Reason: Man in the Image of God

Having examined John Paul's understanding of the multifaceted relationship between faith and reason accentuating its Thomistic heart, I would like now to address the question of what sort of anthropology is necessary for ensuring and sanctioning such a relationship. It is here that I perceive a weakness, maybe even a serious one, within the encyclical. While the pope rightly articulated many necessary points concerning faith and reason and their intricate relatedness, he does not propose an anthropology, with its confirming metaphysical and epistemology constituents, that is needed to support such an understanding. This may due to his belief that it is not his duty to articulate such a philosophical and theological program. As the pope himself notes: "It is my task to state principles and criteria which in my judgement are necessary in order to restore a harmonious

[7] *ST* I, q. 1, a. 5, ad 2.

[8] *ST* I, q. 1, a. 8.

and creative relationship between theology and philosophy" (§62).

Nonetheless, I believe that John Paul made a tactical error at the onset of his encyclical. He began by appraising the human search, both within the east and the west, for truth and meaning (see §1). I am sure he did this so as to begin from the point of human reason itself and not from some preconceived position of faith. Moreover, those without faith might also enter more easily into the discussion by first taking up the issues from within this very basic and universal human experience. However, having begun at the level of the universal human experience of searching for truth, John Paul never arrived at the point of fully providing a philosophical or theological basis for this human desire to know the truth or for the human ability actually to attain the truth.

While Plato and Aristotle, within their differing epistemological theories, may have argued that human beings could come to the truth, yet they too never asked the question of why such is the case. Within their respective anthropologies they highlighted the difference between man and what they considered the Ultimate: Plato, the immutable transcendental forms; Aristotle, the self enclosed pure Self-Thinking Thought. God, and not philosophers, would have to tell man why he is able to know the truth. Man, left to himself, could never tell himself why he is able to obtain knowledge. The answer lies not in the difference between God and man, but in their mutual likeness. "Then God said, 'Let us make man in our image, after our likeness'" (Genesis 1:26). (It is astonishing that there are only two allusions to this passage within the whole of the pope's encyclical [see §§80 and 90].) Human beings possess the nobility of being able to come to the truth because human beings possess the nobility of being created in the image and likeness of God. It is here that faith has primarily befriended reason for faith has revealed to man why he is indeed rational, capable of knowing the truth. But, then, this says something too about God in himself as Creator of the world and human beings.

On the first day of creation God established the science of metaphysics for, in bringing beings into existence, he founded the science of being, the science of that which is. Moreover, by giving existence to that which did not exist, God revealed that he is the fullness of being. God, then, within the completeness of his ontological nature as the fullness of being, embraces the full science of metaphysics. On the sixth day of creation God established the science of epistemology for in making man in his image and likeness he created a being that possessed the ability to know what is. There now exists a symmetry between God and man founded upon man being created in God's likeness. God in himself embraces both the fullness of being and thus the fullness of the science of metaphysics, and, equally, in knowing the fullness of the ontological reality that he is, he embraces the fullness of the science of epistemology. Man, created in his image and likeness, thus, like God, embraces, in a created and human manner, both the science of metaphysics and the science of epistemology in that he, like God, is able *to know that which is*. This, it seems to me, is the authentic foundation both for the integrity of reason with its ability to obtain metaphysical knowledge and the integrity of faith with its ability to receive and know the revelation of God. Moreover, such an understanding establishes their mutually complementary befriending interrelationship, for reason is not only open to revelation, but it is also able to befriend faith in searching the metaphysical depths of what is revealed and so received in and guided by faith (see §97).

The above also founds and accentuates John Paul's theme of the need for conversion. Sin has blemished and distorted the image of God within man, thus imperilling his ability to know the truth. It is now only through faith in Christ, with its concurrent reception of the Holy Spirit of truth, that human beings are once more re-created in God's image and likeness and so able once more confidently to assume their full stature as rational beings. This now becomes faith's supreme act of charity bestowed upon reason.

Faith and Reason: Man in the Image of the Trinity

The depth of man's being created in God's image and likeness is only reached when placed within a Trinitarian context. While space does not allow a full treatment, I would like to note a few salient features taken from Aquinas. For Aquinas, man, as the image of God, is not simply seen within God's oneness, but rather, following Augustine, specifically and authentically within God being a trinity of persons.

> Likewise, as the uncreated Trinity is distinguished by the procession of the Word from the Speaker, and of Love from both of these . . . ; so we may say that in rational creatures wherein we find a procession of the word in the intellect, and a procession of the love in the will, there exists an image of the uncreated Trinity.[9]

There are two points here that strengthen and deepen what was said above. First, the fact that man's intellect bears the likeness of the Word's procession from the Father accentuates the intellect's ability to know the truth, and specifically metaphysical truth. As the Word embodies and knows the whole of the Trinity's metaphysical reality, so man's intellect, which bears the Word's likeness, is equally able, in a human manner, to attain to the truth of being. Again, the pope could have theologically more firmly

---

[9] *ST* I, q. 93, a. 6.

grounded man's ability to know the truth had he noted that man's intellect, bearing the image of God, assumes a similarity to the Father's Word in that the nature of both resides in their ability to embrace, in their own distinctive manner, the truth.

Second, as the Spirit proceeds as the love of the Father and Son, so human love proceeds from the will as a love for what is true. Here, I think we find another lacunae in the pope's encyclical. While great emphasis is placed on reason's ability to know the truth, there is little said of the will's predisposition to love the truth. Bringing this theme into play would have allowed the pope to address what might be at the heart of the contemporary disparagement of reason. Contemporary men and women often possess no love for the truth for fear of what truth will demand. This again, though, underscores John Paul's call for conversion for only faith will enkindle the will's loving desire to know the truth.

Third, Aquinas recognized that being in the Trinity's image and likeness is threefold in nature.

> First, inasmuch as man possesses a natural aptitude for understanding and loving God; and this aptitude consists in the very nature of the mind, which is common to all men. Secondly, inasmuch as man actually or habitually knows and loves God, though imperfectly; and this image consists in the conformity of grace. Thirdly, inasmuch as man knows and loves God perfectly; and this image consists in the likeness of glory.[10]

Aquinas's first two ways in which human beings are created in the image of God are similar to what I articulated above, though now placed within a more Trinitarian context. The last is in keeping with John Paul's own emphasis, and it will be on this point that I will conclude this essay.

For John Paul the culmination of faith and reason's desire for the truth lies in the contemplation of the Trinity (see §§13 and 93). Here the relationship between faith and reason most fully befriend one another and so are most fully united, for here faith places before reason what reason most fully desires and loves—the fullness of Truth itself. This finds its completion in the beatific vision, where human beings reside in the everlasting communion of knowledge and love with the Father, the Son, and the Holy Spirit. As John Paul states:

> The ultimate purpose of personal existence, then, is the theme of philosophy and theology alike. For all their difference of method and content, both disciplines point to that "path of life" (Ps 16:11) which, as faith tells us, leads in the end to the full and lasting joy of the contemplation of the Triune God (§14).

[10] *ST* I, q. 93, a. 4.

Fides et Ratio, Analytic Philosophy, and Metaphysics of Goodness

FERGUS KERR, OP
Oxford University
Oxford, England

OBVIOUSLY THE ENCYCLICAL *Fides et Ratio* is one of the many great documents of this pontificate which will be cited for decades to come. That needs no demonstration. It seems, however, to pay little if any attention to the ways in which philosophy has been practised in the mainstream Anglo-American tradition for the past half century.

Addressing primarily his fellow bishops (§§6, 50), Pope John Paul II surveys the state of modern philosophy (§§46–48, 88–90); notes the neglect of philosophy by some (many?) Catholic theologians and in some (many?) Catholic institutions (§§61–62); insists on the indispensability of philosophy for the understanding and expounding of Catholic Christian doctrine (e.g., §§5, 65, 77); and invites philosophers to respond to the vocation of true philosophy (§106) as a search for wisdom—indeed, with respect to philosophers who are themselves Catholic, inviting them to see the Blessed Virgin Mary as "the table at which faith sits in thought." and thus to cultivate the practice of *philosophari in Maria* (§108). More specifically, he recommends a return to metaphysics as the "philosophy of being" (§§76, 97–98). Above all, he hopes that philosophers would show less reluctance to confront the Big Questions: "the problem of evil and suffering, the personal nature of God and the question of the meaning of life or, more directly, the radical metaphysical question, "Why is there something rather than nothing?" (§76). Throughout the encyclical the pope highlights "the deep-seated distrust of reason" (§55), which he sees as characteristic of modern thought in general: the central issue for his pastoral concern since it has effects, evidently, in Catholic institutions.

Those who study St. Thomas Aquinas in the environment of Anglo-American analytical philosophy, rather than in that of "postmodern" phenomenological and hermeneutic philosophies, have, of course, much to learn from the encyclical; yet it is not very evident that the author and his advisers have paid enough informed attention to our tradition to engage with it seriously. While "a certain positivist cast of mind" frames much English-speaking philosophy—that is undeniable—few if any mainstream analytic philosophers would regard their work as "postmodern" or subscribe to the doctrines of post-Nietzschean nihilism (§91). Anglo-American philosophy may be lumped under scientism (§88) and pragmatism (§89)—a ticketing which would not be incorrect or bizarre; yet, if so, that is to ignore the struggles *against* varieties of these positions that have preoccupied philosophers in the analytic tradition for many years. If we were to regard great philosophers like Bertrand Russell and William James as progenitors of scientism and pragmatism respectively, caricaturing a bit, we should also want to say that the later work of Ludwig Wittgenstein (properly understood!) engages with both but leaves nothing standing of either scientism or pragmatism. For those of us who work in universities in which analytic philosophy dominates, the modern philosophy with which *Fides et Ratio* deals seems "Continental," post-Nietzschean and post-Heideggerian—a way of philosophizing barely acknowledged as philosophy at all in many Anglo-American philosophy departments! Rightly or wrongly—perhaps to some extent wrongly but perhaps to a greater extent rightly—philosophers trained in the analytic tradition are always startled at the seriousness with which the work of Heidegger, for example, is taken by many Catholic theologians. It is not difficult to find analytic philosophers, themselves devout Catholics, who despair of making much headway in some of Pope John Paul II's earlier writings because of what seems to them the impenetrable jargon of the phenomenological tradition.

The pope expresses gratitude to modern philosophers for many insights such as "penetrating analyses of perception and experience, of the imaginary and the unconscious, of personhood and intersubjectivity, of freedom and values, of time and history" (§48)—a predominantly if not entirely phenomenological agenda, alluding to Husserl, Scheler, Merleau-Ponty, Lacan for *l'imaginaire*, Ricoeur, Heidegger, and so on.

A handful of philosophers in the analytic tradition, welcoming the message of the encyclical, have endorsed the pope's regret that philosophers refrain from tackling the "big questions" (e.g., David Braine, John Haldane, Janet Martin Soskice, Anthony Kenny). Few non-Catholic colleagues would suppose that the encyclical was addressed also to them but, in the unlikely event that they saw a copy, many would agree that philosophers should be much less reluctant to consider the Big Questions.

The heirs of Nietzsche and Heidegger seem to the analytical eye, on the other hand, to indulge only too uncritically in grand meta-narratives as well as to encroach on matters most anglophone philosophers prefer to leave to theologians.

Stephen Mulhall, however, in one of several fine recent books by Oxford-trained philosophers, includes the last paragraph of the encyclical among the three quotations with which he prefaces his argument, contending in the course of his argument that the concerns of Wittgenstein, Heidegger, and Kierkegaard—indeed the concerns of philosophy altogether—are unintelligible ultimately without reference to *theological* concerns.[1]

This is, admittedly, a daringly ambitious book by Oxford standards. On the whole, philosophers in the analytic tradition prefer not to engage in questions that they regard as primarily religious.

One reason for this, obviously, is that the philosophy of religion, originally as a response to the challenges of skepticism, scientism, and logical-positivist verificationism, has developed into a specialist subject area with its own journals and ever-expanding literature, such that most philosophers engaged in other fields of interest, even including ethics and metaphysics, are reluctant to intervene (and even if they personally are Christians). There is so much intellectually demanding discussion in philosophical theology of a generally analytical bent that, paradoxically, it has become largely inaccessible to other analytic philosophers, let alone to philosophers of other schools.[2]

Moreover, as the encyclical notes (§30), philosophy has been professionalized. From being contemplation of truth and a search for the ultimate goal and meaning of life, philosophy has often settled for much less—"some philosophers have abandoned the search for truth in itself and made their sole aim the attainment of objective [*sic,* not "subjective"

---

[1] Stephen Mulhall, *Inheritance and Originality: Wittgenstein, Heidegger, Kierkegaard* (Oxford: Clarendon Press, 2000); but see also, as indications of recent work by mainstream Oxford philosophers, A. W. Moore, *Points of View* (Oxford: Oxford University Press, 1997); Hugh Rice, *God and Goodness* (Oxford: Oxford University Press, 2000); Bede Rundell, *Why there is Something rather than Nothing* (Oxford: Clarendon Press, 2004)—none of which is "talk about talk," as the old jibe about philosophy at Oxford used to go.

[2] If the intellectual quality, or even the existence, of this work is doubted then the place for beginners to start is *A Companion to the Philosophy of Religion*, ed. Philip L. Quinn and Charles Taliaferro (Oxford: Blackwell, 1997), surveying much more than the analytical allegiance of the editors might suggest.

as in the Libreria Editrice Vaticana translation!] certainty or a pragmatic sense of utility" (§47).[3]

While this means that excellent work is done, as the encyclical also notes (§§5, 48), it means as well that participation in philosophical reflection, or even understanding of what is going on at the cutting edge, has become increasingly difficult for the amateur, or the outsider, in analytic philosophy. Sometimes, even philosophers adept in Thomistic thought seem to lack the training in philosophical logic to be able to engage. It would, on the other hand, be unfair to regard all analytical philosophers as logic-chopping technicians for whom their professional activities have no bearing on their "private" lives. For all that, however, we should have to acknowledge the absence of the "sapiential dimension" in their work: Their philosophizing seldom looks like "a practical wisdom and a school of life" (§37).[4]

It is a long-standing complaint that analytical philosophy deals only with trivial matters, or, to put it less pejoratively, restricts itself to piecemeal analyses of manageable topics. When the encyclical speaks of philosophers for whom "philosophy is expected to rest content with more modest tasks such as the simple interpretation of facts or enquiries into restricted fields of human knowing or its structures" (§55), it is not unreasonable to judge, as James McEvoy does, that the target is the dominant "analytic" tradition in English-speaking philosophy[5]—but can this really be so?

The text runs as follows: "An example of this is the deep-seated distrust of reason which has surfaced in the most recent developments of much of philosophical research, to the point where there is talk at times of "the end of metaphysics." Philosophy is expected to rest content with more modest tasks such as the simple interpretation of facts or an enquiry into restricted fields of human knowing or its structures."[6]

---

[3] [V]eritatem ipsius causa inquirere desistentes, sibi hoc unum statuerunt ut objectivam certitudinem practicamve utilitatem obtinerent. (Since it is not so clearwhat is defective about seeking "objective certainty," and the encyclical elsewhere is much concerned with the deficiencies of subjectivism, it may be the official Latin text that contradicts the author's intention.)

[4] It would have been difficult even to explain what this might mean but now we have Pierre Hadot, *Philosophy as a Way of Life*, edited with an introduction by Arnold I. Davidson (Oxford: Blackwell, 1995). Davidson holds a chair in philosophy at the University of Chicago.

[5] *Restoring Faith in Reason: A New Translation of the Encyclical Letter Faith and Reason of Pope John Paul II together with a commentary and discussion,* ed. Laurence Paul Hemming and Susan Frank Parsons (London: SCM Press, 2000), 177.

[6] "Talis est, exempli gratia, radicalis de ratione diffidentia. Quae recentes multarum inquisitionum philosophicarum explicationes contendunt. Hac de re compluribus ex partibus audita est vox de 'interitu metaphysicae': est voluntas ut philosophia tenuioribus muneribus contenta sit, quae tantum versetur in factis interpretandis

Thus, in much recent philosophy there is a "radical diffidence about reason." We hear of "the end of metaphysics." It is a matter of *will* that philosophers restrict themselves to "more modest tasks"—which turn out to be "interpreting facts," or "investigating a number of the assured arguments of human knowledge or its structures."

Well, these observations seem somewhat off the mark if they are aimed at analytical philosophy. "The end of metaphysics," for example, is a slogan that most observers would associate with either Rudolf Carnap or Heidegger. In neither case did philosophy restrict itself to "modest tasks": On the contrary, Carnap's "scientific philosophy," and Heidegger's post-metaphysical *andenkendes Denken*, totally different from one another as they are, indeed at opposite ends of the spectrum, seem, to most analytical philosophers, the most extravagantly ambitious projects in twentieth-century philosophy!

Philosophy as "interpreting facts" McEvoy takes to be *positivism*. He allows, however, that this would not pass as a satisfactory account of what has been happening for many years in Anglo-American analytic philosophy: "[P]erhaps there is in general less consciousness in Rome of what goes on in English-speaking philosophy"—conceding, in effect, that only the German tradition from Nietzsche, Husserl, et al. and its ramifications, is really in view in the encyclical.

The reason for this, McEvoy goes on to suggest, is that "positivism excepted, [English-speaking philosophy] must seem (and on the whole it undoubtedly is), much less ideological than were some prominent currents of continental European philosophy in the course of the twentieth century."

That is a very interesting judgment. Obviously, apart from the scientistic behaviorism in much philosophical anthropology, nothing in the profile of twentieth-century English-speaking philosophy compares with Marxism or post-Nietzschean nihilism as "worldviews." On the other hand, no doubt, ideologies can be much more subtle and diffused: It would not be difficult to detect the liberal-capitalist individualism lurking in much Anglo-American analytic philosophy.

In short, analytic philosophy in the sense of current debates is never seriously confronted or even much mentioned in the encyclical—which means decades of fine work in most universities in the English-speaking world.

One cannot help regretting this. "Whereas almost all of Continental philosophy has gone 'post modern,' Anglo-American philosophy continues to defend truth and objectivity," as John Greco says. "Ironically,

---

vel investigationibus de quibusdam certis argumentis humanae cognitionis vel ejusdem de structuris."

analytic philosophy has become the natural ally of Thomism and Catholic philosophy."[7]

Unfortunately, few on either side have noticed this.

The encyclical is far from negative about recent developments. The great merit of modern philosophy, indeed, is the focus on philosophical anthropology, on human subjectivity (§5). The down side of this, however, is the tendency to concentrate on *knowing* at the expense of the investigation of *being*: "While, on the one hand, philosophical thinking has succeeded in coming closer to the reality of human life and its forms of expression, it has also tended to pursue issues, existential, hermeneutical or linguistic, which ignore the radical question of the truth about personal existence, about being and about God."[8]

As everyone knows, philosophy since Descartes has been concentrated on questions relating subjectivity, consciousness, knowing, etc., in continental as well as Anglo-American philosophy.

It is also true that the existentialist, hermeneutic, and linguistic schools bring philosophers, in various ways, closer to "human life and its forms of expression," a fair enough rubric, anyway, for what analytic philosophers do.

It is also true, as already noted, that analytic-philosophical considerations bypass or neglect the big question about "the *truth* of human life, of existence and of God himself" (emphasis added). Philosophy, after all, the encyclical insists, is concerned above all with the question of *truth* (§§25–33).

Fair enough—yet, for analytical philosophers, it might seem that the history of anglophone philosophy in the second half of the twentieth century could be written round the question of truth introduced onto the agenda, principally, by Michael Dummett in an epoch-making essay in 1959.[9]

---

7 John Greco, "Thomism and the Future of Catholic Philosophy," *New Blackfriars* 80 (1999): 182.

8 "[C]um hinc philosophica investigatio iam in illam viam se inserere potuit, quae propiorem eam reddit ad hominum vitam eiusque formas expressas, illinc tamen eadem inquisitio explicare iam vult deliberationes existentiales, hermeneuticas vel linguisticas quae alienae sunt a fundamentali hac quaestione de veritate cuiusque hominis vitae, exsistentiae atque Dei ipsius."

9 Michael Dummett, *"Truth," Proceedings of the Aristotelian Society* 59 (1957): 141–62; reprinted in his *Truth and Other Enigmas* (London: Duckworth, 1978). For an introduction to the status quaestionis today, see Truth ed. Simon Blackburn and Keith Simmons (Oxford: Oxford University Press, 1999): an anthology of the classical interventions from F. H. Bradley, H. H. Joachim, William James, and Bertrand Russell, via Frege, F. P. Ramsey, Wittgenstein, Tarski, and Quine, then the Oxford debate between P. F. Strawson and J. L. Austin (1950), through to

Some analytic philosophers may well distrust the idea of propositions that are universally and absolutely true or false; others may be attracted to the notion that truth is born of consensus (§56)—but they have to contend with colleagues who utterly reject such views. Indeed, this is the decisive point: In analytic philosophy these last fifty years there has been *no* generally accepted theory of truth. On the contrary, many different accounts of truth have been tabled over the years. First-year philosophy students have to consider the range of options between coherence and correspondence theories of truth. At the most sophisticated level, in the debates in metaphysics over realism and anti-realism, the question of truth is central. Dummett's contribution has been to reconstruct the ancient debate between realism and idealism in terms precisely of truth, arguing that the debate is best construed as between those who hold that there may be truths that transcend our methods of verification and those who hold by contrast that it makes no sense to posit such truths (inclining toward positivism nowadays rather than absolute idealism).

Quasi-verificationist, redundancy, and eliminativist theories of truth circulate in the literature. These may indeed predominate. In some versions they may sometimes resemble post-Nietzschean disenchantment with the very idea of truth, if of course in an entirely different terminology. This does not mean, however, that philosophers have altogether given up realist conceptions of truth and objectivity. Far from it. Major philosophers such as Donald Davidson, Hilary Putnam, and Thomas Nagel, as well as Michael Dummett, have been working for decades on the classical problems of truth and objectivity, much more respectfully and assiduously, one might think, than some of their better known coevals in the continental tradition.[10]

Again, "current developments in hermeneutics and the analysis of language yield great results, helpful for the understanding of faith, since they bring to light the structures of our thought and speech and the meaning which language bears" (§84)—but if "the analysis of language" *(variae sermonis humani pervestigationes)* might sound like a reference to "linguistic analysis," and thus to Anglo-American philosophy, it has to be said that, if these investigations "lay bare the structure of human thought and expression and all the meaning enclosed in language," many leading philosophers, starting with the later Wittgenstein and J. L. Austin, would jib at such an account of their work. In fact, the allusion is probably to semiotics, semantics, linguistics, Saussure, and such like—again very much a continental agenda.

---

recent work by well-known Anglo-American philosophers. (Michael Dummett, by the way, is a devout Catholic.)

[10] Jürgen Habermas excepted.

Finally, in this summary account of possible references, there is this passage: "[L]ogic, philosophy of language, epistemology, philosophy of nature, anthropology, a more profound investigation of the affective character of knowledge and an existential approach to the analysis of freedom." This sounds very much like what analytic philosophers have been doing over the past thirty or forty years. These developments are all good, "yet since the nineteenth century the affirmation of the principle of immanence, which is a sort of basis to the claims of rationalism, has provoked the profoundest doubting of claims once thought indisputable . . . so currents of irrationalism have arisen, while at the same time critical judgement has shown the emptiness of the claims of the absolute domination of reason . . . some more subtle writers have labeled the age 'post modern'. . . the expression comes from aesthetics, social and technological agendas, it remains ambiguous, nevertheless the reasons and reflections which refer to the area of post modernity always merit serious consideration."

To anyone familiar with the analytic tradition this seems a comment once again entirely about post-Nietzschean philosophy in the continental tradition.

Partly, no doubt, when we look for an explanation of this absence of interest, it may be supposed that, for observers of modern philosophy from a continental perspective, as perhaps those who helped Pope John Paul II to draft the encyclical, analytical philosophy is regarded as basically logical positivism.

Historically, positivism in the style of Comte, its progenitor, never took hold in English-language philosophy; it was very much a "continental" adventure (often openly anti-Catholic).

Logical positivism was a different matter. This movement was also, of course, "continental" in origin: Rooted in the work of the Vienna Circle (Carnap, Weigl, Neurath, and others), it was translated to Oxford by A. J. Ayer, in his *Language, Truth and Logic* (1936) and, more widely, and much more influentially, by members of the group (Carnap and Feigl) who found refuge from Nazism in the United States.

The most characteristic doctrine of logical positivism is the verification principle: the denial of literal or cognitive meaning to any statement that is not empirically verifiable. In terms of the encyclical, however, it was never limited to "simple interpretation of facts." Nor could it be described as resting content with a quite modest task. On the contrary, logical positivism is one of the most ambitious projects in twentieth-century philosophy (the scientism mentioned in §88).

Rudolf Carnap (1891–1970) taught at Chicago and Los Angeles from 1935 onward. He had immense influence on the development of philosophy in North America. In his first great work, *Der logische Aufbau der Welt* (1928), he combines an empiricism much more governed by the hard sciences than any empiricism espoused by British philosophers in the wake of Locke or Hume. Powering himself with the logical apparatus provided by Frege and Russell, Carnap produced logical positivism in its most classical form. This phenomenalistic reduction of all objects of knowledge delivered the solipsistic basis of the construction of the external world that the encyclical seems to allude to (§82)—against which, however, much analytic philosophy has contended for half a century.

The greatest American-born philosopher of the second half of the twentieth century, Willard van Orman Quine (1908–2002) spent a postgraduate year in Europe with Carnap and (in Warsaw) with Tarski. He dominated American philosophy for the next forty years, developing his own distinctive approach in logic, semantics, epistemology, and philosophy of science, much too complex to reduce to a simple formula, yet always unmistakably indebted (as he would not have denied) to logical positivism.

Quine held that the only languages that are suitable for literal and true description of the world are those of mathematics and science. He had a holistic view of verification, conceiving of a body of knowledge in terms of a web touching experience at the edge but with each point connected by a network of relations to other points. He is famous for the view that epistemology should be naturalized, with the object of investigation being the relationship, in human beings, between the inputs of experience and the outputs of belief. While nuancing would be required in a longer account, it seems not unfair to describe Quine's philosophy as scientism and behaviorism.

That twentieth-century American philosophy has been shaped by Carnap and Quine is undeniable—but from the beginning their views have been resisted. In England, in particular, where Carnap left little trace, the asylum-seeking Austrians who took up permanent residence, Wittgenstein and Friedrich Waismann, were both vigorously and steadfastly opposed to scientism and behaviorism. Ayer's little book had an unjustifiably intimidatory effect on philosophical theology, perhaps into the 1960s; but it rapidly lost credibility among philosophers in Cambridge, Oxford, and elsewhere. Theologians were just slow to catch up. By 1947, however, in Oxford at least, Ayer was more celebrated for the destructive analysis of his book *The Foundations of Empirical Knowledge* (1940), which was pursued in lectures by J. L. Austin, the paradigm of the "linguistic analyst."[11]

---

[11] These lectures, frequently repeated, given at the University of California in 1958 and for the last time in Oxford in 1959, the year before his early death, were

For all the absence of any sustained logical positivism, it is not mistaken to believe that, from the 1920s onward, philosophers in the United Kingdom, and eventually all over the English-speaking world, often scoffed at "metaphysics." Thus, one might conclude, philosophers brought up in the analytic tradition could have little or nothing to contribute to renewal of the philosophy of being within the Christian metaphysical tradition (cf. §97).

We need, however, to ask what it was that was rejected.

At Cambridge both G. E. Moore and Bertrand Russell were once enthusiastic admirers of Hegel, as were most philosophers in Oxford also and in the Scottish universities, before 1914. Skepticism about the claims of German idealism as represented by Hegel, Schelling, and Fichte, was already under way (not unconnected with hatred of "German imperialism"). By the 1930s, while philosophers continued to study and admire Plato and Aristotle, often attracted by their metaphysical writings, the word "metaphysics" had largely become associated with German idealism—and had become an extremely negative and pejorative term.

There is a significant difference between Moore and Russell in their anti-metaphysical philosophies. For Moore metaphysics could not survive appeal to common sense; for Russell, on the other hand, the appeal was to logic: "The business of philosophy, as I conceive it, is essentially that of logical analysis, followed by logical synthesis. . . . Although . . . comprehensive construction is part of the business of philosophy, I do not believe it is the most important part. The most important part, to my mind, consists in criticizing and clarifying notions that are apt to be regarded as fundamental and accepted uncritically. As instances I might mention: mind, matter, consciousness, knowledge, experience, causality, will, time. I believe all these notions to be inexact and approximate, essentially infected with vagueness, incapable of forming part of any exact science."[12] In many ways Russell's early work could easily count as "metaphysics," though he preferred to call it "logic."

Wittgenstein early and late reacted against Russell's conception of philosophy. He came to think that his own *Tractatus Logico-Philosophicus*

reconstructed by his colleague G. J. Warnock and appeared in 1962 as *Sense and Sensibilia*—the classical demolition of one of the most typical conceptions of perception as requiring some intermediary entity (impressions, sense data, etc.) between the perceiver and the object perceived; it should be of great interest to students of St. Thomas; it is at least as important as the so-called "speech act theory" developed from Austin's William James Lectures at Harvard, *How to do things with words,* also published posthumously in 1962.

12 Bertrand Russell, "Logical atomism," in *Contemporary British Philosophy*, ed. J. H. Muirhead (London: Allen and Unwin, 1924).

was a piece of "metaphysics," understood pejoratively—contending, in his later work, that "what *we* do is bring words like being, knowledge, intentionality and so on back from their metaphysical use to how they are used in the language in which they are at home" (*Investigations* §116; emphasis added).

This may well sound anti-metaphysical but there again one needs to ask what the objectionable metaphysical uses are. Wittgenstein is, after all, on record expressing his respect for the profundity of Kant and Berkeley. His later work wrestles indefatigably with Descartes, Hume, William James, and Russell, as well as the logical positivism of the Vienna Circle. He attacks both subjectivism and scientism—but since these were, for him, metaphysical fantasies generated by fantasies of language he could not think of metaphysics except negatively.

By 1959, however, in the work of Peter Strawson, metaphysics was already back on the agenda in British philosophy, at Oxford specifically, and as a Good Thing—both "descriptive metaphysics" and "revisionary metaphysics."[13]

True, when Anglo-American philosophers publish books of metaphysics these days, it is most commonly metaphysics at the service of naturalism or physicalism. Their adherents would regard these as substantive metaphysical views of the world. It may well be, then, in the English-speaking world, if we do not turn our backs on analytic philosophers, that the substantive metaphysics that we need for Catholic Christian theology is what we work out dialectically against—for example—any version of physicalism. This is the view that the real world is nothing more than the physical world. Often, perhaps usually, this comes out as the doctrine that everything that can be truly said is said in the language of physics. The nearer we get to the basic physical constituents the more we have of the truth of how things are. In philosophical psychology the more we know about how the brain works the more we understand about people.

Compared with some of the post-Nietzschean accounts of the world as constructed or projected into existence by the human mind, with the doctrines of cultural relativism that often accompany this, one might be allowed to think that grounding one's view of the world on the physical world, for all the scientistic and reductionist assumptions in this enterprise, offers a much more solid and congenial starting point for discussion for those who believe the world to be created. At least physicalist metaphysics will be unlikely to lend credence to relativistic doctrines according to

---

13 Peter F. Strawson, *Indivividuals: An Essay in Descriptive Metaphysics* (London: Methuen, 1959).

which the world is how we make it up, or according to which there is no one true version of the world at all. Engaging in dialectic with some versions of physicalism, that is to say, might be more fruitful than trying to understand even sober forms of cultural relativism. It would not be unprecedented. St. Thomas Aquinas himself, after all, introduces the conception of the natural order that he needs for expounding Christian doctrine precisely by recapitulating the history of pre-Aristotelian naturalism, incorporating and transcending it.

The encyclical is pretty sketchy about the details of the recommended philosophy of being—*perquisitiones in ipsum "esse"* (§5). We really need an appendix of exemplary books or papers.

It is clear what the question is: "[T]he question of the meaning of things and of their very existence . . . the quest for meaning which has always compelled the human heart . . . the question of life's meaning and. an answer to it" (§§1, 3).

One example of what this yields positively is "the basic form of philosophical knowledge which is evident to this day in the postulates which inspire national and international legal systems in regulating the life of society" (§3)—thus human rights, natural rights, and so on.[14]

More in tune with standard expectations, the pope makes the following request: "Consider for example [so this isn't intended as an exhaustive list] the principles of non-contradiction, finality and causality, as well as the concept of the person as a free and intelligent subject with the capacity to know God, truth and goodness. . . . Consider as well certain fundamental moral norms which are shared by all" (§4).

In other words, we are to consider the topics that are, as it happens, already on the agenda nowadays in any department of analytical philosophy. Moreover, in any good university bookstore there will be shelves of textbooks introducing metaphysics, philosophical anthropology, and ethics, discussing all these issues, perhaps even including the question of the knowability of God—though that, as we have already noted, would usually be little developed but left to the specialists in the philosophy of religion.

More specifically, in connection with St. Thomas (§44), we are directed to consider the realism that recognizes the objectivity of truth and produces not merely a philosophy of "what seems to be" but a philosophy of "what is," very much a concern in analytic philosophy (phenomenalism versus realism, in the jargon).

---

[14] Of course a philosophy of human rights emerging from the philosophy of being would not be greeted with unanimous delight by all Catholic thinkers about these matters, some of whom would agree with Jeremy Bentham's famous dismissal of the very idea of natural rights as "nonsense upon stilts."

Specifically again, the pope refers to the need for a discipline of ethics which is neither subjective nor utilitarian, which looks to philosophical anthropology—and at the same time involves a metaphysical treatment of the good (cf §98). (We shall come back to that.)

In these recommendations we certainly pick up themes central to controversies in mainstream analytic philosophy, for the past half-century. Yet, we have a problem. What is this philosophy of being, *philosophia respiciens "esse"* (§76)? In detail, what is *philosophia essendi* (§97), which, "within the perspective of the Christian metaphysical tradition, . . . is an active or dynamic philosophy which presents truth in its ontological, causal and communicative structures, retrieving its impetus and perennial impulse in the very fact that it is upheld by the act of 'being' and as a result it possesses a complete and general access to a solid universe of things and goes beyond every limit to arrive at Him in whom the consummation of all things is attained."

Here, in a footnote, we are referred to the pope's address at the Pontifical University of St. Thomas in Rome, in November 1979. Here, we are advised, the philosophy of St. Thomas needs to be studied attentively and accepted with conviction by reason of its spirit of openness and of universalism—"an openness to the whole of reality in all its parts and dimension, without either reducing reality or confining thought to particular forms or aspects (and without turning singular aspects into absolutes), as intelligence demands in the name of objective and integral truth about what is real. . . . The basis and source of this openness lie in the fact that the philosophy of St. Thomas is a philosophy of being, that is, of the *actus essendi* whose transcendental value paves the most direct way to rise to the knowledge of subsisting Being and pure Act, namely to God."

Once again, then, the metaphysics of being that the pope has in mind does not stop short of theistic considerations. Indeed, he goes much further: "[W]e can even call this philosophy the philosophy of the proclamation of being, a chant in praise of what exists . . . *filosofia della proclamazione dell'essere, il canto in onore dell'esistente*."[15] This wonderful phrase takes us back to G. K. Chesterton's wonderful little book on St. Thomas (1933), in which he speaks of the praise of Being, by St. Thomas, as the praise of God as the creator of the world. In short, on this understanding of the question of being, there is no metaphysics that stops short of natural theology, no philosophy of being that does not culminate in a song of praise, no ontology without doxology.

---

[15] *Angelicum* 57 (1980): 121–46.

Philosophers, Catholics included, working in the analytic tradition, are likely to find the move from philosophy of being to chanting the praises of being almost unthinkable.

There are splendid expositions of the philosophy of St. Thomas, by Joseph Owens and John F. Wippel to name only the most obvious; but for colleagues in departments in which analytic philosophy sets the standards of rigor, clarity, and sobriety, I can think of no recent book in English that I could recommend as exemplifying metaphysics as praise of being (whatever one may find in French, German, Spanish, Italian, or Polish).

It might be argued, on the other hand, that no textbook can take the place of a course of lectures—that metaphysics is, precisely, not a body of knowledge to be imparted (like British history, physiology, or quantum mechanics) but an activity—a way of being in the world—into which one is best initiated in face-to-face exchange, conversation, discussion, "dialogue" (not forgetting prayer and penance, cf. *Fides et Ratio* §105, the wonderful citation from St. Bonaventure's *Itinerarium Mentis in Deum*).

This might not be uncongenial. Wittgenstein, after all, maintained that "philosophy is not a body of doctrine but an activity" (*Tractatus* 4.112)—a conviction only confirmed in his later work.

On the other hand, as noted, there are dozens of textbooks of metaphysics currently available, mostly the byproduct of courses taught in English-speaking universities. Books cannot do it all but they can help. In principle, it surely seems, there is no reason why there should not be textbooks outlining the philosophy of being, as there used to be expositions of *philosophia ad mentem sancti Thomae*.

And yet—according to Christopher Martin, who has clearly worked through them, the textbooks of Thomistic philosophy, "though crammed with valuable Thomist content . . . do . . . by their very form as textbooks falsify the nature of philosophy as an inquiry."[16]

As John Haldane has insisted, it is a mistake to regard analytic philosophy as inherently anti-metaphysical, skeptical, and nihilist—rather, he says, it "has a claim to be the prime continuant of Western philosophical rationalism."[17]

On the other hand, talk about "being" remains baffling for most analytic philosophers. Haldane's lecture never once mentions the word "being."[18]

---

16 Christopher Martin, *New Blackfriars* 80 (1999): 190.

17 John Haldane, *New Blackfriars* 80 (1999): 170.

18 Indeed in this entire issue, authored by Timothy Chappell, Dagfinn Føllesdal, Bas C. van Fraassen, John Greco, Bonnie Kent, Christopher Martin, Ralph McInerny, Hayden Ramsay, Nicholas Rescher, Thomas D. Sullivan, Charles Taylor, Linda Trinkhaus Zagzebski, and Haldane himself, no one sees any need to mention the word "being"!

Indeed, none of the philosophers whom he assembled to reflect on Thomism in the context of analytical philosophy felt any need to mention the word—whether they avoided it deliberately or quite without thinking (which would be even more revealing).

We have some way yet to go, in the Anglo-American tradition, to feel free to speak of "Being." We need, the pope says (§83), a philosophy of genuinely metaphysical range, "capable, that is, of transcending empirical data, in order to attain something absolute, ultimate and foundational in its search for truth." There is a "requirement," as he says, which is "implicit in sapiential and analytical knowledge alike" "a requirement for knowing the moral good, which has its ultimate foundation in the Supreme Good, God himself."[19] We need "a philosophical ethics which looks to the truth of the good, to an ethics which is neither subjectivist nor utilitarian. Such an ethics implies and presupposes a philosophical anthropology and a metaphysics of the good."[20]

For most philosophers in the analytic tradition this metaphysics of the good seems to move too rapidly into Christian theology. There may be residual Protestant Christian suspicions of the Catholic doctrine of grace building on nature (cf. §43), the idea that philosophy as sapiential should be consonant with biblical wisdom such that philosophers may be summoned to engage in the search for the natural foundation of this meaning, which corresponds to the religious impulse innate in every person (§81). In effect, if some such genesis is a plausible story, reluctance on the part of analytical philosophers (including some who are Catholics in "private" life) to extend their reflections into a philosophical consideration of *actus essendi* may be an unwitting endorsement of the dualism between reason and revelation, nature and grace, so decisive for the parting of the ways in western Christianity since the sixteenth century. After all, analytical philosophy is most at home in the universities that long ago slipped out of communion with the Catholic Church: It is perhaps to be expected that analytical philosophers would on the whole prefer to regard the question of God as purely a matter of faith.

---

19 "[O]pus est philosophia naturae vere metaphysicae, que excedere nempe valeat empirica indicia ut, veritatem conquirens, ad aliquid absolutum ultimum, fundamentale pertingat. Haec postulatio iam implicita reperitur in cognitionibus indolis sapientialis tum etiam analyticae; est necessitas praesertim cognitionum de bono morali cujus extremum fundamentum est Bonum supremum, Deus ipse. . . . Ubicumque praesentem quandam appellationem ad absolutum et transcendens detegit homo, inibi ei aperitur indicatio metaphysicae rerum interpretationis: in veritate ac pulchritudine, in bonis moralibus ac personis ceteris, in esse ac in Deo."

20 "[H]aec postulata ethica ratio importat atque ante flagitat philosophicam anthropologiam nec non metaphysicam bonorum tractationem."

Obviously, also, most analytical philosophers take it for granted that Kant was right, in the *Critique of Pure Reason* (1781) to rule out the versions of metaphysics that purport to establish doctrines about the nature of the soul, the constitution of an independent order of space and time, and the knowability of God. In another way, that is to say, this is only to entrench the gulf between reason and revelation, and thus leave all talk of God to the faithful.

Paradoxically, of course, for the Thomist, at least "of the strict observance," this gulf between reason and revelation—more specifically between a philosophy engaged in coming to terms with the allurements of physicalism and the assumption so happily made by many theologians that all talk of God is indeed pure fideism—could easily become the common ground on which discussion might arise. True, the encyclical *Fides et Ratio* keeps insisting on the way in which metaphysics, and specifically the philosophy of *esse*, should be allowed to spread over into fundamental theology; one might, on the other hand, be happy to delay the introduction of theistic considerations in favor of saying as much as possible within the ambit of a naturalistic ontology and philosophical anthropology. Since analytic metaphysicians are unlikely to turn to natural theology in great numbers in the proximate future, we really have no alternative—unless, of course, we prefer to keep aloof.

Yet, if a philosophy of *esse* seems unlikely to emerge soon, we may already have the makings of a metaphysics of the good, such as the pope envisages.

Of course God is identified by St. Thomas as *ipsum esse subsistens*. In the *secunda pars* of the *Summa theologiae*, however, as often elsewhere, in what we might call his outline of philosophical anthropology (the subject as moral agent), it is God as *beatitudo* on whom the focus lies. God as the sovereign good, *summum bonum,* the good that generously and graciously diffuses itself in creating the world (and so on).

We surely could, in a totally non-Christian academic environment, get ethics going in terms of human orientation to the Good—which is, anyway, basically what several philosophers in the analytic mode have been doing for decades.

Iris Murdoch, to start with, in her lecture "The sovereignty of good over other concepts," then in the Gifford lectures she gave in Edinburgh, *Metaphysics as a guide for morals*, says that of course we cannot believe the Christian story any longer. How could God (under any description) ever become one of us: a man, a Jewish prophet, in an out of the way part of the world, in the year 4 B.C. (etc)—"the scandal of particularity"? Yet, she insists, we surely don't invent our ethical standards for ourselves: There are certain givens. We can't do just what we like with our nature, certain features are given; we don't make up morality as we go along, or from scratch, or as whatever suits us.[21]

For Murdoch, then, there is no biblical revelation—yet on the other hand there is no settling for nihilism either. For Murdoch we need to get back to Plato: Morals need metaphysics; it is a frighteningly practical matter for her. The social order is collapsing because people don't acknowledge certain standards, which are effectively Plato's forms of the good, the true, and the beautiful. We have to free ourselves of centuries of Christian interpretation of Plato: Just let us get back to a pre-Christian understanding of how human lives are always already, mysteriously, directed, motivated, by a congenital insatiable desire for the true, the good, and the beautiful. In the professional philosophical literature Murdoch is a precursor, an example of realism in ethics—moral realism, one way of heading off subjectivism, projectivism, emotivism, and so on.[22]

For the realist in ethics, we don't invent our standards and paradigms of the good, or project them out of our own resources, we *discover* them. Of course we have to work at this, it is a training, an asceticism—Murdoch insists on this very strongly. It is like Plato's metaphysical ascent story in the *Symposium*, always her model even when she doesn't say so—you gradually painfully move from attraction to this or that finite particular good or value or ideal and are drawn on, onward and upward, to uncover, unveil, the ultimate truth and beauty.

The problem (to my mind) with Murdoch's Plato is that, while of course he is pre- and non-Christian, he is nevertheless a profoundly religious thinker. (Surely Murdoch is correct: that Plato is "just a philosopher" is a very modern idea.) The ascent by asceticism to vision of the form of the Good, even in this life (not that for her there is any other), is an appeal to a religious conception that scares off many analytical philosophers.[23]

---

21 Iris Murdoch, no doubt much better known as a (too prolific?) novelist, published three important papers before she abandoned her academic career: "The Idea of Perfection," "The Sovereignty of Good over Other Concepts," and "On 'God' and 'Good' " in the 1960s, reprinting them as *The Sovereignty of Good* (London: Routledge & Kegan Paul, 1970). Her Gifford lectures at Edinburgh in 1982 eventually appeared as *Metaphysics as a Guide to Morals* (London: Chatto & Windus, 1992), something of a "loose and baggy monster."

22 See J. L. Mackie, *Ethics: Inventing Right and Wrong* (1977); Simon Blackburn, *Being Good: An Introduction to Philosophy* (2001).

23 Nevertheless Murdoch's early papers have exerted a great deal of influence: see, for example, Alasdair MacIntyre, *After Virtue* (1981); Sabina Lovibond, *Realism and Imagination in Ethics* (1983) Charles Taylor, *Sources of the Self: The Making of the Modern Identity* (1989); *Iris Murdoch and the Search for Human Goodness,* ed. Maria Antonaccio and William Schweiker (1996); Maria Antonaccio, *Picturing the*

However—there were *three* young women philosophers in Oxford in the 1950s, colleagues and friends, each engaged in quite distinct ways in chipping away at the foundations of the dominant forms of ethics.

Elizabeth Anscombe, in a famous essay on modern moral philosophy, barely mentions utilitarianism,[24] regarding it as beneath serious attention, placing the focus on Kant, deontology, versions of ethics that, as she contends, depend consciously or otherwise on divine law doctrines. Since moral philosophers have mostly all stopped believing in God as a lawgiver (she attributes this, perhaps a little hastily, to the Reformation, denying that Christ is our judge), they should also drop talking about obligation, conscience, duty and responsibility, and so forth, about what you "ought" to do. All this is dependent on biblical doctrines (God as the one to whom we are accountable, to whom we are indebted, etc.)—without biblical theism there is no basis for deontological ethics. Thus, having given up God, let philosophers return to Aristotle—to rediscover a philosophical anthropology that includes a metaphysics of the good.

The third young philosopher in Oxford in the 1950s was Philippa Foot.[25] In a stream of important papers, starting in 1961 with "Goodness and choice," including two important critiques of Nietzsche, she has played a decisive role in the revival of so-called "virtue ethics."

Foot's first (and no doubt last!) book of 120 pages summing up her life's work, *Natural Goodness,* appeared in her 80th year—and the first person she mentions in the preface is Anscombe: "It will be obvious that I owe most to the work of Elizabeth Anscombe and to early discussions with her." Interestingly, indeed quite movingly, Foot's gratitude as a philosopher goes above all to the devout Catholic Anscombe, and one cannot doubt that Foot herself is manifestly a happy-go-lucky pagan. They are on the same side against subjectivism, emotivism, among others; and they agree that Aristotle's naturalistic ethics is where we should now start.

What Foot is doing then is getting back to the idea that there is a close connection between human happiness and virtue but she is doing it as if Christianity never existed.

Human: The Moral Thought of Iris Murdoch (2000); Hilary Putnam, *The Collapse of the Fact/Value Dichotomy and Other Essays* (2002).

24 "Modern moral philosophy," originally in *Philosophy* 33 (1958), reprinted in *Collected Philosophical Papers*, vol. III (Oxford: Basil Blackwell,1981), 26–42, introducing the term "consequentialism," 36 ("a shallow philosophy").

25 Philippa Bosanquet, granddaughter of Grover Cleveland and long since divorced from M. R. D. Foot the historian, has published two collections of papers, *Virtues and Vices and Other Essays in Moral Philosophy* (1978) and *Moral Dilemmas and Other Topics in Moral Philosophy* (2002) besides *Natural Goodness* (2001).

Once we understand how human goodness depends on the nature of our species—she puts "life" at the center, takes "life" as her focus—then we can see that the claim a human action or disposition is good or bad of its kind is simply a claim about a given feature of a certain kind of living thing. Describe the kind of animal we are and you will see this.

Foot inveighs against subjectivism, the dominant conception of ethics in analytic philosophy for sixty years, as she allows (A. J. Ayer, J. L. Mackie, Simon Blackburn). All these forms of "non-cognitivism" in morals she traces to the philosophy of David Hume and thus the fact/value dichotomy. But do we always separate facts from values? On the contrary, reflection on common experience indicates that we do not; indeed we are usually interested in the facts only because of their significance. Following one of the later Wittgenstein's methods, Foot reminds us of what she hopes we shall agree is the kind of thing we say in ordinary everyday circumstances.

Referring us to another famous essay by Anscombe, "On promising,"[26] Foot asks us to recall that it is facts about human life that make it necessary for human beings to make promises, to be able to bind each other to action through institutions, practices, customs, and so on, such that there few other ways in which one person can reliably get another to do what he or she wants. This is another typical Wittgensteinian move, inviting one to move away from dwelling on one's own inner experience to look at the practices and institutions that one inhabits and without which one would have no interesting inner experiences anyway.

Promising is not "a convention," if by that you mean a rule we could alter or do without; it is what Anscombe calls an "Aristotelian necessity," meaning by this that, just as it is necessary for plants to have water, for birds to build nests, for wolves to hunt in packs and so on, all depending on what the kind of plants or animals need, in their natural habitats, and the ways of making out that are within their physical and mental repertoire, such things determine what it is for members of that species to be as they should be, and to do what they should do. This "should," this "ought," is now grounded in the "necessities" of the nature of that species—it is not an "ought" issuing supernaturally from divine command nor on the other hand is it merely a convention that human beings could choose to alter at will.

We humans don't need to be able to dive like gannets, Foot says; nor to see in the dark like owls; but our remembering and focusing, our memory and concentration, have to be such as to allow us to pick up language; our

[26] G. E. M. Anscombe, "On Promising and its Justice, and whether it need be respected in *foro interno*," originally in *Critica* 3 (1960), reprinted in *Collected Philosophical Papers*, vol. III (Oxford: Basil Blackwell, 1981), 10–21.

balance such that we eventually learn to stand and walk; our sight such that we can recognize faces at a glance; and so forth. Human parents are just defective if they do not teach their young the skills human young need to survive—as a lioness teaches her young. Of course it is vastly more complicated, human beings are very different from other beings. Yet, Foot anticipates, anyone who thinks about it can see that, for human beings, teaching their young what promising is, for example, and a whole lot of other social skills, is *necessary*—"how could we manage, for example, if there were no way of making appointments, being punctual"—simple ordinary everyday things—"how could we survive without justice?"

The moral virtues, then, are "Aristotelian necessities": The kind of life we humans live necessitates practices, dispositions, cultivated and settled, skills, virtues, such as being able to make and keep promises. Morality is grounded in our biological nature. What is "good" is what is "necessary" for our kind of animal to flourish, indeed to survive.

There is no problem about how to justify morals, either claiming that a course of action is right because it produces the happiest consequences, or because we hear God commanding it. For Foot it is right because it is what you need to do given the kind of animal you are. There is no problem about what is "morally good," indeed you can take the word "moral" out of our discourse—it adds nothing, you don't need it, it only adds confusion; it is not in Aristotle.[27]

This is not to say that objections cannot be brought, or difficulties imagined, against Foot's argument. Obviously, her neo-Aristotelianism offers a persuasive way of avoiding the range of different doctrines from utilitarianism via emotivism to fideistic divine command ethics, all of which, in their way, attempt to do without the concept of human nature and its orientation to the good.

This naturalistic view of ethics, as she calls it, Foot finds in Thomas Aquinas: The nature of our kind requires, enables, and allows us to do this and that, to be this or that, and that is how we flourish, that is how we are happy, that is how we are good—in short, goodness, happiness, virtue, and human nature are inseparable. These concepts are internally related, they form a structure that it is not too difficult to envisage as the ground on which to develop a metaphysics of the sovereignty of Good.

---

[27] The word "moral" has been so blighted by Kantian deontological talk and (even more) by guilt-inducing pietism that perhaps the best course is to suspend the use of the word, as Anscombe virtually suggests, until it has been freed of that overlayer and returned to something more like Thomas Aquinas's usage: The word "moralis" equals "voluntarius" or "humanus"—an action is "moral" if it is freely chosen in accordance with our rational nature.

What Thomas Aquinas adds to this naturalistic account is, of course, that we are created in the image of God, God understood in faith as Trinity of persons, this communion of bliss which by grace human beings may be invited, called, to participate in. Foot shows no interest in going that far: She shows no sympathy with Iris Murdoch's quasi-religious Platonism nor is she ever dismissive of religion in the way in which some influential moral philosophers are (Mackie and Blackburn). (Perhaps her many conversations with Anscombe left Foot respectful of beliefs she never felt attracted by herself.) Thomas Aquinas's discussion, in the *secunda pars*, is "a wonderful piece of moral philosophy," as she says;[28] opening up the possibility, anyway, of an analytical-philosophical ethics of the good that would not be too difficult to relate, however cautiously, to a metaphysics of being.

In conclusion, though there is much for analytical philosophers who are themselves Catholics to learn from the encyclical *Fides et Ratio*, the perspective of the document seems to conceal the fine work done in the Anglo-American analytical tradition over at least the last half century. In particular, it is the clash of views, the conflict of positions, in metaphysics as in ethics, that characterizes this tradition. Many of these views are as incompatible with the truths of Catholic Christian faith as any in the nihilistic and relativistic tradition of post-Nietzschean philosophy. On the other hand, physicalism in metaphysics and naturalism in ethics offer highly congenial starting points for discussion between analytical philosophers and Thomists. While we have discovered, in recent years, that there is much more to "Thomism" than "Aristotelianism," the possibility lies open for a reengagement with Aristotle's philosophy in ways that could bring Thomists and some analytical philosophers together to find common ground, in the midst of the "crisis of meaning" which Pope John Paul II discerns (§81).[29]

---

28 *Natural Goodness,* 73.

29 For related discussion, see my "Aquinas and Analytic Philosophy: Natural Allies?," *Modern Theology* 20 (2004): 123–39. For an exemplary demonstration of philosophical work that demonstrates complete command both of analytical philosophical and Thomist ways of thinking see John P. O'Callaghan, *Thomist Realism and the Linguistic Turn: Toward a More Perfect Form of Existence* (Notre Dame, IN: University of Notre Dame Press, 2003).

John Paul II and Aquinas on the Eucharist

MATTHEW LEVERING
Ave Maria University
Naples, Florida

IN NUMEROUS recent writings marking the turn of the Millennium, Pope John Paul II exhorted humankind "[t]o contemplate the face of Christ."[1] In his encyclical *Ecclesia de Eucharistia*, John Paul II specifies that we should contemplate "the 'Eucharistic face' of Christ."[2] Such contemplation, he argues, will renew both the Church's life and the theology of the Eucharist. The contemplative believer will recognize Christ's "many forms of presence, but above all in the living sacrament of his body and his blood,"[3] and thereby be united with him more deeply in the faith, hope, and love that unite and build up the Church. As the pope writes, "*The Church draws her life from Christ in the Eucharist;* by him she is fed and by him she is enlightened."[4] The "enlightenment" that the Church expresses in her theological understanding of the Eucharist depends upon the spiritual nourishment gained by Eucharistic contemplation of Christ. Contrasting this contemplative insight with current distortions in Eucharistic theology, John Paul II notes, "At times one encounters an extremely reductive understanding of the Eucharistic mystery. Stripped of its sacrificial meaning, it is celebrated as if it were simply a fraternal banquet. Furthermore, the necessity of the ministerial priesthood, grounded in

---

1 *Ecclesia de Eucharistia,* §6; cf. *Rosarium Virginis Mariae* (2002); *Novo Millennio Ineunte* (January 6, 2001), especially §16ff.; *Incarnationis Mysterium* (1998), especially §1–4; *Tertio Millennio Adveniente* (1994), especially §1–8, 55.

2 *Ecclesia de Eucharistia,* §7. I should note at the outset that *Ecclesia de Eucharistia* repeats, two decades later, the main points made in Pope John Paul II's apostolic letter *Dominicae Cenae (On the Mystery and Worship of the Eucharist),* which was promulgated on February 24, 1980.

3 *Ecclesia de Eucharistia,* §6.

4 Ibid.

apostolic succession, is at times obscured and the sacramental nature of the Eucharist is reduced to its mere effectiveness as a form of proclamation."[5] The pope is thus concerned, among other things, to foster contemplative understanding of the Eucharist as a sacrifice.

Why does he consider the sacrificial aspect central to the "Eucharistic face" of Christ? This article will explore this question by means of three steps. First, I will examine the work of David Power, who advocates modifying the concept of Eucharistic "sacrifice" in light of his understanding of communion. Second, aided by Aquinas's *Commentary on the Gospel of St. John*, I will explore the concept of communion in its classic expression in the Gospel of John. In light of this biblical depiction of "communion," the final section of the essay will argue—drawing upon the *Summa theologiae* and *Ecclesia de Eucharistia*—that understanding the Eucharist as cultic sacrifice illumines the reality of salvation in which we are united with Christ's Cross in order to join in the Trinitarian communion of his risen life.

The Eucharist as Communion: John Paul II and David Power

In order to highlight the issue at stake, I will begin by comparing the encyclical's brief comments on the Eucharist as communion with the approach of David Power. In the *Ecclesia de Eucharistia*, John Paul II remarks, "The Extraordinary Assembly of the Synod of Bishops in 1985 saw in the concept of an 'ecclesiology of communion' the central and fundamental idea of the documents of the Second Vatican Council."[6] The Church exists to foster the communion between human beings and the triune God. Within this communion, a common love binds together human beings, who love each other in loving their Creator. The Eucharist is the perfect sacrament of communion. In receiving the Eucharist, we are united to the Son and share in his relationship (communion) with the Father in the Holy Spirit. As the locus of our Trinitarian communion with God, the Eucharist contains our common good.

In this regard, the pope quotes the Byzantine theologian Nicholas Cabasilas, who praises the Eucharist because in it "unlike any other sacrament, the mystery [of communion] is so perfect that it brings us to the heights of every good thing: here is the ultimate goal of every human desire, because here we attain God and God joins himself to us in the most perfect union."[7] Having mentioned this point, however, the pope

[5] Ibid., §10.

[6] Ibid., §34.

[7] Ibid.

does not linger upon it, although he does return briefly to the Eucharist's power in promoting communion. Rather, he moves on to the implications of the fact that the Eucharist presupposes for its celebration ecclesial communion through baptism and the sacramental priesthood. In contrast to certain overzealous ecumenical or interreligious endeavors, as well as to efforts within the Church to bypass the ministerial priesthood, the pope affirms that without the outward and visible communion of the Church, Eucharistic communion is impossible, since the latter depends upon the existence of the former.

In contrast to "sacrifice," with its connotations of suffering and blood, "communion" evokes friendship. Why then does the pope prioritize "sacrifice" rather than "communion" for understanding the sacrament of the Eucharist? Writing a decade before the pope's encyclical, David Power makes the argument for the priority of the notion of "communion" in an especially clear fashion. Power first claims that traditional sacrificial understandings of the Catholic priesthood are a mistake. In the biblical writings and the writings of the earliest Fathers, Power holds, one encounters clearly "the metaphorical nature of Christian sacrificial language."[8] The Christian "sacrifice" is at this earliest period simply a sacrifice of praise and thanksgiving, like the thanksgiving offerings of the Old Testament.

Christ's "sacrifice," similarly, is understood not in terms of cult but in terms of his embodying praise and thanksgiving to the Father. Christ is the ultimate "sacrifice" not in a cultic sense, but in the analogous sense of bringing an end to cultic sacrifice. Power writes, "Later theology pointed to the death of Christ as the highest sacrifice in which all other sacrifices are fulfilled and for that reason rendered obsolete. That was not the meaning of the word as it was applied to the Eucharist and to the death of Christ in early writers, nor the meaning of taking the language of offering into the thanksgiving prayer itself."[9] Rather, Christ's self-offering constitutes as an alternative path to the sacrificial system, because in his communion with the Father he embodies a relationship to God more harmonious than the cultic sacrificial system could have imagined. For Power, "All ritual offerings ceased because of the way in which the Word Incarnate had wrestled with humankind's alienation from God in death and sin. Christ's pasch and its Eucharist were not one, albeit the highest form, in a series. They were outside the series, a totally different kind of reality. One could call them sacrifices because they realized superabundantly the end and purpose of

[8] David N. Power, OMI, *The Eucharistic Mystery: Revitalizing the Tradition* (New York: Crossroad, 1997 [1992]), 320.

[9] Ibid., 321.

sacrifice. To do this is to take sacrifice apart and to point to a different reality as the way to God. . . ."[10]

In tandem with this analogous or metaphorical understanding of sacrifice in early Christianity, the earliest Christian authors did not envision the presider as a cultic priest engaging in a sacrificial act.[11] Originally the presider was not called a "priest." The titles given him—"*presider, supervisor,* or *bishop*"—gave a "functional designation" to his role of leadership.[12] In leading the community's celebration of Christ's triumphant wrestling with human alienation (Christ's reversal of the sacrificial system), the presider needed no cultic title. In time, however, the title "priest" was applied to the presider—but only, Power cautions, in the metaphorical sense of leading the sacrifice of praise.[13] Similarly, the development of notion of the "priest" acting *"ex persona Christi"* signified solely that Christ's power, not the priest's, brought about "whatever was done by way of sanctification and blessing."[14] Yet, these developments made possible grave misunderstanding of the priest's role, as "the minister" came to be seen in terms of (at first metaphorical) cult.[15] By the time of John Chrysostom, Power finds, "sacrifice" and the role of the priesthood were once again being misunderstood in their cultic, "mythological" sense, rather than their proper metaphorical sense of thanksgiving for God's reversal of humankind's dependency upon sacrifice.[16]

Having briefly narrated this grave historical distortion of sacrificial language in the fourth century, a distortion that has lasted to the present day, Power then proposes that "the language of priesthood and sacrifice needs to be once more demythologized."[17] In order to accomplish this, he explains the mythic understanding of priesthood and sacrifice: "We have to understand first why Christians, as all other humans, resort so readily to this cultic and mythic world. It is one thing to repudiate the cultic sense and the need for victims that it seems to sanction. It is another to understand what it is in human life that seems to cry out for this mode of commerce with the divine."[18] As he explains it, rural peoples traditionally imagine a world of spirits—in Christianized countries, this role is taken by saints and the Virgin Mary—who needed to be propitiated in order for the commu-

[10] Ibid.

[11] Ibid., 320–21.

[12] Ibid., 321.

[13] Ibid.

[14] Ibid.

[15] Ibid.

[16] Ibid.

[17] Ibid., 322.

[18] Ibid.

nity to survive and thrive. For such peoples, the Mass serves to honor and placate such spirits.[19] Such peoples view Christ's suffering as appeasing God: "Remembrance of Christ himself and of his passion and suffering was often combined with the persuasion that his suffering appeased God and so rendered the surrounding world benevolent."[20] Urban and technological peoples experience a similar need, in their case the need to impose order in the face of the confusing presence of injustice and unexpected events.

In light of this (fallen) human desire to impose order and wellbeing by exacting a sacrifice, Power argues that Christians should reclaim the original meaning of sacrificial discourse as metaphorically expressing the solidarity and communion attained by Christ. In contrast to the violence of sacrifice, Christ's Cross signifies the response of loving non-violence in the face of violent oppressors. God, revealed as love, no longer can be seen as in need of appeasement through blood-sacrifice. Power thus holds that "it is the power of the Christian use of the language of sacrifice as a language of reversal that has to be brought again to the fore. It reverses the quest to restore order by preparing victims and appeasing a threatening anger, whether that of God or that of spirits that abide in the universe."[21] For Power, sacrificial language can be retained in Christianity only once its meanings, distorted in the fourth century, are replaced by solidarity and communion. Properly understood, the Eucharist is "a communion of solidarity in love in God's Spirit that withstands human judgment and prevails in the midst of suffering."[22] In the Eucharistic meal, all the fruits of the earth are recognized as sacred:[23] Food and drink now represent "a gift of God and a communion in godly love when it is eaten in faith" rather than something for which the spirits must be propitiated.[24]

Similarly, Christ's body and blood need no longer appear as the sole "sacrifice," since the recognition of solidarity and communion "reverses the attempt to set aside special times and acts of worship by revealing that the people freed in Christ are themselves 'sacrifice,' that true worship is a life lived in faith and according to the gospel and in Eucharist celebrated as such."[25] God emerges, after the distortion of so many centuries, as a

19 Ibid.

20 Ibid.

21 Ibid.

22 Ibid.

23 Ibid.; cf. 341, where Power argues against limiting Eucharistic celebration to bread and wine: "It seems to be a matter of institutional ideology that there is still insistence on the use of wheaten bread and grape wine." Bread and wine are appropriate to Mediterranean/western culture, but not to numerous other cultures.

24 Ibid.

25 Ibid., 322–23.

God of communion, love, and solidarity. Christ's manifestation of this reality embodied a complete reversal of the sacrificial religions of the ancient world: "His love proclaimed reverses the order of religion in which the judgment of God demands satisfaction to one in which a communion with a forgiving and loving God is possible."[26] Indeed, Power warns urgently that continuing to use the language of sacrifice, without making explicit this reversal, threatens the very heart of Christian faith in a loving God and hope in eternal salvation. In contrast to the earliest Christian practice, the cultic understanding of the Eucharist grossly distorts humankind's relationship with God by causing people to remain wedded to juridical fear, lacking true hope of communion.[27] Given these dark shadows cast upon pre-Vatican II Catholicism by a distortion of the meaning of Christian "sacrifice," Power urges that the theology of the Eucharist should focus upon the ritual meal of bread and wine, with its expressions of thanksgiving for God's gracious gifts "in the communion of a common table that knows no discrimination," as "summed up in the symbolic reality of their transformation into the gift of Christ's body and blood."[28] Power's language here, of course, is strikingly Protestant in its implications.

The Gospel of John: Communion and Sacrifice

What is the relationship between communion and sacrifice in the New Testament? No greater depiction of "communion" is found in the Bible than the lengthy discourse in the Gospel of John in which Jesus, before washing the disciples' feet, instructs his disciples at the last supper:

> As the Father has loved me, so I have loved you; abide in my love. If you keep my commandments, you will abide in my love, just as I have kept my Father's commandments and abide in his love. These things I have spoken to you, that my joy may be in you, and that your joy may be full. This is my commandment, that you love one another as I have loved you. Greater love has no man than this, that a man lay down his life for his friends. You are my friends if you do what I command you. No longer do I call you servants, for the servant does not know what his master is doing; but I have called you friends, for all that I have heard from my Father I have made known to you. You did not choose me, but I chose you and appointed you that you should go and bear fruit and that your fruit should abide; so that whatever you ask the Father in my name, he may give it to you. This I command you, to love one another. (Jn 15:9–17)

---

[26] Ibid., 323.

[27] Ibid.

[28] Ibid., 324. The referent of "their" is ambiguous in Power's text.

Commenting upon this passage, St. Thomas Aquinas begins by proposing Christ as our model. He states, "For just as the love which the Father has for him is the model or standard of Christ's love for us, so Christ wants his obedience to be the model of our obedience."[29] To abide in Christ's love, we must imitate his obedience to the Father's commandments. According to Aquinas, this means two things: submitting to death, and committing no sin. In other words, there must be in us no impediment to God's love. Sin constitutes such an impediment, as does prideful unwillingness to pay the due penalty of sin (death). Aquinas explains that Jesus says, " 'I abide in his love,' because there is nothing in me, as a human being, opposed to his love."[30] Yet, how are we to share in Jesus' condition of having no impediment to God's love? As Aquinas notes elsewhere, in commenting upon Aristotle's Nichomachean Ethics, "Friendship is destroyed especially when one friend finds in the other something opposed to their friendship. But this is impossible in friendship between the virtuous."[31] How are we to share in the perfect virtue of Christ's charity?

Drawing upon the Old Testament, Aquinas first affirms an ontological reason for hope that we might share in Jesus' condition: namely, God's causal love, which overflows both in creation and new creation. The Trinity rejoices from eternity in the reality of being participated by human creatures: "Now love is the cause of joy, for everyone takes joy in what he loves. But God loves himself and creatures, especially rational creatures, to whom he grants an infinite good. So Christ rejoices in two things from all eternity: first, in his own good and that of the Father: 'I was delighted every day, playing before him' [Prov 8:30]; secondly, he delights in the good of the rational creature: 'delighting in the sons of men' (Prov 8:31), that is, in the fact that I am shared in by the children of men. He rejoices in these things from eternity: 'As the bridegroom rejoices over the bride, so shall your God rejoice over you' (Is 62:5)."[32] Christ has joy in us. Indeed, as Aquinas later states, Christ has an "intense desire for the salvation of the human race."[33] For Aquinas, Christ's words from the Cross, "I thirst" (Jn 19:28), express this intense desire. In urging his disciples to abide in his love, Christ refers to the joy he will have in

[29] St. Thomas Aquinas, *Commentary on the Gospel of St. John,* Part I, trans. James A. Weisheipl, OP and Fabian Larcher, OP (Petersham, MA: St. Bede's Publications, 1999): Chapter 15, Lecture 2, §2003 (398).

[30] Ibid.

[31] Aquinas, *Commentary on Aristotle's Nichomachean Ethics,* trans. C. I. Litzinger, OP (Notre Dame, IN: Dumb Ox Books, 1993 [1964]): Book VIII, Lecture 4, §1592 (490).

[32] Aquinas, *Commentary on the Gospel of St. John,* §2004 (398).

[33] Ibid., §2447 (577).

them if they obey: "that my joy may be in you, and that your joy may be full" (Jn 15:11). As Aquinas says, "our Lord wants us to become sharers of his joy by our observing his commandments."[34] God wills to draw us into his Trinitarian life of wisdom and love.

On biblical and metaphysical grounds, then, Aquinas holds that God wills to make us sharers of his joy. Christ's obedience is the model for ours; in order to share in God's joy, we too must submit willingly to death and be without sin. This sinless submission is possible for us because of Christ's Cross. Aquinas states, "Christ loved us in the correct order and efficaciously. His love was orderly because he loved nothing in us but God and in relation to God: 'I am the mother of beautiful love' (Sir 24:18), and efficacious because he loved us so much that he delivered himself for us: 'Christ loved us and gave himself up for us, a fragrant offering and sacrifice to God' (Eph 5:2)."[35] Objectively speaking, Christ has removed the impediment to God's love in us. He has restored a right relationship between human beings and God, and all human beings can now travel this path in Christ. His charity, embodied by his sacrificial death, which restored the order of justice, opens the path of our charity. Nonetheless, how can we make our own the redemption won by the Cross? Christ has restored the proper order between human beings and God, but how can particular human beings share in this right order? How can we "abide" in him by truly imitating his love as his friends? It will be no surprise that, according to Aquinas, Christ makes possible our conversion (from servants to friends of God) by the grace of the Holy Spirit: "Servitude is opposed to friendship; and he rejects this by saying, 'No longer do I call you servants.' It is like saying: although you were formerly servants under the law, now you are free under grace: 'You have received the spirit of adoption' [Rom 8:15]."[36] The efficacious sign of our reception of grace is that we come to share in God's wisdom, the wisdom of sacrificial love. Aquinas states, "For the true sign of friendship is that a friend reveals the secrets of his heart to his friend. . . . Now God reveals his secrets to us by letting us share in his wisdom: 'In every generation she [Wisdom] passes into holy souls and makes them friends of God and prophets' (Wis 7:27)."[37]

To abide in Christ—to be able as his friends to obey his commandments and imitate his sacrificial love—is thus a gift of grace whereby we receive the divine Wisdom, the Word of God, that enables us to know and

[34] Ibid., §2004 (398).
[35] Ibid., §2008 (400).
[36] Ibid., §2014 (402).
[37] Ibid., §2016 (403).

to love as Christ knows and loves. Aquinas quotes Gregory the Great, " 'All the things he has made known to his servants are the joys of interior love and the feasts of our heavenly fatherland, which he excites in our minds every day by the breath of his love. For as long as we love the sublime heavenly things we have heard, we already know what we love, because the love itself is knowledge."[38] In receiving the Wisdom of God, we discover that true wisdom is love. This is so, as Aquinas has remarked earlier in the *Commentary*, because the Word of God is not a mere word, but a Word that "breathes forth love."[39] The hearer of this Word truly learns when he or she hears with love: "For that person learns the word who grasps it according to the meaning of the speaker."[40]

The goal of this receptive learning of the Word consists in our bearing the ecclesial fruit of the eternal life of the community of the blessed. Aquinas interprets Christ's wish "that that your fruit should abide" (Jn 15:16) to mean "that the society of the faithful would be led into eternal life and their spiritual fruit flourish: 'He gathers fruit for eternal life' (Jn 4:36)."[41] Christ desires eternal life for us, and so he gives us his Wisdom—that is, himself—that inspires love. He does this in two ways: through the gift of faith, and through the sacrament of the Eucharist. As Aquinas remarks in his *Commentary on John* as regards the Eucharist, "whatever is an effect of our Lord's passion is also an effect of this sacrament. For this sacrament is nothing other than the application of our Lord's passion to us."[42] Christ's gift of himself in the Eucharist flows from his desire to unite human beings to himself; he enables us to "love one another as I have loved you" by enabling us to share Eucharistically in the self-giving love of his sacrifice on the Cross. The Eucharist enables us to abide in the divine Wisdom of his Pasch. Abiding in and with him, in the joy of the life of the Trinity, we accomplish his intense desire, his thirst, that "my joy may be in you, and that your joy may be full" (Jn 15:11).

John Paul II and Aquinas on Sacrifice and Communion

If this "abiding" is also at the same time an obeying of Christ's commandment to "love one another as I have loved you," then it is a real sharing

---

38 Ibid., §2018 (404). The quotation is from Homily 27. Cf. *Catena Aurea*, Vol. 4, Part II (St. John) (Albany, NY: Preserving Christian Publications, 1995 [1842]), 486.

39 Aquinas, *Commentary on the Gospel of St. John,* Part I, trans. James A. Weisheipl, OP and Fabian Larcher, OP (Albany, NY: Magi Books, 1980): Chapter 6, Lecture 5, §946 (376).

40 Ibid.

41 Aquinas, *Commentary on the Gospel of St. John,* Part II, §2027 (407).

42 Ibid., Part I, §963 (382).

in his sacrificial self-offering. Put another way, if in receiving the Wisdom of God in the Eucharist we are truly and fully participating in his love, then we must be participating in the greatest love of his "[laying] down his life for his friends." Does this mean encountering Christ in the sacrament, and rejoicing in our communion with him in his Body, without needing to be united with him under a (cultic) sacrificial aspect? Or does this mean participating liturgically in his one sacrifice, and thereby ourselves sacrificially offering up his saving sacrifice (now as the Church's sacrifice) for our sanctification?

In order to illumine why the "abiding in Christ"—the communion described in John's Gospel—brought about by the Eucharist depends upon the Eucharist's character as a cultic sacrifice, the remainder of this essay will explore Aquinas's theology of the Eucharist in the *Summa theologiae* and John Paul II's encyclical *Ecclesia de Eucharistia*. I will seek to show how the communion brought about by the Eucharist depends upon the Eucharist's character as a sacrifice, and thereby to show the links between Christ's sacrifice on the Cross and the unity or communion of the Church.[43] I will focus upon four aspects of Aquinas's and John Paul II's Eucharistic theology: the sacrificial character of the Eucharist, sacramental representation, the participation of believers in Christ's sacrifice by means of the Eucharist, and the doctrine of transubstantiation as the foundation of Eucharistic communion. For both Aquinas and John Paul II, our communion or "abiding in Christ" comes about through our sacramental representation of, and thus sharing in, Christ's cultic sacrifice—a sharing that conforms us to Christ's image by enabling and including our gift of self within his sacrificial self-offering to God. As John Paul II writes, "The Eucharist is indelibly marked by the event of the Lord's passion and death, of which it is not only a reminder but the sacramental representation. It is the sacrifice of the Cross perpetuated down the ages."[44]

The Eucharist as Sacrifice

What does it mean to call Christ's death a "sacrifice"? According to Aquinas, "[a] sacrifice properly so called is something done for that honor

---

43 For further development of this thesis, see my *Sacrifice and Community: Jewish Offering and Christian Eucharist* (Oxford: Blackwell, 2006).

44 *Ecclesia de Eucharistia,* §11. The footnote to this text cites *Sacrosanctum Concilium* §47: "[O]ur Savior instituted the Eucharistic Sacrifice of his body and blood, in order to perpetuate the sacrifice of the Cross throughout time, until he should return." Cf. the Council of Trent, Session 22: "Teaching and canons on the most holy sacrifice of the mass," chs. 1–2.

which is properly due to God, in order to appease him."[45] Why would God be appeased by Christ's bloody death? The answer is that the Creator-creature relationship involves, on the side of the creature, an "order of justice." The order of justice is another name for the right relationship of the creature to the Creator. The creature owes honor and love to the Creator, as the Creator's due in return for the gift of creation. The sin of Adam and Eve violated this order of justice. Instead of loving the Creator above all things, Adam and Eve chose self-aggrandizement (pride) rather than self-gift. In violating the order of justice, Adam and Eve also violated the order of being. Not only were their wills disordered, but also their very being was disordered. Having turned away from the divine Giver of being, they (and all humankind with them) lost being. Their corruption of soul caused bodily corruption, ultimately death. By violating the order of justice, they brought down upon themselves the just penalty of death.

Let us return to Aquinas's definition of "sacrifice": "something done for that honor which is properly due to God, in order to appease him." Because of his supreme love for God and for human beings in relation to God, Christ on the Cross undergoes the penalty of suffering and death and thereby restores the order of justice—the right relationship with God the Creator—that human rebellion had violated. As such, Christ's sacrifice is pleasing to God, because it shares in the goodness of justice. Elsewhere, Aquinas points out that "[a] *sacrifice*, properly speaking, requires that something be done to the thing which is offered to God, for instance animals were slain and burnt, the bread is broken, eaten, blessed."[46] This is so because a sacrifice is an outward sign of inward gift of self to God, and the outward sign must convey the radical nature of the gift.[47] Not merely the Cross, but also the sacrament of the Eucharist is a sacrifice in this sense, because something is done to the bread and wine.

In answer to an objection that Christ has been sacrificed once and for all and thus is not sacrificed in the celebration of the Eucharist, Aquinas states, "As Ambrose says [commenting on Hebrews 10:1], *there is but one*

---

[45] *ST* III, q. 48, a. 3. Cf. Council of Trent, Session 22, ch. 2: "For the Lord is appeased *[placatus]* by this offering, he gives the gracious gift of repentance, he absolves even enormous offences and sins. For it is one and the same victim offering himself by the ministry of his priests, who then offered himself on the cross: it is only the manner of offering that is different" (translation in *Decrees of the Ecumenical Councils*, Volume II, ed. Norman P. Tanner, SJ [Washington, DC: Georgetown University Press, 1990], 733). Trent adopts the scholastic (and Thomistic) understanding of God as "appeased" by Christ's sacrifice and thus by the Church's sacrificial sharing in Christ's sacrifice.

[46] *ST* II–II, q. 85, a. 3, ad 3.

[47] Cf. *ST* II–II, q. 85, aa. 1–2.

victim, namely that which Christ offered, and which we offer, *and not many victims, because Christ was offered but once: and this latter sacrifice is the pattern of the former.*"[48] Christ is sacrificed only once, on the Cross. Yet his one sacrifice becomes the *Church's* sacrifice also, when the Church offers up the one sacrifice. Aquinas notes, "This sacrament is both a sacrifice and a sacrament; it has the nature of a sacrifice inasmuch as it is offered up; and it has the nature of a sacrament inasmuch as it is received."[49] In the celebration of the sacrament of the Eucharist, through the ministerial priesthood, the whole Church offers sacramentally the sacrifice of Christ to the Father in the Holy Spirit. The whole Church receives his sacrifice as a sacrament. As both a sacrament and a sacrifice, the Eucharist enables the Church to offer up and share in Christ's sacrifice.

As a sacrifice to God, the sacrament of the Eucharist possesses the spiritual sweetness of divine justice. Aquinas affirms that "the soul is spiritually nourished through the power of this sacrament, by being spiritually gladdened, and as it were inebriated with the sweetness of the Divine goodness, according to Cant. v. 1: *Eat, O friends, and drink, and be inebriated, my dearly beloved.*"[50] Indeed, Aquinas suggests that Christ himself experienced this inebriation or delight in receiving the sacrament. Describing a "delectation of spiritual sweetness" over and above the increase of habitual grace (which Christ did not need), he proposes that "although grace was not increased in Christ through his receiving this sacrament, yet He had a certain spiritual delectation from the new institution of this sacrament. Hence He Himself said (Luke xxii. 15): *With desire I have desired to eat this Pasch with you. . . .*"[51] The "delectation" comes from the joy found in offering oneself to God in self-giving love. Aquinas quotes Ephesians 5:2, "He delivered Himself for us, an oblation and a sacrifice to God for an odor of sweetness."[52] As a sacrifice (the Church's offering of Christ's sacrifice), the Eucharist enables us to share sacrificially in Christ's expiation for sins; yet since the Eucharist remains ultimately Christ's work, we can enjoy "spiritual sweetness" with Christ rather than despairing over our inadequacy. As a sharing in Christ's sacrifice, the

---

[48] *ST* III, q. 83, a. 1, ad 1.

[49] *ST* III, q. 79, a. 5. Cf. the anathematizing by the Council of Trent of the idea that the Eucharist was only a sacrament (Session 22, Canon 1): "If anyone says that a true and proper sacrifice is not offered to God in the mass, or that the offering is nothing but the giving of Christ to us to eat: let him be anathema" *(Decrees of the Ecumenical Councils,* Vol. II, 735).

[50] *ST* III, q. 79, a. 1, ad 2.

[51] *ST* III, q. 81, a. 1, ad 3.

[52] *ST* III, q. 83, a. 1, obj. 2.

Eucharist conveys the life of grace, "spiritual refreshment, and charity,"[53] and nourishes the union in charity that is the "union between Christ and his members," the Mystical Body of Christ.[54]

In *Ecclesia de Eucharistia*, regarding the Eucharist's sacrificial character, John Paul II turns first to Luke 22:19–20, in which we find Christ's words of institution. Against those who would deny the cultic character of Christ's sacrifice for sins, the pope notes that Christ "did not merely say: 'This is my body', 'this is my blood', but went on to add: 'which is given for you', 'which is poured out for you'. . . . Jesus did not simply state that what he was giving them to eat and drink was his body and his blood; he also expressed *its sacrificial meaning* and made sacramentally present his sacrifice which would soon be offered on the Cross for the salvation of all."[55] The Eucharist is not merely an offering of thanksgiving and praise, let alone a Christian reversal of ancient cultic sacrificial practices, as David Power suggests. Rather, the Eucharist is a participation in the sacrificial character of Christ's Cross, his pouring out of his blood as a sin offering to God for the redemption of the world. In making this point, the pope, in sharp contrast to Power, approvingly quotes St. John Chrysostom.[56]

Christ's Cross is, according to the pope, primarily a gift of self to the Father: a sacrifice offered, as is required by the nature of liturgical sacrifice, to God. The pope explains, "Certainly it is a gift given for our sake, and indeed that of all humanity (cf. Mt 26:28; Mk 14:24; Lk 22:20; Jn 10:15), yet it is first and foremost a gift to the Father: 'a sacrifice that the Father accepted, giving, in return for this total self-giving by his Son, who 'became obedient unto death' (Phil 2:8), his own paternal gift, that is to say the grant

---

53 *ST* III, q. 79, a. 1.

54 *ST* III, q. 79, a. 5. Cf. the Council of Trent, Session 13, ch. 2, describing Christ's purpose in instituting the sacrament of the Eucharist: "Therefore, our Saviour, about to depart from this world to the Father, instituted this sacrament in which he as it were poured out the riches of his divine love toward humanity, *causing his wonderful works to be remembered* [Ps 110:4], and he bade us cherish his memory as we partook of it and *to proclaim his death until he comes* [1 Cor 11:26] to judge the world. He wished this sacrament to be taken as the spiritual food of souls, to nourish and strengthen them as they lived by his life who said, *he who eats me will live because of me* [Jn 6:58], and as an antidote to free us from daily faults and preserve us from mortal sins. He further wished it to be a pledge of our future glory and unending happiness, and thus a sign of that one body of which he is the head and to which he wished us all to be united as members by the closest bonds of faith, hope and love, so that we should all speak with one voice and there might be no division among us" (*Decrees of the Ecumenical Councils,* Vol. II, 694).

55 *Ecclesia de Eucharistia,* §12.

56 Ibid.

of new immortal life in the resurrection.'"[57] It follows that the Eucharist, in which the Church offers up Christ's sacrifice in sacramental mode, is "a sacrifice in the strict sense, and not only in a general way, as if it were simply a matter of Christ's offering himself to the faithful as their spiritual food."[58] John Paul II thus makes clear that the meaning of "sacrifice," as regards both Christ's Cross and the Eucharist, is cultic in the sense of a sin offering to God, not metaphorical in the sense of thanksgiving and praise. He concurs, in short, with Aquinas.[59]

Sacramental Representation

In the sacrament of the Eucharist, the Church's offering of Christ's sacrifice—her liturgical sharing in Christ's sacrificial act—occurs through sacramental representation. Aquinas affirms that "the celebration of the sacrament is an image representing Christ's Passion, which is His true sacrifice."[60] A sacrament is a sign. In the sacrament of the Eucharist, what is sacramentally represented is Christ on the Cross, that is, the sacrificial separation of Christ's blood from his body. Since a sacrament causes (by God's power) what it signifies, the sacrament causes the change of the bread and wine into Christ's body and blood. In so doing, the sacrament retains its sign-character: In sacramental representation Christ becomes present not in his natural or "proper" mode of being (in which he is over five feet tall and so forth), but in his sacramental mode of being (in which he exists under the sacramental sign or species).[61]

All aspects of the Church's sacramental sign are therefore important. Aquinas affirms that the altar represents the Cross upon which Christ was sacrificed in his natural mode of being; the sacrifice of the Eucharist

[57] Ibid., §13; the quotation is from *Redemptor Hominis*, §20.

[58] Ibid.

[59] As well as with the Council of Trent, whose doctrine here follows Aquinas.

[60] *ST* III, q. 83, a. 1.

[61] Aquinas's views on the sacramental mode of being converge, not surprisingly, with those of the Council of Trent. See, for example, Session 13, ch. 1: "In the first place, the holy council teaches and openly and without qualification professes that, after the consecration of the bread and the wine, our lord Jesus Christ, true God and true man, is truly, really and substantially contained in the propitious sacrament of the holy eucharist under the appearance of those things which are perceptible to the senses. Nor are the two assertions incompatible, that our Saviour is ever seated in heaven at the right hand of the Father in his natural mode of existing, and that he is nevertheless sacramentally present to us by his substance in many other places in a mode of existing which, though we can hardly express it in words, we can grasp with minds enlightened by faith as possible to God and must most firmly believe" (*Decrees of the Ecumenical Councils,* Vol. 2, 694).

offers up Christ in his sacramental mode of being on the altar.[62] Likewise, "the priest also bears Christ's image, in Whose person and by Whose power he pronounces the words of consecration. . . . And so, in a measure, the priest and the victim are one and the same."[63] The priest offers up, *in persona Christi*, Christ's sacrifice for the people. The people by their prayers join in the sacramental offering of Christ's sacrifice: The whole Mystical Body, united to Christ by the Holy Spirit, offers up Christ's sacrifice to the Father. Indeed, the sacrament signifies both Christ and Christ's Mystical Body: In the offering up of Christ's sacrifice, the Church (Mystical Body) is built up in the image of Christ's self-giving charity. As Aquinas explains, "there is a twofold reality *(res)* of this sacrament . . . : one which is signified and contained, namely, Christ Himself; while the other is signified but not contained, namely, Christ's mystical body, which is the fellowship of the saints."[64]

Although John Paul II does not undertake the lengthy analysis of sacramental representation that one finds in the *Summa theologiae*, nonetheless he affirms the same tenets throughout. He states that the Eucharist is "not only a reminder but the sacramental representation" of Christ's Passion and death, and he affirms the substantial change of the bread and wine into Christ's body and blood (transubstantiation) as well as the real presence of Christ in the Eucharist.[65] By holding that the Last Supper is already the celebration of the Eucharist—Christ's body and blood in sacramental mode are consumed by Christ and the disciples—John Paul II further underscores the importance of reflection upon Christ's mode of being in the Eucharist, namely by sacramental representation under the species of bread and wine.[66] At the Last Supper, Christ can consume his own body and blood only if his Eucharistic body and blood are present through sacramental representation. Christ is present at the Last Supper in two modes, his natural mode and his sacramental mode.

Participation of Believers in Christ's Sacrifice

When treating of the Eucharist as a sacrifice, Aquinas notes that the discussion has two aspects: "[I]n the celebration of this mystery, we must take into consideration the representation of our Lord's Passion, and the participation of its fruits. . . ."[67] The "representation of our Lord's Passion"

---

62 *ST* III, q. 83, a. 1, ad 2.
63 *ST* III, q. 83, a. 1, ad 3.
64 *ST* III, q. 80, a. 4.
65 *Ecclesia de Eucharistia,* §11, 15.
66 This point about the Last Supper is likewise affirmed by both Trent and Aquinas.
67 *ST* III, q. 83, a. 2.

is the sacrifice, and the "participation of its fruits" is our communion in charity with Christ and each other. As the note of "participation" makes clear, communion with God (and each other) in Christ through the Holy Spirit cannot be separated from Christ's sacrifice. It is our offering of Christ's sacrifice that enables, in the sacrament of the Eucharist, our sharing in its fruits of ecclesial unity and communion.

The Church's offering of Christ's sacrifice, her sharing in Christ's holy sacrificial act, culminates in her reception of, or communion in, the sacrifice. Arguing that the priest who consecrates the sacrament of the Eucharist must also receive the sacrament, Aquinas states, "Now whoever offers sacrifice must be a sharer in the sacrifice, because the outward sacrifice he offers is a sign of the inner sacrifice whereby he offers himself to God, as Augustine says *(De Civ. Dei x)*."[68] Indeed, Aquinas goes on to say that "it is by partaking of the sacrifice that he has a share in it, as the Apostle says (1 Cor. x. 18)."[69] When the Church sacramentally represents Christ's sacrifice, she receives what she has sacramentally represented. Our stature as "participators in His sacrifice"[70] is fully attained when "through the Eucharist we eat Christ."[71] In the celebration of the Eucharist we do not only represent Christ and his mystical body; by communing in the sacrificial meal, we are transformed into the Christic image that we have taken on by our sacramental act of representation. Aquinas explains that "the Eucharist is the sacrament of Christ's Passion according as a man is made perfect in union with Christ who suffered."[72] Note that the union accomplished by the sacrament of the Eucharist is not simply with "Christ," but with "Christ who suffered." Our union with Christ is found in union with Christ's sacrifice: "[S]piritual food changes man into itself, according to that saying of Augustine (Conf. vii), that he heard the voice of Christ as it were saying to him: *Nor shalt thou change Me into thyself, as food of thy flesh, but thou shalt be changed into Me*."[73] In this union with Christ who suffered, a union that can occur through either sacramental or spiritual eating, the believer is "changed into Christ" and "incorporated in Him."[74]

What does it mean to be united to Christ by being "changed into Christ"? It means to come to share, through his sacrifice, in his relation-

68 *ST* III, q. 82, a. 4.
69 Ibid.
70 *ST* III, q. 22, a. 3, ad 2.
71 *ST* III, q. 73, a. 5, ad 1.
72 *ST* III, q. 73, a. 3, ad 3.
73 *ST* III, q. 73, a. 3, ad 2.
74 Ibid.

ship to the Father in the Holy Spirit. The Eucharist presses us forward in the imitation of Christ's love. Recalling John Damascene's comparison of the Eucharist to Isaiah's burning coal (Isaiah 6) and Gregory the Great's observation that God's love is continually working great things, Aquinas argues that "through this sacrament, as far as its power is concerned, not only is the habit of grace and of virtue bestowed, but it is furthermore aroused to act, according to 2 Cor. v. 14: *The charity of Christ presseth us*."[75] In the sacrament of the Eucharist, we are conformed to Christ both externally, through sacramental representation, and internally, through charity aroused to act—active self-giving love.[76] This active self-giving love, restoring the relationship of justice between humankind and God, makes Christ's sacrificial death pleasing before God. As Aquinas notes, Christ's "voluntary enduring of the Passion was most acceptable to God, as coming from charity."[77]

In *Ecclesia de Eucharistia*, Pope John Paul II emphasizes the connection between sacrifice and communion: The communion meal of the Last Supper is already a sacrificial meal. Quoting the *Catechism of the Catholic Church*, he states, " 'The Mass is at the same time, and inseparably, the sacrificial memorial in which the sacrifice of the Cross is perpetuated and the sacred banquet of communion with the Lord's body and blood.' "[78] Our communion flows from our sharing in Christ's sacrifice. This sharing is not merely subjective, as if by our thanksgiving and praise we succeeded in sharing in the consciousness of thanksgiving that Christ experienced on the Cross. On the contrary, God makes sacramentally present Christ's cultic sacrifice to us in the Eucharist, and thereby enables us to receive the fruits of Christ's sacrifice. John Paul II remarks, "The Church constantly draws her life from the redeeming sacrifice; she approaches it not only through faith-filled remembrance, but also through a real contact, since *this sacrifice is made present ever anew*, sacramentally perpetuated, in every community which offers it at the hands of the consecrated minister. The Eucharist thus applies to men and women today the reconciliation won once for all by Christ for mankind in every age."[79] In the sacrament of the Eucharist, the Church offers the one and only sacrifice of Christ. Christ offered himself for our sins at Calvary; the Church daily offers sacramentally this once-and-for-all

---

75 *ST* III, q. 79, a. 1, ad 2.

76 See also *ST* III, q. 79, a. 4, and numerous similar texts.

77 *ST* III, q. 48, a. 3.

78 *Ecclesia de Eucharistia*, §12; cf. *Catechism of the Catholic Church*, §1382.

79 *Ecclesia de Eucharistia*, §12.

offering on the altars throughout the world, so that humankind may be one in the communion of his risen life.[80]

The pope thus rules out the strictly metaphorical sense of sacrifice that would focus, as Power does, on the memorial meal. The Church's sacramental offering of Christ's sacrifice is her mode, given her by Christ, of sharing in Christ's sacrificial self-offering and thereby being conformed to his image in the unity of his Body. As the John Paul II put it, "In giving his sacrifice to the Church, Christ has also made his own the spiritual sacrifice of the Church, which is called to offer herself in union with the sacrifice of Christ." Here the he quotes *Lumen Gentium*: " 'Taking part in the Eucharistic Sacrifice, which is the source and summit of the whole Christian life, they offer the divine victim to God, and offer themselves along with it.'"[81] In affirming the sacrificial character of Christ's Cross and of the Eucharist, however, the pope is careful not to cut off the Eucharist from the Resurrection. Christ's self-giving sacrifice bridges the sinful alienation between self-aggrandizing humankind and the self-giving God of love, and thereby opens the path of eternal life. The pope states, "The Eucharistic Sacrifice makes present not only the mystery of the Saviour's passion and death, but also the mystery of the resurrection which crowned his sacrifice."[82] As the risen Lord, Christ offers himself to us in the Eucharist truly as the "bread of life" (Jn 6:35, 48) in whom we find eternal life.[83] The celebration of the Eucharist thus unites the sacrificial aspect of the Cross with the triumphant aspect of the Resurrection. As John Paul II emphasizes, however, the "life" of communion is found only through Christ's sacrifice, because through Christ's sacrifice God restores the relationship between human beings and himself and invites us into the "communion" of divine self-giving love, in the life of the risen Lord.

Transubstantiation and Communion

Recall how David Power, who rejects conceptualizing the change of the Eucharistic elements in terms of "efficient causality" and "substantial change" and who instead prefers to envision the Eucharist as God's special presence mediated through language and ritual,[84] speaks of the "transformation" of the bread and wine:

---

[80] The pope here (§12) quotes with approval Chrysostom's use of cultic sacrificial language. Recall that for Power, Chrysostom represents the fourth-century distortion of the allegedly original metaphorical meaning of sacrificial language.

[81] *Ecclesia de Eucharistia,* §13; cf. *Lumen Gentium*, §11.

[82] *Ecclesia de Eucharistia,* §14.

[83] Ibid.

[84] Cf. David Power, *The Eucharistic Mystery,* 320–24.

> The acknowledgment of a gracious and gratuitous presence in the midst of the people is what is expressed in thanksgiving and ritual sharing. Such acknowledgment is meant to find its focal point in the bread and wine set on the table in the middle of the assembly. In the bread and wine of the people there is the presence of a God who is revealed by being veiled under these symbols, just as the divine love continues to be revealed under the veil of Christ's suffering. The gratuity of God's presence at the heart of creation, the gratuity of God's advent in Jesus Christ, and the gratuity of the Spirit dwelling in the hearts of the people who convene as one are expressed in thanksgiving over these realities of daily life and in the communion of a common table that knows of no discrimination. All this is summed up in the symbolic reality of their transformation into the gift of Christ's body and blood.[85]

Aquinas, in contrast, places the emphasis upon *Christ's* friendship with us, rather than upon our harmonious expression of thanksgiving at the common table. Christ's charity, as manifested by his bodily presence in the Eucharist, fuels our faith, hope, and love. Referring to John 6, Aquinas states that "in our pilgrimage He does not deprive us of His bodily presence; but unites us with Himself in this sacrament through the truth of His body and blood. . . . Hence this sacrament is the sign of supreme charity, and the uplifter of our hope, from such familiar union of Christ with us."[86] Aquinas notes that Christ's bodily presence in the Eucharist comes about not by "local motion" of Christ's body and blood from one place to another, but by change on the side of bread and wine, namely substantial change of the bread and wine. Aquinas affirms that "this is done by Divine power in this sacrament; for the whole substance of the bread is changed into the whole substance of Christ's body, and the whole substance of the wine into the whole substance of Christ's blood. Hence this is not a formal, but a substantial conversion; nor is it a kind of natural movement: But, with a name of its own, it can be called transubstantiation."[87]

John Paul II adopts the same Christological emphasis as does Aquinas. Before describing the Eucharistic banquet, John Paul II describes ontologically Christ's real presence brought about by God's power in the "sacramental re-presentation of Christ's sacrifice, crowned by the resurrection."[88] The pope affirms "the perennially valid teaching of the Council of Trent: 'the consecration of the bread and wine effects the change of the whole substance of the bread into the substance of the body of Christ

---

85 Ibid., 324.
86 *ST* III, q. 75, a. 1.
87 *ST* III, q. 75, a. 4.
88 *Ecclesia de Eucharistia,* §15.

our Lord, and of the whole substance of the wine into the substance of his blood. And the holy Catholic Church has fittingly and properly called this change transubstantiation.' "[89] Only Eucharistic theology that retains this ontological principle of transubstantiation, the pope suggests, can do justice to the Church's Eucharistic faith.[90] This is so because Christ's sacrifice achieves its "saving efficacy" in us when we commune in his sacrificial body and blood.[91]

Transubstantiation is not simply a theoretical doctrine: It has radical import for the Christian life. Sharing in the crucified Lord brings about communion, because his sacrifice takes away sins that destroy communion. The pope writes, "The Eucharistic Sacrifice is intrinsically directed to the inward union of the faithful with Christ through communion; we receive the very One who offered himself for us, we receive his body which he gave up for us on the Cross and his blood which he 'poured out for many for the forgiveness of sins' (Mt 26:28)."[92] We commune in Christ's sacrifice, and thereby share in his justice as members of his Body. Through his righteousness, we are conformed to his active self-giving charity and are raised by God to share in the Trinitarian life that the risen Lord enjoys. In other words, by communing in the justice of his sacrifice, we commune in his self-giving life, which is the manifestation of the life (love) of the Trinity. The pope states, "We are reminded of his words: " 'As the living Father sent me, and I live because of the Father, so he who eats me will live because of me' (Jn 6:57). Jesus himself reassures us that this union, which he compares to that of the life of the Trinity, is truly realized. *The Eucharist is a true banquet,* in which Christ offers himself as our nourishment."[93] It is by sharing in Christ's cultic sacrifice that we "abide with him" in the communion of the banquet.

Just as Christ's Cross results in the outpouring of his Spirit, now that the impediment of sin has been removed, so also sharing in the Eucharistic sacrifice brings about an influx of the Holy Spirit, from whom comes true communion in active self-giving love.[94] In this gift, which is a sharing in Christ's risen life in the Spirit, we receive a pledge of the eternal "life" that the Son receives from the Father. David Power states, "Eucharistic memorial both obliges us and permits us to live the given moment in eschatological hope. This is not to be translated into a time-plan for the future but

89 Ibid.; cf. Council of Trent, Session 13, ch. 4.
90 *Ecclesia de Eucharistia,* §15.
91 Ibid.
92 Ibid., §16.
93 Ibid.
94 Ibid., §17.

it allows us to keep hope alive in the expectation of the unexpected intervention of divine love. Where sin abounds, grace does more abound. Which is to say that in the midst of absurdity we are to look for a saving love."[95] Aquinas puts it rather differently. For Aquinas, along with fueling our "eschatological hope," the sacrament of the Eucharist causes the attaining of eternal life through Christ's Cross, by giving us spiritual strength, that is to say active charity: "[T]his sacrament does not at once admit us to glory, but bestows on us the power of coming unto glory. And therefore it is called *Viaticum*, a figure whereof we read in 1 Kgs 19:8: *Elias ate and drank, and walked in the strength of that food forty days and forty nights unto the mount of God, Horeb*."[96] Similarly, John Paul II argues that the Eucharist gives us more than "eschatological hope," although it certainly bestows such hope. As a sharing in Christ's sacrificial body and blood, the Eucharist is also a sharing in risen Lord, who embodies the self-giving wisdom and love of the life of the Trinity. Therefore, the Eucharist gives "real contact," in Christ's Spirit-filled body and blood, with the life of the Trinity. Christ is living. The pope notes, "Those who feed on Christ in the Eucharist need not wait until the hereafter to receive eternal life: *They already possess it on earth*, as the first-fruits of a future fullness which will embrace man in his totality. For in the Eucharist we also receive the pledge of our bodily resurrection at the end of the world: 'He who eats my flesh and drinks my blood has eternal life, and I will raise him up at the last day' (Jn 6:54)."[97]

As the book of Revelation teaches, the Eucharistic liturgy unites us to the heavenly liturgy of the triumphant followers of the Lamb. John Paul II says, "The Eucharist is truly a glimpse of heaven appearing on earth."[98] Yet, this communion, the glory of heaven, comes about through the sacrificial justice of Christ's Cross, in which the Eucharist enables us to share. Eucharistic communion (abiding in Christ) is a communion of charity manifested by the willingness to lay down one's life sacrificially in conformity to Christ (Jn 15). Communion and sacrifice once again are inseparable. As the pope says, "We need but think of the urgent need to work for peace, to base relationships between peoples on solid premises of justice and solidarity, and to defend human life from conception to its natural end. And what should we say of the thousand inconsistencies of a 'globalized' world where the weakest, the most powerless and the poorest appear to have so little hope!"[99] If the Eucharist is a glimpse of

[95] Power, *The Eucharistic Mystery,* 348.

[96] *ST* III, q. 79, a. 2, ad 1.

[97] *Ecclesia de Eucharistia,* §18.

[98] Ibid., §19.

[99] Ibid., §20.

heaven on earth, this is so because the communion of heaven, in Christ's Body, is radical self-giving love that manifests perfect justice. Christ connects his Eucharistic sacrifice with the sacrificial love of believers by instructing his disciples to wash each other's feet (Jn 13), and St. Paul draws the connection between the Eucharistic meal and charity in his letter to the Corinthians (1 Cor 11).[100] The pope affirms, "Proclaiming the death of the Lord 'until he comes' (1 Cor 11:26) entails that all who take part in the Eucharist be committed to changing their lives and making them in a certain way completely 'Eucharistic.'"[101] Going beyond expressions of "thanksgiving and ritual sharing,"[102] such radical Christian action flows from participation in Christ's cultic sacrifice, his self-offering to God. As Aquinas remarks, "The reality *(res)* of this sacrament is charity, not only as to its habit, but also as to its act, which is kindled in this sacrament."[103]

Conclusion

Although much more could be said, I have said enough to show why John Paul II and Aquinas—whose ideas flow from the Church's tradition and are mediated to John Paul II through the Council of Trent and other ecclesial teaching—are agreed upon the necessary conjunction of cultic sacrifice and communion in theological understanding of the Eucharist. In light of an alternative posed by David Power, I have sought to answer the question: Why should union or communion with Christ, in the Eucharist, be a union in sacrifice understood in the cultic sense? In concluding, let us recall our analysis of John 15. Christ calls human beings to abide in his love, and thereby to enjoy the communion of friendship with the Trinity. Specifically, he teaches that we must "love one another as I have loved you" (Jn 15:12). Such love is sacrificial, as Christ makes explicit: "Greater love has no man than this, that a man lay down his life for his friends" (Jn 15:13). This sacrificial love is the "love" in which we must "abide." If we do so, we become no longer Jesus' servants, but his friends. Jesus notes that the servant "does not know what his master is doing." In contrast, Jesus' disciples are now his friends because he has revealed to them what their divine Master "is doing," that is to say, God's self-giving love. We can love as Christ loved because the Eucharist inflames our charity and enables us radically to offer our lives to God in

---

100 Ibid.

101 Ibid.

102 Power, *The Eucharistic Mystery,* 324.

103 *ST* III, q. 79, a. 4.

Christ, thereby sharing in Christ's (cultic) justice. The knowledge that we gain of Christ through the Eucharist is a knowing of God as self-giving or sacrificial love; it is truly "to know the love of Christ which surpasses knowledge, that you may be filled with all the fulness of God" (Eph 3:19). This fulness, which we receive by sharing in his sacrifice, is divine communion. By his communion with us in his Eucharistic sacrifice, Jesus himself chooses and appoints us so that we might bear this fruit of sacrificial love, a community of self-giving love in Christ (Jn 15:16).[104]

---

[104] I am grateful to Therese Scarpelli for comments on earlier drafts of this article.

Theological Aesthetics in Aquinas and John Paul II

FRANCESCA ARAN MURPHY
University of Aberdeen
Aberdeen, Scotland

WRITING THIS ESSAY, I have on my desk a photo of the Pope standing in the snowy Italian mountains. He is quoted alongside, saying: "Every time that I have the opportunity to rest in these mountains . . . I thank God for the majestic beauty of creation. I thank him for his own Beauty, of which the universe is a reflection, capable of fascinating attentive souls, urging them to praise its greatness."[1] In 1999, John Paul II addressed a "Letter to Artists." That is going to be my basic text, but "beauty" is an often unnoticed presence in many of the Pope's encyclicals. Even when he isn't explicitly speaking about beauty, an aesthetic way of looking remains a conditioning characteristic of John Paul's thought. Aesthetic vision conditions and modifies his thinking about ethics and metaphysics. Because he envisages of God and humanity as beautiful, he sees creation and salvation ecologically.

When John Paul speaks of the beauty of the mountain as a reflection of the Beauty of God, he is conceiving of beauty as a transcendental property of being. Mountains reflect the beauty of God because their grandeur sends our minds beyond those great snowy hunks of rock. Transcendentals are beyond-pointers: They are elements found in finite realities which are themselves *infinite*; and because they are infinite, they are analogous to God.[2]

---

[1] John Paul II, Message to Benedictines for 1500 Anniversary, July 11, 1999, on the "Catholic Convervation Centre" Website, www.conservation.catholic.org/index.htm.

[2] Jacques Maritain, *Art and Scholasticism and other Essays,* translated by J. F. Scanlan. (London: Sheed and Ward, 1930), 30–31; Maritain, *Creative Intuition in Art and Poetry* (Princeton, NJ: Princeton University Press, 1953), 162–63.

Everyone knows the encyclicals *Veritatis Splendor* and *Fides et Ratio* encourage theologians and philosophers to explore the transcendental properties of truth and goodness. But John Paul does not isolate the transcendentals from each other. *Fides et Ratio* actually refers to a *triad* of transcendentals, that is, goodness, truth and *beauty*.[3] "Faith . . . stirs reason," that encyclical says, "to move beyond all isolation and willingly to run risks to that it may attain whatever is beautiful, good and true. Faith thus becomes the convinced and convincing advocate of reason."[4] Taken in *isolation*, analytic reasoning, with the idea of truth as correspondence is not entirely convincing: What makes the mountain range of metaphysics *attractive* to explorers, and *convincing* to those of us who read the traveler's tales, is the *beauty* of truth and goodness. Jacques Maritain described beauty as "the radiance of all the transcendentals united."[5]

The modern tradition of Thomistic aesthetics which Maritain represents focussed its attention on the beauty of art and on artistic making. John Paul's notion of beauty and aesthetic experience is wider than that which relates simply to the visual and literary arts. On one occasion, deprecating the notion that art is merely escapist fantasy, John Paul II gave these examples of beautiful things: "an act of justice, a gesture of forgiveness, sacrifice for a great ideal lived with joy and generosity."[6] Whereas twentieth-century neo-Thomist philosophers like Maritain wrote separate treatises on metaphysics, ethics, and aesthetics, John Paul makes truth, goodness and beauty into mutually supportive parts of a single theological ecology.

In writing about this pope's philosophy or theology, one usually questions whether one should be speaking about "Karol Wojtyla" or John Paul II. On the one hand, one ought to say "the Pope" or "John Paul II," because papal Encyclicals are not personal articulations of one man's philosophy, but a development of the Church's tradition. Papal writings are not "philosophy" or "theology," they are doctrine. On the other hand, the encyclicals are the work of *the man who was to become* John Paul II. This is especially obvious when one is dealing with his philosophy and theology of beauty. Back of much that the *pope* says about beauty is the *man* who was a poet and dramatist. The plays and the poems are like an apprenticeship for encyclicals in which the Pope grapples with the biblical

[3] "Wherever men and women discover a call to the absolute and transcendent, the metaphysical dimension of reality opens up before them: in truth, in beauty, in moral values, in other persons, in being itself, in God." John Paul II, *Fides et Ratio,* §83.

[4] Ibid., §56.

[5] Maritain, *Creative Intuition,* 162.

[6] John Paul II, "Beauty Opens Spirit to Mystery of God," August 2002.

images and parables with the hands of a poet. Take *Salvifici Doloris*, which sets out from the premise that " 'suffering' " is *"essential to the nature of man."*[7] When the author of the encyclical suddenly describes "the cross of Christ" as "a source from which flow rivers of living water,"[8] the electric shock can send us back to the "Song of the Brightness of Water," a young priest's poems about Christ's meeting with the Samaritan woman, at the well.[9] The "Letter to Artists" observes that the biblical stories have "fired the imagination of painters, poetics, musicians, playwrights and film-makers";[10] encyclicals like *Salvifici Doloris, Veritatis Splendor,* or *Dives in Misericordia* are remembered as much for the imaginative way they get inside the parables and the Johannine discourses as for their theology. John Paul sees the biblical parables as an extension of the fact that Christ is "the icon of the unseen God."[11]

Aesthetics is about perception, the science asking what makes artworks *perceptible. Theological* aesthetics is about the perceptibility of God. As the "Letter to Artists" notes, Christianity overspills the Old Testament prohibition on images of God, when, "in the mystery of the Incarnation, the Son of God becomes *visible* in person."[12] Christian theological aesthetics takes its rise from biblical texts like "Who sees me, sees the Father." John 14.9 is the "base" text of the encyclical *Dives in Misericordia.* When he states there that "Believing in the crucified Son means 'seeing the Father,' means believing that . . . love is more powerful than . . . evil. . . . The cross is like a touch of eternal love upon the most painful wounds of man's existence"[13] John Paul is not developing the Christian tradition of the beauty of God in an "impersonal" way. He is speaking as one who has meditated *as an artist* on the meaning of suffering; as someone who has experienced suffering as beauty.

In his "Letter to Artists," the Pope reminds his friends that Paul Claudel called Scripture an " 'immense vocabulary,' " a treasury of symbols, "from which . . . Christian culture and art have drawn." Perhaps he has his tongue in cheek when he adds that, "A figure like Job, to take but one example . . . still arouses an interest which is not just philosophical but literary and artistic as well."[14] For, in occupied Warsaw, in 1940, a nineteen year old

[7] John Paul II, *Salvifici Doloris,* §2.

[8] Ibid., §28.

[9] The "Song of the Brightness of Water" is found in Karol Wojtyla, *Collected Poems,* trans. by Jerzy Peterkiewicz (London: Hutchinson, 1982), 49–58.

[10] John Paul II, "Letter to Artists" (1999), §5.

[11] Ibid., §12.

[12] Ibid., §5.

[13] John Paul II, *Dives in Misericordia,* §§7 and 8.

[14] John Paul II, "Letter to Artists," §5.

actor-playwright wrote a play based on a biblical story. As he told his mentor, Mieczyslaw Kotlarczyk, "I have written a new drama, Greek in form, Christian in spirit, eternal in substance, like *Everyman*. A drama about suffering: *Job*. Some people here quite like it. It is partly the result of my reading of the Old Testament. I have read . . . Job, the Book of Wisdom, . . . the Prophets."[15]

Wojtyla's play is not about a righteous individual up on stage: Prologos tells the audience that it's about *them*:

> Behold my people,—
> and listen to the Word of the Lord,
> you who are downtrodden
> you who are flogged,
> sent to the camps, you—
> Jobs—Jobs.

As in a Greek tragedy, the gory stuff happens offstage. Job has invited his friends to a feast. But, one after another, three messengers break in to tell how "heaven sent" pillage, fire and wind have stripped Job of his wealth, his flocks, and his children. He asks his friends if they see God as he does:

> In what I say I see one thing,
> which, being blind, you cannot see:
> how souls are struggling with grief
> whether they are righteous or sinful,
> and in this world I do not see
> equal chances in that struggle.
> Where? Where? It is a mystery.
> How will it balance, as it must?
> I look and see: He is Harmony.
> I look and see: He balances all.
> Nothing will mar the Harmony of tone;
> nothing will overthrow eternal laws.
> I look and see: He is the Truth.
> I look and see: He is Beauty.
> How will it balance, as it must?
> Can you see it? Can you see it?[16]

Job sees the beauty, or justice, of *God*. But simultaneously, Job experiences the disparity between that divine justice and the disordered world that he

[15] "Job," in Karol Wojtyla, *The Collected Plays and Writings on Theatre*," translated with introductions by Bolewslaw Taborski (Los Angeles: University of California Press, 1987), 19.

[16] Ibid., 53.

himself represents in his innocent suffering. His greatest need is to *see* "how it balances." But the picture is torn in half. Job sees double, perceiving God as justice and injustice. As voyeurs upon this scene, the friends and chorus see neither the beauty nor the disharmony. Job's suffering makes him "look further," and perceive God more clearly.[17] And so, only Job can demand

> Show Divine Justice now
> to a humbled man.[18]

Job cannot figure why one *innocent* like himself should suffer. A first step toward righting his sight is to acknowledge that his own "justice" or innocence is incommensurable with God's. Elihu tells him:

> You must not call yourself just
> before Him; even His angels
> do not dare show Him their faces—
> before such Beauty heaven trembles.[19]

But talk of "justice" is not enough. *Salvifici Doloris* describes the book of Job as "*sufficient argument* why the answer to the question about the meaning of suffering is not to be unreservedly linked to the moral order, based on justice alone. . . . [S]uch an answer . . . seems to trivialize and impoverish *the concept of justice* which we encounter in Revelation."[20] Redemption "creates a new dimension . . . different from that which determined the meaning of suffering within the limits of justice."[21] Faith makes this new dimension aesthetic, that is, it makes it *visible*. In the play of *Job*, the answer to Job's demands to *see* divine justice is mediated through Elihu, whom the playwright turns into a visionary prophet. Elihu looks upon God, and, looking into God, he *sees* "The Just One," walking the slow steps to Calvary:

> The flagellant is walking, whipped,
> the King in scarlet, up that mountain
> where You make my spirit walk,
> where You are forcing me to go
> and make me watch—O Eternal One—
> You let me tell Your people . . .
> how Your Chosen Son suffers.[22]

---

[17] Ibid., 57.
[18] Ibid.
[19] Ibid., 64.
[20] John Paul II, *Salvifici Doloris,* §11.
[21] Ibid., §14.
[22] "Job," in *The Collected Plays*, 66.

Participating in Elihu's vision, Job now *sees* "the Bright One," and is able to say, "I see that the Redeemer lives."[23] The play of *Job* is about how to use the verb "to see" in relation to God. A detached "eye," or aesthetic vision, searches for "balance," "proportion," "justice." It can't keep together a "beautiful" God with suffering. Because it embodies suffering humanity, Job's vision can begin to understand that "[i]n becoming man, the Son of God . . . has . . . unveiled a new dimension of beauty."[24] A crucial "turning point" in *Salvifici Doloris* is the discussion of the "suffering servant" passages, in Deutero-Isaiah; the encyclical quotes in full Isaiah's picture of the man who "had no form or comeliness . . . and no beauty that we should desire him." John Paul emphasizes the aesthetic or imaginative immediacy of the prophet's vision: "Isaiah," he says, presents "an image of the sufferings of the Servant with a realism as acute as if he were seeing them with his own eyes: the eyes of the body and the spirit. In the light of the verses of Isaiah, the passion of Christ becomes almost more expressive and touching than in the descriptions of the evangelists themselves."[25]

Like a Greek tragedy, *Job* is staged round a sacrificial altar. Composed fifty years later, John Paul's "Letter to Artists" is a development of the same insight. The letter draws, not only on modern Thomistic aesthetics, but also on the Eastern Orthodox conception of artifacts as "icons" of God. The attitude that humans need in order to see a picture as a mirror of the divine is cultivated in sacred groves, not in museums. The "Letter" comments that

> By analogy with what occurs in the sacraments, the icon makes present the mystery of the Incarnation. . . . This is why the beauty of the icon can best be appreciated in a church where in the shadows burning lamps stir infinite flickerings of light. As Pavel Florensky has written: "By the flat light of day, gold is crude, heavy, useless, but by the tremulous light of a lamp or candle it springs to life and glitters in sparks beyond counting—now here, now there, evoking the sense of other lights, not of this earth, which fill the space of heaven."[26]

The Eastern tradition has recognized that, to see a mountain as a reflection of God, one needs to look at it not only aesthetically, but with a religious feeling that makes the universe a God-built cathedral.

---

[23] Ibid., 68; "in the Vulgate, Job says, 'For I know that my Redeemer lives, and at last . . . I shall see God. . . .' " John Paul II, *Salvifici Doloris,* §14.
[24] John Paul II, "Letter to Artists," §5.
[25] John Paul II, *Salvifici Doloris,* §17.
[26] John Paul II, "Letter to Artists," §8.

The "Letter to Artists" characterizes artistic creation as an "echo of the mystery" of divine creation.[27] That sounds rather "Platonistic," and, because his aesthetic is a "Platonic" one, Maritain is a good mediator between west and east. He is certainly the modern Thomist to whom the "Letter to Artists" is most clearly indebted. As Maritain has it, Plato envisages the artist's "inspiration" into an irrational force, a "Muse": the aim of Maritain's idea of "creative intuition" was to incarnate Plato's Muse within the human mind.[28] In Maritain's theory of poetic knowledge, artists conceives the "form" of the beauty which they intend to create, by intuiting the transcendental of beauty within concrete, particular facts. As Maritain describes it, "Poetic intuition is directed . . . towards some singular existent. . . . But . . . it goes beyond . . . because it has no conceptualized object, it tends and extends to the infinite." "Things," Maritain claims, "ceaselessly pass beyond themselves, and give more than they have, because from all sides they are permeated by the activating influx of the Prime Cause. . . . [T]his mutual communication in existence and in the spiritual flux from which existence proceeds . . . is . . . in the last analysis what the poet receives and suffers, and grasps in the night of his Self, or knows as unknown."[29] This suggests that an artist's vision of beauty sees in the fruits of creation the divine creative act at work within them. Maritain claims that poetic intuition "grasps" reality within the "Self" on the analogy that, when God creates, he does so by virtue of his own "creative Idea," his own divine self-knowledge.[30] John Paul's "Letter to Artists" shows a close kinship with this "epistemology" of artistic knowledge. He writes:

> Every genuine artistic intuition goes beyond what the senses perceive and, reaching beneath reality's surface, strives to interpret its hidden mystery. The intuition itself springs from the depths of the human soul, where the desire to give meaning to one's own life is joined by the fleeting vision of beauty and the mysterious unity of things. All artists experience the unbridgeable gap between the work of their hands . . . and the dazzling perfection of the beauty glimpsed in the ardor of the creative moment: . . . I wish to remind each of you that . . . the close alliance that has always existed between the Gospel and art means that you are invited to use your creative intuition to enter into the heart of the mystery of the Incarnate God and at the same time into the mystery of man.[31]

[27] Ibid., §1.

[28] Maritain, *Creative Intuition in Art and Poetry,* 91.

[29] Ibid, 126–27.

[30] Ibid., 112–14.

[31] John Paul II, "Letter to Artists," §§6 and 14.

What we call "Thomistic aesthetics" derives from two modern scholarly projects. In the first place, twentieth-century historians of ideas have researched the history of aesthetic theory. Some, like Edgar de Bruyne and Umberto Eco, focussed on the Middle Ages and Thomas. Others, like Tatakiewicz and Munroe Beardsley, slotted what they call "mediaeval aesthetics" into wider surveys of aesthetic theory. Secondly, there have been modern Thomists, like Maritain, Thomas Gilby, and Armand Maurer, who have created "Thomistic" theories of art, creativity and beauty. Both groups begin by studying the bits and pieces about beauty and about making artifacts in Thomas's writings. The "inventors" of a Thomist aesthetic have gone on create an "art-theory," an aesthetics and a "calology." Because modern people are specially interested in artists, and art works, they have applied what Thomas says about beauty to novelists and novels, painters and paintings. So, for example, Thomas says knowledge of the beautiful is a kind of practical knowledge, and the neo-Thomists theorized about how artistic knowing or poetic experience flows from connaturality between the artist and the beauty he intends to create.[32] Or, again, the Mediaevals variously spoke of beauty as having three features, integrity, form, and a certain "light" or "splendor," a quality of attractiveness.[33] So Maritain and others have applied this to music, to painting, and to fiction, trying to identify what would constitute the "integrity," "form," and "splendor" in a novel or a painting. What they are trying to lay out is what would make an art work "beautiful" in a "Thomist" sense, thus creating a "Thomist aesthetic."

There are reasons to think that this construction of a "Thomist aesthetic" is a dubious endeavor. It is somewhat reminiscent of the way of presenting world religions that begins with a package of concepts like sacred space, sacred time, sacred texts, and finds these concepts exemplified in each of the world religions, as if the concepts created the religions, rather than the particular religions producing and nourishing their own shaping ideas. With regard to pulling a philosophical aesthetics out of Thomas Aquinas, the basic problem is anachronism. The science of "aesthetics," as a philosophical theory dedicated to figuring out what makes art works beautiful, was invented by a German philosopher called Friedrich Baumgarten, in the eighteenth century. As Etienne Gilson liked to point out, St. Thomas Aquinas never expressed any interest in artistic creativity, and his sole reference to poetry describes it as "defective in truth."[34] Above all, St. Thomas Aquinas never looked at a painting, let alone looked from a painting to

[32] Maritain, *Art and Scholasticism,* 11, 47–50; *Creative Intuition in Art and Poetry*, 46–50.

[33] Maritain, *Art and Scholasticism,* 24; *Creative Intuition in Art and Poetry,* 160–62.

[34] Etienne Gilson, *Matières et formes: poiétiques particulières des arts majeurs* (Paris: J. Vrin, 1964), 16–18, and 225.

God. It is not that Thomas literally never set eyes on a picture or a sculpture or a stained-glass window, but that he never "looked" at an art work in the "museum" sense of "looking" which belongs to post-Enlightenment art critics and aestheticians. When we use words like "beauty" or "aesthetics," they have picked up all the specialist, art-related connotations which they have for moderns, but did not have for Thomas.

Our ways of seeing are conditioned by the pictorial imagination of visual artists. Mediaeval Christian paintings simply use landscape as a backdrop for the human or divine scenes in the foreground. Humanity and divinity were where the action was; landscape was one step above gold leaf. By the fifteenth century, there is enough interest in trees and flowers to paint them accurately. But it was not until the eighteenth century that whole pictures were given over to landscapes, now depicted as free-standing entities, displayed for their own sake. The problem of "anachronism" in "Thomistic aesthetics" is not just that our idea of beauty is "art" related, and his was not. The other side of the coin is that we use the word "beautiful" about many things—like mountains—which it did not occur to Thomas to describe in aesthetic terms. Arguably, one had to see mountains as paintings before one could describe mountains as beautiful, because the painting gives the mountain a sense and meaning, a form and a light, which hadn't previously been articulated.

By putting the secular science invented by Baumgarten together with various of Thomas's statements about beauty, "neo-Thomistic aesthetics" created a curious hybrid, an entity that is outwardly Christian without being explicitly theological. The project only makes *philosophical* sense if one does like John Paul, in the "Letter to Artists," and consciously sets the idea of creation as "icon" in a religious context. John Paul recognizes the way imagination focuses our gaze. One can see this in his comment that, "From the time that we were first able to see pictures of the world from space, a perceptible change has taken place in our understanding of our planet, and of its immense *beauty* and fragility."[35]

A modern theological aesthetics might be better off putting words into Thomas's mouth than running a search through the *Summae* for the word "beauty," applying it to art objects, and calling that "Thomist aesthetics." Because, just as Thomas uses the word "beauty" differently to the way we do, so, conversely, sometimes when he ignores the vocabulary of aesthetics, what he is aiming at is what we would name as beauty. And one would *miss Thomas's point* if one did not add a word and a perception which he seldom articulates.

---

[35] John Paul II, "Message for the World Day of Peace" (1987).

A case in point is Thomas's fifth argument for the existence of God, the argument from the purposive functioning of nature. In *Fides et Ratio*, John Paul seems specifically to recast this as an aesthetic and calological argument. He writes, that in the "Book of Wisdom,"

> the sacred author speaks of God who reveals himself in nature. . . . Having affirmed that . . . human beings can "know the structure of the world . . . the cycles of the year and the constellations of the stars, the natures of animals and the tempers of wild beasts" (Wis 7.17, 19–20) . . . that he can philosophize—the sacred text makes a significant step forward. Making his own the thought of Greek philosophy . . . the author affirms that, in reasoning about nature, the human being can rise to God: "From the greatness and beauty of created things comes a corresponding perception of their Creator" (Wis 13.5). This is to recognize . . . the marvelous "book of nature," which, when read with the proper tools of human reason, can lead to knowledge of the Creator.[36]

Beauty is usually the ugly duckling of the transcendentals for St. Thomas. But, in *Fides et Ratio*, it turns into a swan, with the two wings of faith and reason. For here, John Paul interprets Thomas's metaphysical 'ecology' of creation in the light of Scriptural beauty. He seems to be claiming that Thomas's "Fifth Way" comes down to a sort of "eco-aesthetic" vision.

Fides et Ratio repeats the distinction made in Thomistic aesthetics that God creates out of nothing, whereas human craftsfolk use "something that already exists," to which they "give form and meaning."[37] In *Centesimus Annus*, John Paul relates this theme to ecology. He claims that humans have ceased to see themselves as co-creators with God, and now act as if they were the originators or "owners" of nature: "[I]n all this," he writes,

> one notes the poverty or narrowness of man's outlook, motivated as he by a desire to possess things rather than to relate them to the truth, and lacking that disinterested, unselfish and aesthetic attitude that is born of wonder in the presence of being and of the beauty which enables one to see in visible things the message of the invisible God who created them.[38]

Behind religious aesthetics is the Platonic idea of God as the exemplar of artists. In the "Letter to Artists," this role is ascribed to the Holy Ghost, "the Breath (ruah)" who breathes over the "face of the waters" in the Genesis creation scene. And so, the Pope says, "The Spirit is the mysteri-

---

36 John Paul II, *Fides et Ratio,* §19.

37 Ibid; Maritain, *Creative Intuition in Art and Poetry,* 65; Etienne Gilson, *Painting and Reality* (New York: Meridian Books, 1959), 126.

38 John Paul II, *Centesimus Annus,* §37.

ous Artist of the universe."[39] Drawing on the "affinity between the words 'breath-breathing' and 'inspiration,' " the Letter is not too shy to suggest, "analogically," that all artistic inspiration comes about through " 'moments of grace,' " that is, through the "experience" of the Spirit, the Breath of God.

John Paul brings out his own specific take on "Thomist theological aesthetics" when he pinpoints what the inspiration of the Spirit consists in. He claims that the "Creator Spirit" "awakens energies of mind and heart which enable it to conceive an idea and give it form in a work of art" when the Spirit "reaches out to human genius and stirs its creative power. He touches it with a kind of inner illumination which brings together the sense of the good and the beautiful."[40] John Paul has a particular rapport with the idea of "the good and the beautiful" coming together, in artistic inspiration.

In Thomist aesthetics, the kinship between goodness and beauty is expressed by relating both of them to *practical knowledge*, rather than the theoretical knowledge by which truth is understood. It is said that the good and the beautiful are both known through co-naturality, co-naturedness. John Paul perceives the way the good and the beautiful are nested in each other in a pragmatic way, for instance, by discussing this metaphysical topic in relation to ecological concerns. Explaining why we need to need to preserve our rural environments, he says that

> the aesthetic value of creation cannot be overlooked. Our very contact with nature has a deep restorative power; contemplation of its magnificence imparts peace and serenity. The Bible speaks again and again of the goodness and beauty of creation which is called to glorify God. . . . More difficult, perhaps, but no less profound, is the contemplation of the works of human ingenuity. Even cities can have a beauty all their own, one that ought to motivate people to care for their surroundings. . . . The relationship between a good aesthetic education and the maintenance of a healthy environment cannot be overlooked.[41]

The "Letter to Artists" starts with an "header" from Genesis: "God saw all that he had made, and it was very good" (Gen 1.31). John Paul brings out the fact that the Hebrew *"tob,"* means both "good" and "beautiful."[42] The formal difference between ethics and aesthetics is that artistic making

---

[39] Ibid., §15.

[40] Ibid.

[41] John Paul II, "Peace with God the Creator, Peace with All of Creation. Message of John Paul II for the Celebration of the World Day of Peace" (1 Jan 1990), §14.

[42] John Paul II, "Letter to Artists," §3.

involves doing something to something else—spinning a pot on the wheel—whereas ethical action requires doing something to oneself: In art, one's attention is on making some external material beautiful, whereas in ethics, one applies oneself to perfecting or improving the internal material, to making oneself good or virtuous. John Paul sees the distinction, but he splits the difference, noting that "all men and women are entrusted with the task of crafting their own life; . . . they are to make of it a work of art, a masterpiece."[43] He is imaginatively converting the work of moral self-formation into its flip-side of craftsmanship, pot-throwing on your own life. The "Letter to Artists" is a reminder of the "ethic . . . of artistic service, which contributes . . . to the life and renewal of a people."[44]

On the evidence of his literary works, "integrity" is the aspect of beauty that first appeals to John Paul. That is because it readily "converts" into a moral quality belonging to persons. The symbolisms that strike his imagination are ethical ones. Take for example *The Jeweler's Shop*, which symbolizes the meaning of marriage in the rings given to each couple by the jeweler. When Anna goes back to the shop alone to return her ring, it is weightless on the scales. Once handed over, the rings only weigh on the jeweler's scales as a "pair." The character of Adam tells Anna that, "Love is not an adventure. It has the taste of the whole man. It has his weight. And the weight of his whole fate. It cannot be a single moment. Man's eternity passes through it. That is why it is to be found in the dimensions of God, because only He is eternity."[45]

The Jeweler's Shop is a reflection on the Augustinian theme of *amor pondus*, a person's love is their "weight," the destiny, sending them in one direction or another. All of the pope's literary works are poems and plays of ideas, and moral ideas at that. With his concentration on the "weight" of human choice, and his "Augustinian" or phenomenological proclivity for introspective analysis, one might ask whether *aesthetics* is ever as important to John Paul as ethics. Where Maritain speaks of poetic intuition as "the divination of the spiritual in the things of *sense*,"[46] the author of *Job* and *The Jeweler's Shop* seems to be more interested in *internalized* drama. Can an authentic *aesthetics* be as interiorized as John Paul's seems to be? Would it be more true to say that he puts aesthetics in the service of ethics, than that his view of goodness is conditioned by beauty?

---

[43] Ibid., §2.

[44] Ibid., §4.

[45] Karol Wojtyla, *The Jeweler's Shop: A Meditation on the Sacrament of Matrinomy, Passing on Occasion into a Drama,* trans. Boleslaw Taborski (San Francisco: Ignatius Press, 1992), 60.

[46] Maritain, *Art and Scholasticism,* 96.

I find it difficult to see the Pope who called nature "the sister of humanity,"[47] as having a disincarnate aesthetic. The way in which his theological aesthetic qualifies his ethics is by offering it a certain "inwardness" with *nature*. John Paul said that he "proclaimed saint Francis of Assisi as the heavenly patron of those who promote ecology" because

> He offers Christians an example of deep and genuine respect for the integrity of creation. As a friend of the poor who was loved by God's creatures, Saint Francis invited all of creation—animals, plants, natural forces, even Brother Sun and Sister Moon—to give honor and praise to the Lord. . . . It is my hope that the inspiration of Saint Francis will help us to keep ever alive a sense of "fraternity" with all those good and beautiful things which Almighty God has created.[48]

To experience nature as beautiful, one has to achieve "empathy" or kinship with it. That is a mental act in which one imaginatively undergoes the weight of nature, just looking at the weight but suffering it. In the play of *Job*, the hero "becomes" nature as a sacrificial fire. The "Letter to Artists" describes Francis crying out, "You are beauty. . . . You are beauty," "after receiving the stigmata of Christ."[49]

For theological aesthetics, the form which artists construct in their artifacts can be a distant echo of the "form" of Christ, although as Maritain said, "No form of art . . . can encompass beauty in itself as the Virgin contained her Creator."[50] As a dramatist, John Paul tends to imagine "form" in terms of "space," that is, as an interpersonal dynamic tension such as one can see on stage, when actors position themselves in relation to each other. *Salvifici Doloris* begins by describing suffering as a kind of "world," of experience,[51] and goes on to describe it being drawn into a heavenly

---

47 John Paul II, "Nature is our Sister," General Audience, 2000. The piece is worth quoting: "Faced with the glory of the Trinity in creation, we must contemplate, sing, and rediscover awe. . . . Contemplation of the universe also means . . . hearing a paradoxical and silent voice . . . this capacity for contemplation and knowledge, this discovery of a transcendent presence in creation, must also lead us to rediscover our fraternity with the earth, to which we have been linked since creation (cf. Gen 2.7). This very goal was foreshadowed by the Old Testament in the Hebrew Jubilee, when the earth rested and man gathered what the land spontaneously offered (cf. Lv. 25.11–12). If nature is not violated and humiliated, it returns to being the sister of humanity."

48 "Peace with God the Creator, Peace with All of Creation. Message of John Paul II for the Celebration of the World Day of Peace," 1 Jan 1990.

49 John Paul II, "Letter to Artists," §6.

50 Maritain, *Art and Scholasticism,* 46.

51 John Paul II, *Salvifici Doloris,* §8.

"space." The encyclical's final response to the question of suffering is that Christ "annihilates . . . evil in the spiritual space of the relationship between God and humanity, and fills this space with good."[52] The aesthetic gift that John Paul has offered to theology is the tragic insight that reality is only understood from the inside out: "[S]uffering cannot be transformed," he writes, by "grace from outside, but *from within*."[53]

John Paul wrote a poem called "Space which remains in you." The lines are addressed to the Virgin, and the "speaker" is St. John the Evangelist:

> I often return
> to the space which is Your son, your first Son.
> Then thought takes on his Form
> but the eyes remain empty—
> and to the lips words return, the same words
> which he put on
> when he wanted to stay with us.
> These self-same words enfold his space
> better than sight,
> better than memory and heart—oh, Mother,
> then you are with Him again. . . .
> And now—more real than in my lips' whisper,
> than in thought, sight and memory—
> is the space also more really in bread?
> Your arms now remember His space, the little head
> snuggling to your shoulder,
> for the space has remained in You,
> for it was taken from You.
> And shining never empty. So very present in you.
> When with my trembling hands I broke the bread
> to give it to you, Mother,
> I stood for a moment amazed as I saw
> the whole truth through one single tear
> in your eye.[54]

---

[52] Ibid., §17.
[53] Ibid., §26.
[54] Wojtyla, "Space which remains in you," in *Collected Poems*, 65.

Index